Spiritual
Formation *as if the*
Church Mattered

Spiritual Formation *as if the* Church Mattered

Growing in Christ through Community

JAMES C. WILHOIT

FOREWORD BY DALLAS WILLARD

BB

Baker Academic

Grand Rapids, Michigan

Published by Baker Academic
a division of Baker Publishing Group
P.O. Box 6287, Grand Rapids, MI 49516-6287
www.bakeracademic.com

Printed in the United States of America

Library of Congress Cataloging-in-Publication Data

Wilhoit, Jim.
    Spiritual formation as if the church mattered : growing in Christ through community
/ James C. Wilhoit.
      p.   cm.
    Includes bibliographical references and index.
    ISBN 978-0-8010-2776-5 (pbk.)
    1. Spiritual formation. 2. Communities—Religious aspects—Christianity. 3. Church growth. I. Title.
    BV4511.W53 2008
    253.5'3—dc22   2007036589

In memory of

Tim Phillips
1950–2000

A friend from whom I learned much

Contents

List of Figures

Foreword

James Wilhoit has written a book of special urgency for our times. In it he addresses *the* central problem facing the contemporary church in the Western world and worldwide, the problem of how to routinely lead its members through a path of spiritual, moral, and personal transformation that brings them into authentic Christlikeness in every aspect of their lives, enabling them, in the language of the apostle Paul, "to walk in a manner worthy of the calling with which you have been called" (Eph. 4:1 NASV).

We have for most of the twentieth century been in period of time when, in all segments, the Christian churches have been distracted from the central task of teaching their people how to live the spiritual life in a way that brings them progressively to enjoy the character of Christ as their own. But in the last few decades a sense of spiritual shallowness and emptiness, in individual lives as well as in church groups and activities, has led to a renewed use of the ancient language of "spiritual formation." Spiritual formation (really, *trans*formation) is the process, in Paul's language, of "putting on the Lord Jesus Christ, and not organizing our lives around the satisfaction of our natural desires" (Rom. 13:14 author's trans.). In that process we "put off the old man, which is corrupt according to the deceitful lusts, and are renewed in the spirit of our mind; and . . . put on the new man, which after God is created in righteousness and true holiness" (Eph. 4:22–24 author's trans.).

In the period we have recently come through, there has simply been no serious intention of fostering in our church activities such a process of individual transformation of members of the group. Becoming the kind of person who routinely and easily does what Jesus told us to do has generally been considered out of reach and therefore not really necessary for what we, as Christians, are about. Paul, in conformity with the central teachings of the whole Bible, is referring to the type of life transformation from inside to outside—"first clean the inside of the cup and of the dish, so that the outside of it may become clean also," as Jesus said (Matt. 23:26 NASB)—that won the ancient world to Christ. If what we have more recently seen of Christianity in the Western world had been all there was to it in earlier centuries, there simply would be no such thing as Christianity today, or at best it would exist as a museum piece. How the church fell onto such thin times is, no doubt, a subject worthy of thorough examination. But the practical problem is: How do we move back into the powerful form of life which won the worlds of the past and alone can meet the crying needs of our world today? Here is where this book comes in.

The answer to the question is that *the local congregations*, the places where Christians gather on a regular basis, *must resume the practice of making the spiritual formation of their members into Christlikeness their primary goal, the aim which every one of its activities serves.* Another way of putting the same point is to say that they must take as their unswerving objective to be a body of apprentices to Jesus that are devoted to learning and teaching one another how to do, through transformation of the "inner man" (Eph. 3:16 NASB), everything Jesus said for us to do. That is what it means to "put on the Lord Jesus Christ."

Unless this course of action is adopted in the local or neighborhood congregations, the now widespread talk about "spiritual formation," and the renewed interest in practices of the spiritual life in Christ, will soon pass, like other superficial fads that offer momentary diversion to a bored and ineffectual church *primarily* interested only in its own success or survival. This is because it is the local group of apprentices that God has chosen as his primary instrument in his redemptive work on earth. No doubt wisely, for only the personal and corporate dynamics of such a group is suited to be the place where humans learn to "love one another as I have loved you" (John 13:34–35 author's trans.). And so long as the local assemblies do not do this transforming work as their central business, everyone, church and world alike, will assume—as in fact they do now—that there is an acceptable alternative form of Christianity other than spiritual transformation into Christlikeness. Indeed, that is the assumption that produces the now standard form in North America of "nominal" Christianity: the curse of the valid aspirations of humanity and the perennial Golgotha of Jesus' trajectory across human history.

Currently, pastors and leaders of congregations do not seem to understand this. Their education, their models of success, and their understanding of what salvation or life in Christ is supposed to be like, point them in other directions. The result is absence of any overriding intention to devote their central effort toward constant transformation of all members of the group. Indeed, radical transformation is not what our folks are prepared for in "going to church." It is not what is in their "contract" with the preacher or the leadership. Thus you will find here and there congregations that spend months or years trying to develop a "mission" statement. Almost never—never, to my knowledge—do they come out at the point Jesus left with us: to be disciples (apprentices of Jesus in kingdom living) who make disciples and form them in inner Christlikeness in such a way that they easily and routinely do the things Jesus told us to do (Matt. 28:18–20).

To respond to Jesus' instructions in faithfulness to God, pastors, teachers, and leaders must form the intention and make the decision to live out the New Testament vision of apprenticeship to Jesus in the local congregation, as Jesus articulated it in his life on earth and as Paul articulates it in Ephesians 4:1–16: the vision of a body of disciples (not just Christians as now understood) building itself up in love and mutual ministry and life together. Then they can begin to think about what they do "in church" and in life that can effectively carry forward on a regular basis spiritual formation in Christlikeness in all the attendees. They will learn how to deal with the fine texture of relationships and events, within the redemptive body and beyond, in such a way that all might "Grow in the grace and knowledge of our Lord and Savior Jesus Christ" (2 Pet. 3:18 NASB)—no hype!

It is in fact very hard today for pastors and leaders to form this intention and begin to put it into practice. Generally speaking, that is because they do not know how to make the group a context of honest spiritual formation, and they fear that, if they try to do that, they will fail by the current standards of "success." But there is a way forward, and it is *the details* that matter. That is where this book, *Spiritual Formation as if the Church Mattered*, is uniquely helpful. Dr. Wilhoit, with a warm heart and a gentle and intelligent manner, helps us see, in great detail, what we can do to relocate spiritual transformation at the center of *what we do* in gathering as disciples of Jesus. He helps any serious person engage the project from where they are, discover what really works for Christlikeness and what doesn't, and assess outcomes realistically to make needed adjustments as they go. No special equipment, abilities, or training—not even a budget—is required. As disciples, we learn what we need to know as we go. Remember, the churches have always been at their best when they had the least but were simply obedient to Christ.

Dallas Willard

Preface

This book had its beginnings in conversations with my students about the nurture they had received in their churches. These conversations had naturally arisen during advising visits, over lunches, and in classes, and I soon became fascinated by the variety of formational practices that students had experienced. As I reflected on these stories, I began to look for the presence of formational principles in these stories, which led to a more intentional set of interviews with church leaders about patterns and practices of spiritual formation. I came to see that some churches are marked by the presence of a "culture of formation" and while others may have many programs and much activity, they lacked the presence of such a transformative culture.

I write as an evangelical and one who is deeply concerned about the erosion of intentional practices of spiritual formation in many of our churches. My concern is that many of the patterns of nurture that served us well for several generations have quickly been set aside. To be sure, some of these practices of formation may have become stale and unattractive. But it often seems like we have simply abandoned many practices without adopting alternative formational patterns. Some practices of formation that were widely implemented in evangelical churches for several generations but have recently been set aside include: an emphasis on systematic Bible teaching; Bible memorization and reading; Sunday evening services with an emphasis on testimonies, missions, and global Christianity; observing the Sabbath; shared church-wide meals; practicing hospitality; attendance at nurture-oriented summer camps; pastoral visitation; and significant intergenerational socializing. These changes represent a sea change in our formational structures and their effects will take a generation to fully manifest themselves.

This book is not so much about reversing a trend but about a call to intentionality about our formation and to repentance about how we have tried to engineer formation more than we have prayerfully opened our lives and our churches to God's grace. I have sought to provide guidance on community-oriented and educationally-based spiritual formation that has stood the test of time. I am grateful to the teaching and writing of Dallas Willard, who has reminded us that our spiritual formation must not be grounded merely in spiritual abstractions but in the life, teaching, and ministry of Jesus.

I am also grateful to those who have assisted me in this process. Over the past half dozen years, faculty members have met under the leadership of Evan Howard for a gathering of evangelical scholars in Christian spirituality. Comments on various chapters were provided by members of this group: Paul Bramer, Klaus Issler, Michael Glerup, and Evan Howard. Tom Schwanda read through the entire manuscript at an earlier stage and provided valuable comments. I am appreciative of the editorial and theological wisdom that Neil Wilson provided. From the beginning of the writing I have been assisted by Linda Rozema who took a deep interest in the material and consistently found the texts and other resources that were needed to move the project forward. The entire writing process benefited from the careful word processing and manuscript checking that Kathleen Cruise provided. The project was made possible by the support of my family, who took an active interest in the project, listened to pieces over dinner, provided illustrations, and critically read portions. Thank you, Carol, Elizabeth, and Juliana.

1

Formation through the Ordinary

Therefore, go and make disciples of all the nations, baptizing them in the name of the Father and the Son and the Holy Spirit. Teach these new disciples to obey all the commands I have given you. And be sure of this: I am with you always, even to the end of the age.

Jesus, in Matthew 28:19–20 NLT

I know of no current denomination or local congregation that has a concrete plan and practice for teaching people to do "all things whatsoever I have commanded you."[1]

Dallas Willard

It takes time, and the penetration of the truth, to make a mature saint.[2]

Richard F. Lovelace

Spiritual Formation: The Task of the Church

Spiritual formation is *the* task of the church. Period. It represents neither an interesting, optional pursuit by the church nor an insignificant category in the job description of the body of Christ. Spiritual formation is at the heart of its whole purpose for existence. The church was formed to form. Our charge, given by Jesus himself, is to make disciples, baptize them, and teach these new disciples to obey his commands (Matt.

28:19–20). The witness, worship, teaching, and compassion that the church is to practice all require that Christians be spiritually formed. Although formation describes the central work of the church, and despite a plethora of resolutions, programs, and resources, the fact remains that spiritual formation has not been the priority in the North American church that it should be.

A safe food supply, clean drinking and recreational waters, sanitation, and widespread vaccinations have improved the quality of our life. These interventions have eliminated diseases like smallpox and polio. These advances, and scores more, are part of the fruit of the public health movement that came to fruition in the twentieth century. I take many of these for granted, assuming that they are just part of life, but in many parts of the world they are not widely present. Currently 250,000 children die every year from measles, a disease easily prevented through vaccinations. We take for granted public health initiatives of the last century that have had measurable, positive social benefits. In medicine, the two tasks of prevention and cure must work hand in hand. Cures may provoke media attention and buzz; however, it is the preventative and public health interventions that generally provide the real "bang for your buck." Likewise, spiritual formation makes its greatest contribution through quiet, hardly noticeable, behind-the-scenes work that places an emphasis on "prevention" and equipping rather than just on crisis interventions or headline-grabbing public conferences and programs.

Consider the effects of the painstakingly established public health infrastructure in the United States. According to the Centers for Disease Control and Prevention (CDC), "Since 1900, the average lifespan of persons in the United States has lengthened by greater than 30 years; 25 years of this gain are attributable to advances in public health."[3]

The quiet and seemingly ordinary work of public health has made a tremendous difference in our life expectancy and in the overall quality of life. When one looks at the list of the CDC's "Ten Great Public Health Achievements," they appear so reasonable that their implementation seems to be obvious to all. For the list includes now widely accepted "best practices" like vaccination, motor-vehicle safety, safer and healthier foods, and the recognition of tobacco use as a health hazard.[4] Yet society implemented these strategies, which seem so commonsensical today, only after long struggles, careful science that established their efficacy, and the slow and ongoing work of public education.

Some years ago a young physician summarized his medical-care trip to Central America by telling of the long days he worked caring for patients. He concluded his story by saying that he was convinced that he could have done more long-term good with one hundred meters of PVC pipe. So many of the people he treated suffered from medical conditions that were the result of the village's contaminated water supply—a problem that could have been easily remedied.

In this chapter, I want to begin to identify what the spiritual formation equivalent of safe drinking water and vaccinations might be. What are the patterns in Christian community life that make a positive contribution to spiritual formation? What are the community practices that we can so easily overlook or underutilize, but that help create a climate of formation in a church?

For many years I have been listening to the stories of how faithful people have grown in grace. These accounts pulse with deep drama. I've realized that Paul was not using hyperbole when he told the Galatians, "I am again in the pain of childbirth until Christ is formed in you" (Gal. 4:19). These stories are unique—unique as the people who tell them—and I want to be careful not to simply reduce their amazing tales of grace to a few abstract principles. However, themes and patterns do emerge when we look at the stories as a whole. While patterns of formation emerge, there does not exist anything approaching a "technology of spiritual formation." Formation remains a messy and imprecise business, where character, wisdom, and faith play a far greater role than theories and techniques. Ironically, one value of engagement in deliberate formation is that it drives us to prayer because it reminds us, more than popular how-to books do, that true formation comes from grace and by grace, channeled through our humble efforts. This is not to deny what others have observed, that "spiritual formation in Christ is an orderly process."[5] Spiritual formation is certainly a multifactorial process that requires us to constantly ask God what we should be doing, rather than relying on our power and skill.

COMMUNITY SPIRITUAL FORMATION COROLLARY 1

All persons are formed spiritually. It may be in either a positive or negative direction. This formation may involve the cultivation of virtues that promote trust in God and foster social compassion or may leave persons wary, self-protective, and unable to promote the welfare of society.

Either-Or

The influential twentieth-century philosopher-educator John Dewey complained that educators were constantly guilty of "either-or" thinking. Instead of recognizing the need for both experience and educational content in schools, he said these writers tended to emphasize one at the

Christian Spirituality—The Ongoing Results of Formation

Widely Shared Patterns in Stories of Spiritual Growth

1. **Christian spirituality begins with a response to the call of Spirit to spirit.** Issues that appear to be primarily psychological in nature often have a deeper spiritual significance. The first steps of response to the call of Spirit to spirit are often not consciously spiritual.

2. **Christian spirituality is rooted in a commitment to Jesus and a transformational approach to life.** Christian spirituality is not simply a state; we do better to think of it as a process.

3. **Christian spirituality is nurtured by the means of grace.** Scriptures, prayer, the sacraments, and Christian fellowship all serve as media through which we may uniquely receive grace.

4. **Christian spirituality involves a deep knowing of Jesus and, through him, the Father and the Spirit.** Christian spirituality is grounded in knowing, not knowledge. Knowing God requires that we believe that God wants to be known. While God reaches out to us, he is also boundless mystery. Christian spirituality involves the grounding of the human spirit in the divine Spirit.

5. **Christian spirituality requires a deep knowing of oneself.** People who are afraid to look deeply at themselves will be equally afraid to look deeply and personally at God. It is important to remember that self-knowledge is simply the means, not the end, of Christian spirituality.

6. **Christian spirituality leads to the realization of the unique self that God ordained each of us should be.** Properly understood, the denial that is a part of Christian spirituality is not of self but of false selves. Christian spirituality does not call for the renunciation of humanness, trading humanity for divinity. It does not make us less human but more human.

7. **Christian spirituality is uniquely developed within the context of suffering.** Openness to suffering is really openness to life. Suffering is an inevitable part of life, and if we are to be open to any of life, we must be open to it all. Openness to life means living it with willingness, not willfulness. Christ is the epitome of life lived with willingness.

8. **Christian spirituality is manifest by a sharing of the goodness of God's love with others and in care for his creation.** Christian spirituality involves participation in God's kingdom plan for the restoration of the totality of his creation.

9. **Christian spirituality expresses the goodness of celebration in Christian community.** Celebration and community are the unmistakable marks of mature Christian spirituality.

continued ➤

Summary: If spirituality is our response to deep foundational yearnings for meaning, identity, connections, and surrender, what part of our psychological functioning could possibly be excluded from such a quest? If anything is excluded from our spirituality, it will by necessity become a dissociated part of ourself, detached from the rest of our life. Whether this be our body, our unconscious, our emotions, our intellect, our sexuality, or any other part of ourself, the result is always the same—a fragmentation of personhood and an encapsulated spirituality. Christian spirituality either makes us more whole or, if it is contained in some limited sphere of our being, furthers our fragmentation. Only wholeness is worthy of being associated with the Spirit of Christ, who empowers, directs, and gives name to the experience we have been calling Christian spirituality.

Adapted from Care of Souls *by David G. Benner. Used by permission.*[6]

expense of the other. We could count the same as true for writers about the Christian life. In the next three sections we will look at three sets of images of the spiritual life: nurture (agriculture, gardening, human growth, intimacy), the journey (race, battle, struggle), and death and resurrection (dying with Christ, being born again). To capture the complexities and nuances of Christian spiritual formation, the biblical writers employed these images, and we would do well to honor their emphasis on nurture, training, and resurrection.

Images of Christian Life and Nurture

Jesus and John the Baptist challenged their hearers with the need to produce good "fruit" (Matt. 21:43) and "fruit" originating in a true repentance (3:8). Jesus used a maxim in fruit growing to show how one can judge a person's character: "A healthy tree produces good fruit, and an unhealthy tree produces bad fruit. A good tree can't produce bad fruit, and a bad tree can't produce good fruit. . . . Yes, the way to identify a tree or a person is by the kind of fruit that is produced" (7:17–18, 20 NLT). Jesus illustrated how our heart condition affects our response to the gospel by his parable of the sower and the seed. When he explained the meaning of it to his followers, he told them, "But the good soil represents honest, good-hearted people who hear God's message, cling to it, and steadily produce a huge harvest" (Luke 8:15 NLT). The image of Jesus as the true vine (John 15) vividly communicates the spiritual truth that we need to stay spiritually connected to Christ. Incidentally, we often misread this image as being just about "me abiding in Jesus," when the actual image and language has a strong community focus: when the branches are connected to the vine, a marvelous crop of grapes is produced. The concreteness of agriculture makes the more abstract subject of spiritual formation less abstract and more comprehensible.

The biblical writers also used agriculture to capture part of the interplay between human and divine in formation. This is seen when Paul described the work he and Apollos did and then asserted that "God, who makes things grow" (1 Cor. 3:7 Message) is the true cause of all the spiritual growth. Yet in saying this, he does not diminish the importance of their participation. Agriculture requires sustained and systematic work performed at the right time and carried out with an experience-based expertise, but all human efforts are subject to weather, pests, disease, and war. Agriculture illuminates the beautiful symmetry between God and his people that is at play in the process of spiritual formation. Therefore, we go about our formation work doing what we can and being prayerfully receptive, especially about those areas outside our direct influence.

"You happen to be God's field in which we are working" (1 Cor. 3:9 Message). The field is the primary location of the work of farming. To flourish, a field must be cultivated, planted, tended, watered, protected, and harvested. The illustration is a communal or population-based image. The farmer is more concerned with the total crop than with one individual plant. In many of the New Testament agricultural images, the focus is on the big picture, on how abundant the harvest is, and not just on the output of a single plant. Nevertheless, there must be a both-and emphasis on the individual and the group in spiritual formation.

Images of Christian Life as Journey and Struggle

Paul uses imagery drawn from the Hellenic games to illustrate the need for training and discipline in the Christian life.

> Do you not know that in a race the runners all compete, but only one receives the prize? Run in such a way that you may win it. Athletes exercise self-control in all things; they do it to receive a perishable wreath, but we an imperishable one. So I do not run aimlessly, nor do I box as though beating the air; but I punish my body and enslave it, so that after proclaiming to others I myself should not be disqualified. (1 Cor. 9:24–27)

The emphasis of this race image is a call for Corinthian believers to adopt the singular focus of a trained athlete who follows Christ. In Philippians 3:13–14 Paul describes his own athletelike straining to pursue Christ well. "The image of 'straining forward, . . . press on toward the goal' evokes the picture of the racer who looks neither to the left nor to the right to check the progress of the competition or be swayed by any diversion."[7] In the Pastoral Epistles the imagery is developed further: the importance of rigorous training (1 Tim. 4:7–8), endurance (4:8), following the rules so that one is not disqualified (2 Tim. 2:5), and winning an imperishable crown (1 Cor. 9:25). The emphasis in this set of images is on the need for training, discipline, and rigor.

Satan was soundly defeated at the cross as Jesus "disarmed the powers and authorities, . . . triumphing over them by the cross" (Col. 2:15 NIV), and yet biblical writers recognized that Satan is still active and a great cause of distress for Christians. He is busy in his constant work of accusation (Rev. 12:10) and "prowls around like a roaring lion, looking for some victim to devour" (1 Pet. 5:8 NLT). We now live between the time of the cross and the final victory. The church is called to wage battle "against the rulers, against the authorities, against the cosmic powers of this present darkness, against the spiritual forces of evil in the heavenly places" (Eph. 6:12). This struggle against the dark spiritual forces is both a corporate responsibility and a personal one for every Christian.

A concern about the battle imagery for sanctification is that often it is presented in a way that emphasizes struggle and risk such that a life of grace-dependency is diminished. Not many writers are as adroit as John Bunyan in *The Holy War* in capturing the reality of this spiritual struggle without minimizing the place of grace in the midst of the struggle. The armor-of-God imagery from Ephesians is full of battle, struggle, alertness to Satan's craftiness, and God-given grace/power. We are told from the outset of this passage that we are to "be strong in the Lord and in the strength of his power" (Eph. 6:10), and the description "whole armor of God" (6:11) reminds us that the armor is of God's design. God gives the battle armor to those he has called, but apparently the armor could just sit and gather dust. Ephesians therefore admonishes us to "take up the whole armor of God" (6:13). As would be true for a first-century soldier, most of the armor is defensive. The only offensive weapon is Scripture, here described as the sword of the Spirit (6:17).

At an individual level the battlefield is the human heart. In Proverbs we are admonished, "Guard your heart, for it affects everything you do" (Prov. 4:23 NLT). The heart/soul is the center of our being and where our growth is solidified. We are warned not to give a "foothold to the Devil" (Eph. 4:27 NLT) and instructed to wage war against "the Devil's strongholds" (2 Cor. 10:3–4 NLT). The picture here is of a territorial battle that is being keenly contested. The battle will turn as we or the enemies are able to secure footholds and establish strongholds. Again, our temptation may be to see the battle merely in individual terms, but Jesus declared that the "gates of hell shall not prevail against" the church (Matt. 16:18 KJV), the corporate might of the body of Christ.

Images of Christian Life and the Resurrection

The death-rebirth pattern is an archetypal paradigm present through the pages of the Bible. The pattern shows itself in the flood (Gen. 6–9), as God destroys the entire world, except for Noah's family and selected animals, and then brings forth life on the earth out of the barrenness of the destruction. Poignantly summarizing the image, Noah plants a vineyard: "After the Flood, Noah became a farmer and planted a vineyard" (Gen. 9:20 NLT). In the exodus, the people of Israel experience a rebirth, after four hundred years of slavery in Egypt, when they escape from the deathlike grip of bondage, moving out to worship and serve God. The pattern is immediately repeated in the death zone of the wilderness, followed by the birthlike entrance into life in the promised land. This imagery "from death to rebirth underlies most of the OT, preoccupied as it is with lament giving way to praise, servitude to freedom, exile to return."[8]

Certainly the central image of resurrection in the New Testament is that of Jesus' death on the cross and subsequent resurrection. The victory of death secured by the resurrection event is the basis of the Christian's claim to new life. Jesus described the Christian's regeneration as a person being born again (John 3:1–8). When we trust Christ for salvation, God makes us alive. "Even when we were dead through our trespasses, [God] made us alive together with Christ" (Eph. 2:5). The central Christian initiation ceremony of baptism symbolizes death and rebirth. Paul says that believers are "buried" with Christ: "Therefore we have been buried with him by baptism into death, so that, just as Christ was raised from the dead by the glory of the Father, so we too might walk in newness of life" (Rom. 6:4).

This imagery of death and resurrection is often missing in much contemporary spiritual formation literature. The absence of these radical and supernatural components can reduce spiritual formation to little more than religious self-help. This is unfortunate because these are the images reminding us that true formation is first and foremost the work of our forming God. Jesus' death and resurrection make our true formation possible and provide the grace we need to experience true spiritual change.

These three image families—nurture, journey and struggle, and death/ resurrection—capture many of the essential elements of spiritual formation. Though in our personal devotional lives we may find that certain images resonate more deeply with us, it is important in our teaching ministry that we provide a balanced treatment of these images. Other people may be at a point where a cluster of images other than our favorites may help to illuminate the path they need to travel. Additionally, the "whole counsel of Scripture" uses these multiple images in a way that safeguards us from promoting an imbalanced approach to the spiritual life. An effective way to evaluate a community's Christian formation practices is to review the comprehensive set of formation images found in Scripture and compare those to the images used in its worship, teaching, and discipleship.

What Spiritual Formation Is

> The Gospel orients us not so much to an object as to a person. The Gospel, then, is not so much belief *that* as it is belief *in*.[9]
>
> Kenneth J. Collins

Christian spiritual formation refers to the intentional communal process of growing in our relationship with God and becoming conformed to Christ through the power of the Holy Spirit. I need to highlight a few implications in the definition. First, I described it as an intentional process to distinguish it from the broad sense in which spiritual formation refers to all the cultural forces, activities, and experiences that shape people's spiritual lives. In this book I am interested in exploring the more intentional and deliberate side of spiritual formation—what is taught and sought more than merely caught. Second, I have described it as communal because the Christian life is best lived in community, where worship, fellowship, and service are practiced, and spiritual formation takes place in, through, and for community. Spiritual transformation must extend beyond the individual to the church, the family, and society.

Third, I described spiritual formation as a process, thereby implying that formation is a long-term, lifelong venture, and that it results from a multidimensional ministry, not just a technique or program. Consequently, while small groups, teaching, accountability structures, and individual spiritual practices can all have a role in spiritual formation, no single dimension of church life can carry out this task alone. Fourth, the focus of spiritual formation is becoming more like Jesus. Fifth, we can never accomplish this through our own power; we need the empowering of the Holy Spirit.

COMMUNITY SPIRITUAL FORMATION COROLLARY 2

Christian spiritual formation: (1) is intentional; (2) is communal; (3) requires our engagement; (4) is accomplished by the Holy Spirit; (5) is for the glory of God and the service of others; and (6) has as its means and end the imitation of Christ.

Biblical Images of Spiritual Formation

Christian life and nurture. These images emphasize the gradual but certain changes that mark the Christian life that results from nurture. The dominant metaphor used here comes from the growth seen in plants and animals that are well cared for. Also included in this group are images of the interior. In an age obsessed with beauty and impression management, the spiritual life invites us to cultivate and attend first to our interiors.

Potter and clay. "Yet, O LORD, you are our Father; we are the clay, and you are our potter; we are all the work of your hand" (Isa. 64:8).

Apprentice/disciple. "An apprentice does not lecture the master. The point is to be careful who you follow as your teacher" (Luke 6:40 Message).

Vine and branches. "I am the vine, you are the branches. Those who abide in me and I in them bear much fruit, because apart from me you can do nothing" (John 15:5).

Hunger and thirst. "Blessed are those who hunger and thirst for righteousness, for they will be filled" (Matt. 5:6).

Famine/drought. "The time is surely coming, says the Lord GOD, when I will send a famine on the land; not a famine of bread, or a thirst for water, but of hearing the words of the LORD" (Amos 8:11).

Growth. "I planted, Apollos watered, but God gave the growth. So neither the one who plants nor the one who waters is anything, but only God who gives the growth" (1 Cor. 3:6–7).

Human growth. "Like newborn infants, long for the pure, spiritual milk, so that by it you may grow into salvation—if indeed you have tasted that the Lord is good" (1 Pet. 2:2–3).

Plants. "Blessed are those who trust in the LORD, whose trust is the LORD. They shall be like a tree planted by water, sending out its roots by the stream. It shall not fear when heat comes, and its leaves shall stay green; in the year of drought it is not anxious, and it does not cease to bear fruit" (Jer. 17:7–8).

Heart/soul. "Keep your heart with all vigilance, for from it flow the springs of life" (Prov. 4:23).

continued ➤

Christian life as journey and struggle. These images capture the call for personal responsibility, action, and discipleship that mark the Christian life.

> **Journey.** "You will do well to send them on in a manner worthy of God; for they began their journey for the sake of Christ" (3 John 6–7). Early Christians were known as followers of "the Way" (Acts 9:2).

> **Coming home.** "At that time I will bring you home, at the time when I gather you; for I will make you renowned and praised among all the peoples of the earth, when I restore your fortunes before your eyes, says the LORD" (Zeph. 3:20).

> **Brokenness.** "He heals the brokenhearted, and binds up their wounds" (Ps. 147:3).

> **Athletics.** "Athletes exercise self-control in all things; they do it to receive a perishable wreath, but we an imperishable one" (1 Cor. 9:25).

> **Putting on and taking off.** "Let us then lay aside the works of darkness and put on the armor of light" (Rom. 13:12). "As God's chosen ones, holy and beloved, clothe yourselves with compassion, kindness, humility, meekness, and patience" (Col. 3:12).

> **Images of battle and struggle.** "Put on the whole armor of God, so that you may be able to stand against the wiles of the devil. For our struggle is not against enemies of blood and flesh, but against the rulers, against the authorities, against the cosmic powers of this present darkness, against the spiritual forces of evil" (Eph. 6:11–12).

> **The race.** "Let us run with perseverance the race that is set before us" (Heb. 12:1).

Christian life and the resurrection. Basic images to the Christian formation are those of rescue, love, redemption, and justification. While these words have come down to us as theological terms, they are rooted in concrete images like freeing a slave or being declared not guilty in a courtroom. At the heart of these images is God's initiative who, because of his love, has freed us from that which enslaved us.

> **Redemption.** "You were bought with a price; do not become slaves of human masters" (1 Cor. 7:23).

> **Passover.** "Clean out the old yeast so that you may be a new batch, as you really are unleavened. For our paschal lamb, Christ, has been sacrificed" (1 Cor. 5:7).

Cross and redemption. "For the message about the cross is foolishness to those who are perishing, but to us who are being saved it is
the power of God" (1 Cor. 1:18).

Disease/healing. "He himself bore our sins in his body on the cross, so
that, free from sins, we might live for righteousness; by his wounds
you have been healed" (1 Pet. 2:24).

Exile. "They confessed that they were strangers and foreigners on the
earth. . . . But as it is, they desire a better country, that is, a heavenly
one. Therefore God is not ashamed to be called their God; indeed,
he has prepared a city for them" (Heb. 11:13, 16).

Open door. "I know your deeds. See, I have placed before you an open
door that no one can shut" (Rev. 3:8 NIV).

The Gospel and Spiritual Formation

I was nurtured in programs that tended to see Christian education,
discipleship, and spiritual formation as things "that happened after the
gospel was preached and believed." The diagram below captures how
my mentors related the gospel and patterns of Christian nurture.

Figure 1. Gospel as pre-discipleship

In this view, the gospel contained both the indictment of our sin
and the announcement of hope through the cross—a message the
unbeliever certainly needed to hear. This "gospel as pre-discipleship"
was vividly set forth in a sermon I read recently. The pastor described
the gospel as the sure foundation and basement on which we are to
build our spiritual house through discipleship/learning. There is a
good measure of truth in this, but what is dangerous is when we think
the gospel is merely the door by which we enter Christianity, something we leave behind as we grow spiritually. The other disturbing
element of this sermon was its emphasis on "my building my house,"
while little emphasis was placed on grace. Like so many sermons, it
seemed to say: God saved me (gospel); now I need to make myself
holy (discipleship).

The gospel must permeate any program of Christian spiritual formation. Returning to the cross in awareness of our sin, rebellion, and

brokenness is the bedrock of spiritual formation. Spiritual formation's relation to the gospel looks more like this:[10]

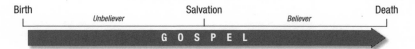

Figure 2. Gospel for spiritual formation

Much of our failure in conceptualizing spiritual formation comes from our failure to keep the gospel central to our ministry. Too often people see the gospel as merely the front door to Christianity, or worse, "heaven's minimum entrance requirement."[11] A bifurcation of salvation into a grace-filled regeneration followed by a human-striving sanctification leads to so many spiritual sorrows. The gospel is the power of God for the beginning, middle, and end of salvation. It is not merely what we need to proclaim to unbelievers; the gospel also needs to permeate our entire Christian experience.

The Gospel and the Christian

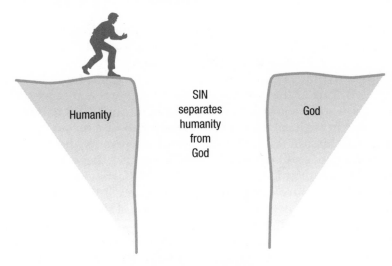

Figure 3. The spiritual chasm

I remember as a young adult having the gospel explained to me in terms of a bridge diagram. In this diagram a chasm separates God and humankind. This gap is the result of sin and is so enormous that humans cannot bridge it through their own efforts and good works. The person who presented it to me did so with great gusto and drew various human bridges (e.g., morality, religion, piety, and good works) on the blackboard and showed that all fell short of crossing the gap.

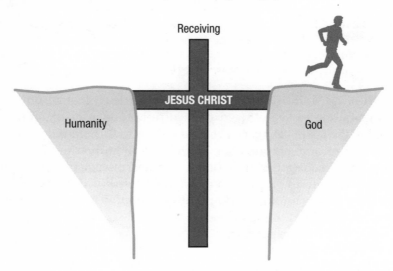

Figure 4. Bridging the gap

The gospel, as I came to believe, was chiefly about bridging this gap. The cross fills the gap perfectly and provides a way to traverse the great chasm. This is certainly true, "For there is one God; there is also one mediator between God and humankind, Christ Jesus, himself human" (1 Tim. 2:5). Part of the glorious news of the gospel is that we do have a mediator, and peace with God is possible through the cross of Jesus Christ. God, in his love, has bridged the gap fully and invites us into fellowship with him. In this picture, however, the person who has crossed the spiritual gap is still running. The cross seems to become a means of transportation rather than God's means of transformation. That was my story: running, doing, serving, but thinking very little about the cross on a daily basis. In Lovelace's words, I was one of those Christians who did not "know enough to start each day with a thoroughgoing stand upon Luther's platform: *you are accepted*, looking outward in faith and claiming the wholly alien righteousness of Christ as the only ground for acceptance, relaxing in that quality of trust which will produce increasing sanctification as faith is active in love and gratitude."[12]

What I did not know then is how hard it is to really live with a sense that the cross fills this gap. The person who showed me this diagram said something like, "Jim, this is true, just like 2 + 2 = 4. It's not about emotions, and you just have to believe it." Not quite. All of my observed reality supports the fact that $2 + 2 = 4$. Yet, much in my life does not seem to support "Jesus paid it all." My inborn pride rebels at this. The pain and guilt that is a bitter fruit of my sin mocks the atonement. Our society, which increasingly ties our worth to productivity, trains us to deny the cross. Learning that the cross is big enough is a lifelong vocation.

From personal brokenness and reflection I have come to see that the gospel is not simply the door of faith: it must also be a compass I daily use to orient my life and a salve I apply for the healing of my soul. It is in returning again and again to the cross that we receive the grace that transforms us.

The metaphor of a gap between God and humans that needs to be bridged is surprisingly widespread. For instance, the chief priest of ancient Rome was called *pontifex maximus*, literally, the chief bridge builder. The sense of a divine-human gap is a universal spiritual intuition; even when people deny having this sense, they live as though they must bridge the gap. However, we must be careful to express the reality of this gap in deep spiritual terms. I have sat with people who had little sense that they were sinners but felt deep agony over their inability to walk free from addictions. A gap was present in their life, but they did not understand it as the classic "sin gap." Rather, it was more akin to a hunger for true freedom.

Many Christians have learned the right answer, "Jesus paid it all," yet live with a nagging sense of shame and guilt. In times of spiritual counsel I frequently listen to persons who can declare the abstract power of Christ to forgive, heal, save, and restore, and yet they are ravaged with guilt and have no perception of God's love. Such people need to learn to rest in their identity as a child of God.

COMMUNITY SPIRITUAL FORMATION COROLLARY 3

The gospel is the power of God for the beginning, middle, and end of salvation. It is not merely what we need to proclaim to unbelievers; the gospel also needs to permeate our entire Christian experience.

I remember hearing as a child the story of a single woman who had adopted an orphan boy from Germany. His parents had been killed during the war, and his postwar experience was horrific. While the woman loved her son deeply, it was only in adulthood that he finally began to love her as a son should. His adolescent years were marked by detachment and rebellion, bringing his long-suffering mother great pain and embarrassment. The death of his parents and the betrayals his family had experienced made it so hard for him to live as a son rather than as an orphan. We are beloved children who regularly "don't get it" and live

Paul on Preaching the Gospel

"To all God's beloved in Rome, who are called to be saints: Grace to you and peace from God our Father and the Lord Jesus Christ. . . . For God, whom I serve with my spirit by announcing the gospel of his Son, is my witness that without ceasing I remember you always in my prayers, asking that by God's will I may somehow at last succeed in coming to you. For I am longing to see you so that I may share with you some spiritual gift to strengthen you . . . hence my eagerness to proclaim the gospel to you also who are in Rome" (Rom. 1:7–15).

Who do we usually think about preaching the gospel to?
- Non-Christians

Who is Paul writing to?
- Roman Christians: "To all God's beloved in Rome, who are called to be saints. . . . Your faith is proclaimed throughout the world" (1:7–8).

Who is Paul eager to preach the gospel to?
- He wants to preach the gospel to the Christians in Rome: "hence my eagerness to proclaim the gospel to you also who are in Rome" (1:15).

What is surprising about this?
- We tend to think that the gospel is just for non-Christians.

Why do Christians need to hear the gospel?
- Over time we simply tend to wander from the truth. As God said to his people through Jeremiah, "You love to wander far from me and do not follow in my paths" (Jer. 14:10 NLT).
- All of us have idols at hand, which we use as substitutes for the cross to gain divine favor. The problem of the Galatians is a problem all of us face: "I am astonished that you are so quickly deserting him who called you in the grace of Christ and are turning to a different gospel" (Gal. 1:6 ESV).

Why does Paul want to preach to Christians?
- He wants to encourage them and strengthen them spiritually. "I can share a spiritual blessing with you that will help you grow strong in the Lord. I'm eager to encourage you in your faith, but I also want to be encouraged by yours. In this way, each of us will be a blessing to the other" (Rom. 1:11–12 NLT).

What is the gospel?
- The power of God for salvation (Rom. 1:16). "It may well be said that, in Paul's view, Jesus Christ is the gospel."[13] The gospel contains the power to become a Christian and is the source of grace/power needed to live the Christian life.

Questions adapted from Discipling by Grace *by World Harvest Mission.*
Used by permission.[14]

instead as spiritual orphans, constantly trying to earn God's love and establish our worthiness.

For years, when I read passages like Romans 1:15—"I am so eager to preach the gospel also to you who are at Rome" (NIV)—I assumed it meant that Paul wanted to come and hold an evangelistic campaign in conjunction with the church in Rome. Indeed, he was an evangelist, but he also had a deep burden that those who were already believers should hear and live by the gospel. He goes on to say that the gospel "is the power of God for salvation to everyone who has faith" (1:16). Salvation describes the complete process of redemption (from turning to Christ through our sanctification and eventual glorification). The gospel contains the power to become a Christian and is the source of grace needed to live the Christian life.

It is clear from the book of Acts and his letters that Paul was committed to the ministry of the gospel in his work. An essential part of spiritual formation is guarding the gospel from the idols and false gospels that are constantly present in our culture and in all of our lives. What was true for Paul, "You are so quickly deserting the one who called you by the grace of Christ and are turning to a different gospel—which is really no gospel at all" (Gal. 1:6–7 NIV), is also true for us: the gospel is under attack.

True spiritual formation will always carry out a twofold task in relation to the gospel. One is the preaching and teaching of the gospel to promote a depth of understanding, greater trust, and spiritual cleansing and healing. This is the mission of actively presenting the gospel so that people can engage it and use it in their lives. Paul describes the effects of this ministry when he says that as the gospel "is bearing fruit and growing in the whole world, so it has been bearing fruit among yourselves from the day you heard it and truly comprehended the grace of God" (Col. 1:6). The language shows that we do not simply learn the gospel when we are converted and then move on from there. For Paul, the gospel continually works in us as we understand more and more of its truth and respond to it. The gospel is at work as we seek to live out its teaching on speaking the truth, turning away from lust, diminishing racially biased judgment, and focusing assessment on character and competence. The gospel calls us to discipleship and contains the power to enable us to follow Christ.

The complementary action to proclaiming the gospel is that of confronting the false gospels and idols, which are always present in our lives. In Galatians we see an example of this. Peter and the apostles had insisted that Gentile believers adopt Jewish cultural forms in order to be "real" Christians, thus maintaining their attitudes of racial superiority. As a result, evangelism, worship, and fellowship suffered. Paul confronted Peter and the apostles about it, calling them to repentance. But when Paul rebuked Peter, he did not say, "Your attitude of racial superiority is immoral" (though it was). Rather, he said, "They were not acting consistently with the truth of the gospel" (Gal. 2:14). The gospel was not growing and bearing fruit in the church because in this area they had not understood God's grace in all its truth. The gospel of grace should end the self-justifying behavior of cultural pride, a form of works righteousness in which the human heart seeks to use cultural differences as measurements of personal worth. Paul applied the gospel, and the result was a renewal, a great leap forward for the church.

In much of the popular writing on spiritual formation there is a tendency to convey a very stunted view of the gospel. We get the idea that what unbelievers need is the gospel, and then, once they accept Christ as Savior, they move on to "needing discipleship," which consists of learning about Christ, developing the fruit of the Spirit, learning how to have a quiet time, and so forth. However, the picture that the New Testament gives is remarkably different. We must remember the description of the gospel as the power of God for the beginning, middle, and end of salvation. Often we do not really understand all the vast implications and applications of the gospel. Only as we apply the gospel more and more deeply and radically—only as we think out all its truth—does it bear fruit and grow. The key to continual and deeper spiritual renewal and revival is the persistent rediscovery of the gospel. *All our spiritual problems come from a failure to apply the gospel*. This is true for us both as a community and as individuals.

The primary motivation behind formation involves understanding the gospel and seeing its fruit grow in our lives. Spiritual formation is a result of the gospel ministry because the way a non-Christian becomes a Christian and the way we grow as Christians are actually the same—believing the gospel more and more. In our culture of self-improvement, which has turned spirituality into a narcissistic pursuit, it seems vital that we do not see spiritual formation as just another route to personal empowerment. Spiritual formation is first and foremost about the gospel. As Peter reminds us, we are to "grow in the grace and knowledge" of the gospel (2 Pet. 3:18), not sit passively in it or take it for granted. Let the power of the gospel transform God's church and his people.

Spiritual Formation Happens

I am encouraged by George Gallup's survey research that finds a sizable group of persons in the United States who have been so transformed by the gospel that others can notice their constructive behavior. He observes that these "highly spiritually committed" people—in addition to the spiritual practices of prayer, forgiveness, and Scripture reading—exhibit laudable social virtues. "These people are much more concerned about the betterment of society. They're more tolerant of other people. They are more involved in charitable activities. And they're far, far happier than the rest."[15] Imagine the benefits to a society and to the witness of the reality of God's kingdom if these numbers were increased. Since I first read Gallup's observation some fifteen years ago, I have been engaged in a quiet "saint hunt." I am looking for people whose spiritual practices and gospel virtues are patently evident. Part of my purpose in writing this book was to report patterns of formation I have observed in what often appeared to be haphazard and messy, real-life spiritual development. I have asked, "What consistent circumstances, patterns of communal nurture, and experiences helped produce many of these genuine, godly folk I have met?" I have sought to learn what contributed to the transformations of the people who have grown in grace.

Meanwhile, I have also witnessed a disquieting trend. So many initiatives aimed at spiritual formation seem to have lost their bearings and have settled for secondary goals. We've learned a new terminology while maintaining the old lack of healthy spirituality. Sadly, many of these spiritual formation programs seem like third-rate manufacturers that crank out mediocre products and never seem to catch on that their manufacturing processes are finely tuned to consistently produce shoddy goods. Yet one must conclude that the program is perfectly designed to bring the disappointing results it consistently gets. As Dallas Willard reminds us, "Your system is perfectly designed to produce the results you are getting."[16]

In summary, real spiritual formation is taking place all around us. Yet most of our Christian peers are not being deeply changed by the gospel in ways that result in Jesus' promised lifestyle of peace, service, and spiritual authority. Our culture and, sadly, many churches seek to squeeze us into the mold of merely being nice and seeking a sensible consumer-oriented faith that meets our needs and avoids offending anyone else.

God and Formation

The practices of faith are not ultimately our own practices but rather habitations of the Spirit, in the midst of which we are invited to participate in the practices of God.[17]

Craig Dykstra

The Bible opens with a description of God's formative work in creation: "In the beginning when God created the heavens and the earth" (Gen. 1:1). And creation, we read, involved a formation process. God created the stuff of the universe, but "the earth was empty, a formless mass" (1:2 NLT). And God was at work forming his creation. The image of God personally forming humankind furthers this picture: "The LORD God formed a man's body from the dust of the ground" (2:7 NLT). The personal creative activity of forming humankind established a bond between God and the first human, Adam. God deepened the bond by preparing a garden, where "he put the man whom he had formed" (2:8). God also "formed every animal of the field and every bird of the air" (2:19). The creation—personally fashioned, crafted, and formed by God—pleased the Artist/Creator. "God saw everything that he had made, and indeed, it was very good" (1:31).

The contrast between the formless primordial cosmos (1:2) and the harmony of the properly formed creative order (1:1–2:25) is an implicit reference point throughout Scripture. God established precedence for formation. Where other religions view good and evil as eternal constants, Scripture presents God as eternal, in contrast to sin, which is a parasitic and temporary condition bent on unraveling and destroying creation.

I have found the term *spiritual entropy* helpful to describe the tendency toward spiritual decay, disunity, and dysfunction that is present in our world. God's love/grace acts powerfully against the entropy in the world.[18]

Love/grace is the powerful force that works against entropy, the basic negative spiritual force in our world. We see how it works in a friendship. Unattended, a friendship will dissolve, but when all parties invest in a friendship through time, trust, and care, it will flourish. We keep a marriage healthy and growing by investing time and energy in it.

God's formative process continues on throughout history. With the entrance of sin into the world, God's formative work took on a redemptive cast as well. In contrast to the formative work of God, chaos/entropy characterizes the rebellion against his rule. Paul later anchors his rebuke of the Corinthians for their disorderly worship by an appeal to God's character: "God is not a God of confusion but of peace" (1 Cor. 14:33 NASB). Chaos marks "any society, culture or institution that divorces itself from the one 'who holds all things together' (Col. 1:17). The connection between spiritual bankruptcy and the decay of the moral/spiritual order is a recurring prophetic theme."[19] The biblical worldview recognizes an ever-present spiritual entropy at work in the fallen world, which requires God's intervention and formative activity. We do not accomplish spiritual formation simply by setting up programs and writing policies. There is nothing "once for all" about formation. It is ceaseless because entropy, sin, the flesh, and our idols never rest in their battle against the human soul and God's kingdom claims on it.

The difficulty of the divine work of formation is illustrated in the events of the exodus. While Moses is on the mountain meeting with God, we read that his brother Aaron "took the gold from them, formed it in a mold, and cast an image of a calf" (Exod. 32:4). The event represents a sad but constant reality in Scripture. God's invitation is to shalom, to peace, to wholeness, but instead of accepting his transformative formation, humans choose to form idols that meet our pressing needs. A theme running through the whole biblical narrative is the constant human rejection of God and ambivalence toward his grace-filled invitation for humanity to be formed (actually transformed) from our brokenness into his beloved children. Humans generally elect the expedient route of forming idols, whether actual or conceptual, instead of submitting to God's gracious formation.

All of our work in spiritual formation must be set against the backdrop of the God who forms us in love. Spiritual formation is part of God's on-going work of creation. God actively sustains the physical world through Christ: "In him all things hold together" (Col. 1:17); Christ "sustains all things by his powerful word" (Heb. 1:3). Thus God's love gives the world the only order we know. As we think about spiritual formation, we must remember that all positive formation in the world has its origin in God's love for humanity. Christian spiritual formation has a specific goal and unique means provided by the cross and the incarnation, but it shares, with all positive formation, the power of love overcoming spiritual entropy/decay. "Let us love one another, for love comes from God" (1 John 4:7).

Formation Is Universal

All persons are being shaped spiritually: their heart or spirit (the core of their being) is undergoing formation. Dallas Willard describes the universal nature of formation as "a process that happens to everyone. The most despicable as well as the most admired of persons have a spiritual formation. Terrorists as well as saints are the outcome of spiritual formation. Their spirits or hearts have been formed."[20] The formation may be in either a positive or negative direction. It may involve the cultivation of virtues that promote social harmony and care or may leave persons wary, self-protective, and unable to promote the welfare of society.

Christians have frequently concluded that since the presence of social virtues does not necessarily indicate a sustaining faith in God, their cultivation is of little spiritual value. This belief has contributed a sad chapter to our social witness and downplayed some important strategies for personal growth. All persons of good will, Christian and non-Christian, should celebrate the presence of virtues that promote a society of shalom and justice. I recall a conversation I had with a missionary couple who were distressed by fellow Christians who made an effort to recycle household waste. To them, it seemed to be a pointless activity because it had no direct salvific benefit and promoted the idea that we could improve society apart from God; they thought that such labor was being "wasted in nonkingdom work." While they represent a small minority, this couple illustrates a tendency to bifurcate formation into that which is radically Christian and beneficial and that which is ordinary and of little importance. Such orientation comes very close to Gnosticism.

We need to see that all true formation has it origins in God, who through Christ is reconciling the world to himself (2 Cor. 5:18–20). We must be very sober about the power of sin, but we need to see Christ, who "sustains the universe by the mighty power of his command" (Heb. 1:3 NLT), as being behind growth in virtue, in love, and in justice. This has a very practical implication. It means that Christians may avail themselves of avenues of change that promote the presence of gospel virtues. Our change does not come in two forms: good Christian church-based change and ordinary change. All true formation has its origin in God, and we must humbly receive it as a gift. I have seen well-meaning Christians reject programs designed to help develop life skills simply because they were "not Christian." We must be discerning, but much of what contributes to our positive spiritual formation may be ordinary activities that, when humbly received from God, are used to weave the wonderful tapestry of our formation.

For Further Reading

Boa, Kenneth. *Conformed to His Image: Biblical and Practical Approaches to Spiritual Formation*. Grand Rapids: Zondervan, 2001. A thorough survey of twelve key dimensions of spiritual formation.

Dykstra, Craig R. *Growing in the Life of Faith: Education and Christian Practices*. 2nd ed. Louisville: Westminster John Knox, 2005. A comprehensive treatment of community spiritual formation.

Lawrence, Brother. *The Practice of the Presence of God; and, the Spiritual Maxims*. Mineola, NY: Dover Publications, 2005. A brief classic presentation on keeping the presence of God in mind and heart.

Palmer, Parker J. *Let Your Life Speak: Listening for the Voice of Vocation*. San Francisco: Jossey-Bass, 2000. A reminder that we are most authentic when we understand and honor our sense of self and calling.

Smith, Gordon. *Beginning Well: Christian Conversion and Authentic Transformation*. Downers Grove, IL: InterVarsity, 2001. He contends that the presence of spiritual immaturity in the evangelical church can be attributed to an inadequate theology of conversion.

Taylor, Jeremy, and Thomas K. Carroll. *Selected Works*. Classics of Western Spirituality. New York: Paulist Press, 1990. A masterpiece on how to live well and die well.

Thompson, Marjorie J. *Soul Feast: An Invitation to the Christian Spiritual Life*. Louisville: Westminster John Knox, 2005. A rich exploration of spiritual disciplines applicable to lay groups seeking spiritual formation.

Willard, Dallas. *Renovation of the Heart: Putting on the Character of Christ*. Colorado Springs: NavPress, 2002. An accessible and comprehensive call for spiritual formation as a way of becoming more like Christ.

2

Curriculum for Christlikeness

Be imitators of me, as I am of Christ.

1 Corinthians 11:1

Therefore be imitators of God, as beloved children.

Ephesians 5:1

Let the same mind be in you that was in Christ Jesus.

Philippians 2:5

When I first looked over my notes of the faithful people whose stories I have heard, I was tempted to say that spiritual formation simply comes from responding well to pain, suffering, loss, and prejudice. That would be an overstatement, but we need to understand the environment in which spiritual formation takes place. Spiritual formation does not take place primarily in small groups and Sunday school classes; instead, it mostly takes place in the well-lived and everyday events of life. Our small groups, retreats, and studies should help us respond wisely to the events of life that form us. In this chapter we will look at a curriculum for Christlikeness. While Jesus was a teacher, he did not teach in a school or publish a formal curriculum. Jesus was a great and captivating teacher who understood that the teaching is worked out not in the classroom but in everyday life.

We must accept the circumstances we constantly find ourselves in as the place of God's kingdom and blessing. God has yet to bless anyone except where they actually are, and if we faithlessly discard situation after situation, moment after moment, as not being "right," we will simply have no place to receive his kingdom into our life, for those situations and moments ARE our life.[1]

At the end of Matthew's Gospel, Jesus gave a final charge to his disciples in what we know as the Great Commission. In his charge, he called his people to the tasks of outreach, discipleship, and education/formation. He told his followers that one of the necessary elements in their formation is to "teach these new disciples to obey all the commands I have given you" (28:20 NLT). The heart of spiritual formation is to teach and train people to follow the wisdom and instructions of Christ through the enabling power of his grace. In fact, "imitation of Christ is both a fundamental means and the glorious end of Christian formation."[2] When we speak of imitation in formation, it is, as Dallas Willard has taught us, more akin to serving an apprenticeship with Jesus than merely mimicking selected actions of his.[3]

Jesus Grew through the Disciplines

Holiness is not a condition into which we drift.[4]

John Stott

We must teach the commands of Christ as "a package deal." These are not mere laws to follow; Jesus invites us to take on his easy yoke: "Take my yoke upon you. Let me teach you, because I am humble and gentle, and you will find rest for your souls. For my yoke fits perfectly, and the burden I give you is light" (Matt. 11:29–30 NLT). These commands are two-sided and contain both the command and the means of change. Spiritual disciplines are Jesus-endorsed spiritual practices (e.g., solitude, fasting, and meditation) that foster positive spiritual change and enable us to become the kind of people who genuinely desire to carry out these commands. When we understand the two-sided nature of Jesus' commands, we no longer view them as heavy burdens but see them as an invitation to a more sensible way of living. Often we pull apart the commands of Jesus from the enabling patterns—the spiritual disciplines, which allow us to do what we could never do through willpower alone.

When I was in college, I experienced such teaching. The commands of Christ and the enabling practices were turned into soul-killing laws. A friend of mine who walked away from the faith during this time told me in effect, "I feel plenty guilty from all my parents' shoulds and shouldn'ts; I don't need a whole boatload more from Jesus."

Jesus is not Moses. Jesus does not just say "You're sick," but he also offers the only efficacious treatment, since he is the great physician of our souls (Matt. 9:12). We follow a doctor's advice because we are convinced that it will bring about positive results, and we follow Jesus' advice because we are convinced that he is the smartest man who ever lived and that his words bring life. Therefore, his way of living is not a burden, but the way of joy and satisfaction. A command given without the means for fulfilling it is just a law, but Jesus has given us commands and the means (grace given through a pattern of living) that will change us. The changes enable us to obey his commands more and more and also conform to the deepest longings of our hearts. Christ provides access *into* a relationship with him, transforms us *through* that relationship, and then affects a still greater union *in* that relationship.

We also need to realize that Jesus is setting forth a way of life for living in God's kingdom. If we want to live under the reign of popular culture, these commands most assuredly will seem odd and irksome. Homer Simpson summed up this outlook when speaking of his religion: "You know, the one with all the well-meaning rules that don't work in real life."[5]

Concrete and specific acts of devotion filled Jesus' devotional life. The devotional acts of Jesus were rich and diverse, consisting of private acts (solitude, prayer retreats), small group practices (pilgrimage, fellowship, teaching, sacraments, worship), and large group meetings (teaching, synagogue worship, healing). He did not simply keep an abstract communion with God but rather carried out his communion through tangible acts of piety and intimacy, which included a constant listening and speaking to the Father. Jesus broke with Jewish tradition and prayed to God as Father on all but one occasion: the agonizing cry of abandonment on the cross (Mark 15:34). He demonstrated that we must see religion not as magic or ritual but as relationship. Just as human relationships are marked by well-developed patterns of interacting, so also our relating to God should be marked by rich, diverse, and consistent patterns.

In the four Gospels one can find over one hundred acts of devotion carried out by Jesus.[6] Some were done in private, others with his disciples, and still others were carried out in public settings. While these acts are in the background in many stories, the Gospels certainly show Jesus as a person deeply concerned with developing his spiritual life through tangible acts of devotion.

We can infer from his use of Scripture that Jesus was a man of meditation and study. The following three passages from Luke provide direct evidence of his prayer life and his practices of solitude and fasting: (1) "He was praying in a certain place, and after he had finished, one of his disciples said to him, 'Lord, teach us to pray, as John taught his disciples'" (11:1). (2) "He would withdraw to deserted places and pray" (5:16). (3) "In the wilderness . . . for forty days he was tempted by the devil. He ate nothing at all during those days, and when they were over, he was famished. . . . Then Jesus, filled with the power of the Spirit, returned to Galilee, and a report about him spread through all the surrounding country" (4:1–2, 14). He adopted an overall lifestyle of personal and corporate communion with his Father.

Many observe Jesus' patterns of devotion and believe they flow out of his divine nature. In other words, the divine part of him naturally sought out God, and the human part just came along for the ride. So here is the really crucial question: Did Jesus' lifestyle of devotion result in his personal holiness and spiritual power? Or were these simply the fruit of his unique divine-human nature?

If we take Jesus' humanity seriously, we are compelled to say that his acts of devotion contributed to the presence of the spiritual power, love, and insight that marked his ministry. It is vital that we affirm that Jesus' spiritual practices were not mere window dressing but had an effect on him and on his world. The Letter to the Hebrews makes this point with exceptional clarity: "In the days of his flesh, Jesus offered up prayers and supplications, with loud cries and tears, to the one who was able to save him from death, and he was heard because of his reverent submission. Although he was a Son, he learned obedience through what he suffered" (5:7–8). Jesus' prayers were heard because of his submission, something learned through acts of humility and devotion. "Ontologically, Jesus' relationship with God the Father is, of course, absolutely unique, but experientially we are invited into the same intimacy with Father God that he knew while here in the flesh. We are encouraged to crawl into the Father's lap and receive his love and comfort and healing and strength."[7]

We can learn about Jesus' spiritual development through personal disciplines and corporate formation from the story of Samuel. This story provides a striking picture of God's sovereign care and the process of spiritual formation. The story begins with a childless wife who pours her heart out to God and is given a child; she takes this special child to the tabernacle as a toddler and gives him for the Lord's service. The tabernacle turns out to be as nurturing as a street-gang hideout, but the Lord literally calls Samuel to himself, and in the midst of hypocrisy and crass religious charlatanism, the boy grows into a righteous man. Scripture succinctly summarizes his development during this time: "Now the boy Samuel continued to grow both in stature and in favor with the LORD and with the people" (1 Sam. 2:26).

Samuel serves as a foil for the priest's two sons, Hophni and Phinehas, who are the very embodiment of narcissism. They steal from the religious pilgrims, seduce women who come to the tabernacle, fail to carry out the religious duties for which they are paid, and treat the Lord with public contempt. Samuel, on the other hand, is open to the Lord and lives in this degrading place "in the presence of the LORD" (2:21). The account gives every impression that the Lord has graciously reached out to Samuel and that Samuel has actively sought the Lord's favor. We leave the story marveling at what the Lord has done in calling, nurturing, and protecting the boy, and at the quality of Samuel's response.

The words written of Samuel, that he "continued to grow in stature and in favor with the LORD and with men" (2:26 NIV), are echoed in Luke's reporting that Jesus "grew in wisdom and stature, and in favor with God and men" (Luke 2:52 NIV). In that passage, Luke has just described Jesus' appearance in the temple at age twelve, when he amazed the teachers with his insight and then returned home with his parents and lived in obedience to them. At this point, Luke has pulled back the veil covering these hidden early years to tell us of the remarkable youth of Jesus and demonstrate that his growth as the Messiah took time and discipline. Eugene Peterson captures this developmental note quite well when he renders this verse: "And Jesus matured, growing up in both body and spirit, blessed by both God and people" (Luke 2:52 Message).

When we take seriously the two natures (divine and human) found in the incarnation, this verse makes perfect sense. Jesus lives a life of thoroughgoing love and service that is perfectly in tune with the wishes of the Father, not simply because the divine has taken over the human, but because through discipline the human has grown in wisdom and grace. We must not make this verse carry too much weight, yet it does echo the language of 1 Samuel 2:26, Proverbs 3:4, and Luke 1:80, which assume human development. Jesus serves as a model because, while vastly different from us, his moral and spiritual life developed through processes that are available to all. A robust view of the incarnation should have no difficulty with affirming the absolute uniqueness of Jesus and that his spiritual and moral growth came through the ordinary means of grace.

The crucial point is that Jesus grew through means that are available to us and which he has given to us as the ordinary way of growing up into the fullness of his love and grace. In saying this we do not denigrate his unique divine nature, nor do we presume that we can literally live with the same power and love as Christ, but we can truly become Christians—that is, little Christs. Orthodox writers have well articulated the radical nature of human transformation through our union with Christ.

The incarnation equally is a doctrine of sharing or participation. Christ shares to the full in what we are, and so he makes it possible for us to share in what he is, in his divine life and glory. He became what we are, so to make us what he is.[8]

What Does "Imitation" Mean?

When we suggest that the way to spiritual transformation lies in following Jesus, some no doubt will point to the impossibility of doing this. They may suggest that we know too little about his private life to be able to copy it. Others will point out that in history we can find persons who claimed, with what seems to be complete sincerity, that they were following Jesus when all the while their lives fell short of Jesus' ethical teachings. Still others will point out that all attempts to follow Jesus are necessarily conditioned by our time and place and thus so provincial that it would be unwise to speak of actually following him. In other words, a future generation may judge any attempt to follow Jesus as quite naive and blind to the actual realities of the social situation. Many even claim that following Jesus simply is not possible this side of the Enlightenment.

In contrast to this skepticism, we must pattern our lives after Jesus and recognize that our perception of his example and our faithfulness in following it will be limited. The difficulty of following him is no argument against the wisdom of this path. Of course, we will do it badly because of sin within us, the sin and the blindness brought about by the age in which we live. The fact that we will inevitably follow Jesus in a way that history may judge as provincial does not remove us from the obligation of patterning our lives after his. With due humility, we can pattern our lives closely enough to his to receive transforming grace, grow in holiness, and be a witness to the transforming power of God's grace.

The imitation of Christ is a means of addressing some of the most basic struggles we face as humans. What does it mean concretely to follow Jesus? Two of the great dangers in setting out to imitate Jesus are: (1) We might fail to see it as a privilege and a means of grace. Remember the joy felt in imitating a loved parent or a mentor? Such should be our feeling in setting out to "do as Jesus did." (2) We might reduce imitation to a limited set of actions. At times, Christians have reduced imitation to receiving the sacraments, pacifism, social action, prayer, doctrinal correctness, separation from the dominant culture, and participating in certain emotive religious experiences. Imitating Jesus' practices of spiritual growth will include the classical spiritual disciplines but must take us far beyond them as well.

Goals within a Curriculum for Christlikeness

To correctly form a curriculum for Christlikeness, we must have a very clear and simple perception of the primary goals it must achieve, as well as what is to be avoided.

Two objectives in particular that are often taken as *primary* goals must not be left in that position. They can be reintroduced later in proper subordination to the true ones. These are *external conformity* to the wording of Jesus' teachings about actions in specific contexts and *profession of perfectly correct doctrine*. Historically these are the very things that have obsessed the church visible—currently the latter far more than the former.

We need wait no longer. The results are in. They do not provide a course of personal growth and development that routinely produces people who "hear and do." They either crush the human mind and soul and separate people from Jesus, or they produce hide-bound legalists and theological experts with "lips close to God and hearts far away from him" (Isa. 29:13). The world hardly needs more of these.

Much the same can be said of the strategies—rarely taken as primary objectives, to be sure, but much used—of encouraging faithfulness to the activities of the church or other outwardly religious routines and various "spiritualities," or the seeking out of special states of mind or ecstatic experiences. These are good things. But let it be said once and for all that, like outward conformity and doctrinally perfect profession, they are not to be taken as major objectives in an adequate curriculum for Christlikeness.

From The Divine Conspiracy *by Dallas Willard.*[9]

Some writers put up resistance to the use of "imitation of Christ" language because they think that this has often led to a human-centered view of sanctification. True imitation respects the tension between the reality that the Holy Spirit ultimately brings about our imitation through conforming us to Christ's likeness and the reality that we must work hard and carefully at imitating Christ by adopting his lifestyle and patterns of life.[10]

In the list of Jesus' commands given below, I have chosen to speak of Jesus inviting us to do certain things. I do not intend to soften the language of command, but rather to recognize that Jesus is inviting us to a certain way of living. He is not content to simply order us to do such and such; he wants "us" far more than our action. He wants all of us.

The listing of Jesus' many invitations may seem long, tiresome, and extensive, since they touch all areas of life. Jesus intends that the disciplines work as a package and impact all of life. They put me in a place of wanting them and engaging in them. When I have accepted the invitation to the place of prayer, worship, study, acts of compassion, integrity, and keeping commitments, I am more open to the work of the Holy Spirit and more open to change. Therefore, the practices contained in disciplining invitations put me in a place that can impact and change the loves and core attitudes of my heart. The practiced invitations of Jesus are a spiritual thoroughfare to God's grace and power and, thereby, a way to expand my love, obedience, and repentance, clarifying my beliefs and deepening my trust in God.

COMMUNITY SPIRITUAL FORMATION COROLLARY 4

Christian spiritual formation seeks to foster a joyful apprenticeship in which we learn to live out the great invitations of Jesus, especially those concerning the life of prayer and love.

We do well to see the invitations of Jesus in the context of the two great commands he gave to love God and neighbor. The focus on loving God and neighbor is the spiritual North Star we follow in seeking to understand Jesus' teaching. The sixteen invitations of Jesus that follow the two great commands come as applications of the call to the twofold love of God and neighbor. At the heart of the "Love God" invitation, we must not simply hear "try harder and harder." Marguerite Shuster has cautioned that "exactly insofar as we get captured by the mystique of imitating Christ and neglect the unglamorous tasks of trusting him and obeying him in the most ordinary moments of our everyday lives, we have forgotten who he is and who we are."[11] We need to hear "Love the loveable Father," "Love the Lover of our soul," and "Receive his embrace," and out of that safe place, as secure spiritual children, we seek to live out these invitations—not to earn love and affection, but to grow in the likeness of one we admire and want to be like.

The Great Invitations of Christ

The Christian stands, not under the dictatorship of a legalistic "You ought," but in the magnetic field of Christian freedom, under the empowering of the "You may."[12]

Helmut Thielicke

The commands of Christ contain words that convict us and expose our self-centered and self-protective strategies of self-improvement (e.g., forgive your enemies) and words that point us to the grace that enables us to do what we could never have done on our own (e.g., the call to pray for our enemies, which in turn enables us to forgive and love them). A number of years ago while reading Scripture, I was struck with my need to forgive someone. It was a spiritual turning point for me; for the first time in my life, I clearly saw the command of Christ—"Forgive!"—and my own inability and unwillingness to carry it out. My perception of the magnitude of the wrong done (now in retrospect I am amazed at how small the injury really was) and the person's lack of remorse made it seem impossible for me to extend forgiveness. In that place of brokenness, where I could see and feel my inability to do what I should do, I did what I could do: I committed myself to pray for the person and the situation. The dedicated prayer led, over a period of time, to my ability to release the person from my anger and thirst for revenge—to experience the freedom of forgiveness.

The Two Great Invitations of Jesus

Jesus invites us to love and obey God.

> "You shall love the Lord your God with all your heart, and with all your soul, and with all your mind." This is the great and foremost commandment. The second is like it, "You shall love your neighbor as yourself." On these two commandments depend the whole Law and the Prophets. (Matt. 22:37–40 NASB)

Jesus invites us to love one another.

> In everything do to others as you would have them do to you; for this is the law and the prophets. (Matt. 7:12)

> A new commandment I give to you, that you love one another, even as I have loved you, that you also love one another. By this all men will know that you are My disciples, if you have love for one another. (John 13:34–35 NASB)

Invitations Flowing out of the Call to Love God and Neighbor

Invitations to steward the gospel

- *Jesus invites us to tell people about the good news and make disciples.*
  Make disciples—Matt. 28:20
  Baptize my new disciples—Matt. 28:19

Feed my sheep—John 21:15–16
Let your light shine—Matt. 5:16

- *Jesus invites us to practice discernment.*
  Beware of false prophets—Matt. 7:15
  Be wise as serpents—Matt. 10:16
  Beware of false teachings—Matt. 16:6, 12
  Beware of covetousness—Luke 12:15
  Do not cast pearls—Matt. 7:6

- *Jesus invites us to a life of integrity.*
  Do unto others—Matt. 7:12
  Keep your word—Matt. 5:37
  Avoid hypocrisy—Matt. 7:5

- *Jesus invites us to use our money wisely.*
  Lay up treasures—Matt. 6:19–21
  Do not serve two masters—Matt. 6:24
  Give sacrificially—Luke 21:2–4

- *Jesus invites us to practice detachment.*
  Deemphasize the material—Matt. 8:20
  Do not worry—Matt. 6:25; Luke 12:22
  Do not store up earthly treasures—Matt. 6:19; Luke 12:17–21
  Let your heart be set on heavenly treasures—Matt. 6:21

Invitations to extend his compassion

- *Jesus invites us to pray for and bless others.*
  Hear God's voice—Matt. 11:15
  Pray for laborers—Matt. 9:38
  Watch and pray—Matt. 26:41
  Let the temple be a house of prayer—Matt. 21:13
  Ask in faith—Matt. 21:21–22
  Commend faith in others—Matt. 16:17; John 20:29
  Bless children—Mark 10:16
  Pray for enemies—Matt. 5:44

- *Jesus invites us to keep relational commitments.*
  Do not commit adultery—Matt. 5:29–30

Honor your parents—Matt. 15:4
Honor marriage—Matt. 19:6

- *Jesus invites us to a life of compassion for the poor and marginalized and to the elimination of prejudice.*
  Bring in the poor—Luke 14:12–14
  Sell all and give to the poor—Mark 10:21
  Judge not—Matt. 7:1

- *Jesus invites us to weep.*
  Weep with the grieving—John 11:35
  Mourn with those who need comfort—Matt. 5:4

- *Jesus invites us to handle conflicts well and forgive one another.*
  Develop a stance of forgiving—Matt. 18:21–22
  Forgive others and secure relationship with God—Mark 11:25
  Set aside a lifestyle of judgment—Luke 6:37

- *Jesus invites us to extend hospitality.*
  Invite poor, crippled, lame—Luke 14:13
  Invite strangers—Matt. 25:35
  Give a cup of cold water—Mark 9:41

Invitations to worship

- *Jesus invites us to worship and to celebrate the sacraments.*
  Worship in spirit and truth—John 4:23–24
  Worship only God—Matt. 4:10
  Take, eat, and drink—Matt. 26:26–27

- *Jesus invites us to create a space for God through solitude.*
  Get away to pray—Luke 4:42
  Make solitude a habit—Luke 5:16
  Keep the Sabbath—Mark 2:27–28

- *Jesus invites us to use our bodies in prayer and worship.*
  Fast in secret—Matt. 6:16
  Lay hands on the sick and heal them—Matt. 8:3
  Anoint the sick—Mark 6:13
  Practice embodied prayer—Matt. 19:13; 26:39

Invitations to think rightly about God

- *Jesus invites us to depend more and more on God and his grace.*
  Attach to Jesus, the vine—John 15:1
  Let God cultivate you to do good—John 15:1, 5

- *Jesus invites us to the joy and freedom of practicing spiritual disciplines.*
  Take his yoke—Matt. 11:29
  Practice secret disciplines (fasting, prayer, giving)—Matt. 6:1–18

- *Jesus invites us to study and meditate on Scripture.*
  Answer temptations with Scripture—Matt. 4:1–10
  Abide in the Word—John 8:31–32
  Hear and act—Matt. 7:24–25

- *Jesus invites us to repentance and to draw close to God and himself.*
  Repent! A required course—Luke 13:3–5
  Repent on earth; bring celebration in heaven—Luke 15:7, 10
  Repent and welcome the kingdom—Matt. 4:17
  Be born again—John 3:7
  Invite Christ into our lives—Rev. 3:20

- *Jesus invites us to believe he is who he claims to be.*
  Believe and so receive eternal life—John 5:24
  Believe in Jesus, the resurrection and the life—John 11:25
  Have faith (trust) in God—Mark 11:22–24
  "Do not fear, only believe"—Mark 5:36

- *Jesus invites us to a life of learning.*
  Learn from me—Matt. 11:29
  Ask, seek, knock—Matt.7:7
  Learn from nature—Matt. 24:32
  Go and learn—Matt. 9:13

A Curriculum for Christlikeness

The fruit of a life *in Christ* is a life *like Christ*.[13]

Andrew Murray

Four Dimensions of Community Formation

Dimension	Description	Community Practices
Receiving	Cultivating spiritual openness and continual repentance	Confession, worship, sacraments, prayer
Remembering	Transformational teaching leading to a deep awareness of our being part of God's community and his beloved children	Teaching, preaching, evangelism, meditation, spiritual guidance, small groups
Responding	Our formation occurs for and through service	Discernment, honoring relational commitment, setting aside prejudices, ministries of compassion
Relating	Our formation takes place in and through community	Hospitality, handling conflict well, honoring relationships, Sabbath observance, attending to pace of life

Woven through the rest of the book, you will find a curriculum for teaching believers to follow Jesus, teaching them "to obey everything that I have commanded you" (Matt. 28:20). The term refers to a lifelong course of study designed to promote spiritual transformation, largely through the teaching of core Christian knowledge, service learning opportunities, training in key spiritual practices, and the continual re-presentation of essential spiritual truths (such as forgiveness, handling conflict, stewardship of time and money, authority in spiritual conflict), coupled with opportunities to be coached through specific applications of the gospel to personal issues. The curriculum, then, is not so much a linear sequence (though it must have some linearity to it) as a spiral, in which topics are re-presented and re-appropriated.

A curriculum must provide concrete guidance for our educational and formational work. I have identified four spiritual commitments, designated as the four pillars of formation; these serve as the framework for cultivating the practice of Jesus' great invitations. They are *receiving, remembering, responding,* and *relating.* These four basic commitments or dispositions summarize the dimensions I found at work in churches and communities of faith where true spiritual formation has taken place. The *receiving* dimension highlights our need to focus on Jesus and be open to his grace for spiritual formation. Christian spirituality's concern that we learn from Christ and receive God's enabling grace separates it from the cultural assumption that any spirituality will do as long as we follow it sincerely. *Remembering* describes the process of learning to remember, deep in our heart, who we are and, more important, whose we are. The next dimension, *responding*, reminds us that the enterprise of formational changes of character and action do not exist for our own private ends but to enable us to serve others and the world through love. Finally, *relating* affirms that spiritual formation takes place best in and through community.

The deep longing for Christlikeness is a longing for God himself and the primary motivator for deep spiritual transformation. Seeking Christlikeness is a lifelong endeavor that requires personal and corporate commitment to both active and passive stances.

Six Myths or False Models of Spiritual Formation

To correctly form a curriculum for Christlikeness, we must have a very clear and simple perception of the primary goals it must achieve, as well as what is to be avoided.[14]

Dallas Willard

Before we turn to looking at this curriculum for following Jesus, it is worth identifying some myths about spiritual growth that often derail the most sincere attempts at spiritual formation.[15] Often these are the result of emphasizing one truth at the expense of others. True spiritual formation, the curriculum for Christlikeness, will always be a rich, grace-filled, multidimensional proposition.

The Quick-Fix Model

I have talked with many people who have the idea that God's primary way, and desired way, of working in our lives is through the quick spiritual fix. They believe that if they are really in the place of growth, God will simply "zap them." This is a very pernicious teaching because it defeats people in the long-run obedience that so often is the path of spiritual growth. Implicit in the stories of the spiritual heroes of the Bible (Abraham, Jacob, David, and Peter) is a spiritual development in growth and wholeness that takes place over a lifetime. Moses was in formation for eighty years before he led Israel out of Egypt. One of the common metaphors for the Christian life in Scripture and for the spiritual writers through the centuries has been that of seeing the Christian life as a long journey.

The Facts-Only Model

This model leads people to believe that the most significant variable in determining whether a person grows or not is their intake of spiritual truth. I have heard this model explicitly taught from the pulpit, but more often it is something that is simply picked up, as people observe that the ministries in the church aimed to support change are all centered around teaching. Christians *must* feast upon truth, and yet that is only one discipline in an array of activities that Christians need to participate in to grow in the likeness of Christ. The image of feasting on truth connotes dining at a banquet with others, following rules of etiquette, eating what is served when it is served, and attending to interests of fellow banqueters, not gorging oneself alone and for one's own comfort.

We must integrate the intake of spiritual truth into all relationships; learned truth must impact one's relationships with both God and people. As Christians study Scripture, they will find multiple instructions to practice truth with one another in relationships. Scripture instructs us: "Submit to one another" (Eph. 5:21 NIV). "Be kind to one another, tenderhearted, forgiving one another" (4:32). "Bear with one another and, if anyone has a complaint against another, forgive each other" (Col. 3:13). "Be devoted to one another in brotherly love. Honor one another above yourselves" (Rom. 12:10 NIV). "Be completely humble and gentle; be patient, bearing with one another in love" (Eph. 4:2 NIV). "Love one another" (John 13:34). "Welcome one another" (Rom. 15:7). "Agree with one another" (1 Cor. 1:10 NIV). "Teach and admonish one another in all wisdom" (Col. 3:16). "Encourage one another and build each other up" (1 Thess. 5:11 NIV). This understanding of information and knowledge as being directly tied to experiences within relationships is what Carol Lakey Hess calls "a retrieval of Aristotle's concept of practical wisdom and its relationship to practice." Hess declares that "knowing is active, practical, and experiential if it is true knowing."[16]

The Emotional Model

This model tells us that we are changed most profoundly when we have deep emotional or spiritual experiences. I have personally seen the power and emotionality of true revival. We will certainly find that true spiritual growth will touch our emotions deeply. However, the emotional model goes so far as to suggest that change primarily comes when our emotions are deeply stirred. Another limitation of this model is that it places an emphasis on positive, feel-good emotions. Indeed, some Christians equate growth with an emotional state that is always positive and are overwhelmed when they find themselves experiencing, as the psalmists did, the darker emotions of loss, grief, and despair over sin. Others assume that it is profitable to be motivated by guilt or an obligating list of "shoulds." Nevertheless, suffering and pain are the needed catalysts for the brokenheartedness that opens us to leave behind our self-made

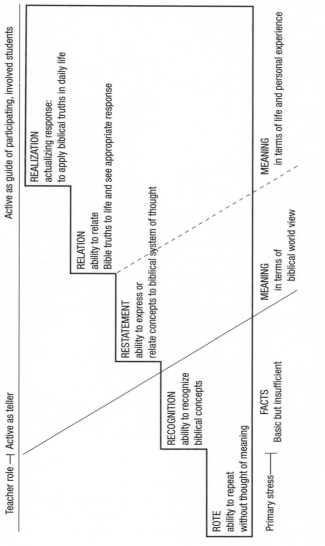

Figure 5. Learning levels

The Bible can be learned at any of these levels.

Creative teaching is teaching to constantly raise students' level of learning toward realization.

From *Creative Bible Teaching*, by Larry Richards. Used by permission.[17]

idols and seek God and his grace. To effect whole formation, the turning of repentance involves the emotions and the intellect, the heart and the mind, the whole person.

The Conference Model

Conferences and special spiritual assemblies can have a powerful effect on a spiritual life. There is a certain validation for teaching that we experience when we see hundreds and thousands of other people submitting to this teaching and hear the testimonies of others as we eat meals together and talk with speakers. However, mountaintop experiences at conferences or similar events might hide two potential problems. First, when they focus on the future, they might reinforce a perspective that what has been part of one's past is not critical or does not need to be redeemed. Second, individuals may be motivated to make resolutions that they are not mature enough to keep over the long term. Conferences are times of renewal or special training, but we must not see them as indispensable spiritual filling stations that become our primary source of nurture and guidance on the journey.

The Insight Model

Coming to see our patterns of sin and patterns of self-protection is so important in the spiritual life. However, insight and introspection are, again, one aspect of spiritual growth, and we can never reduce these to the essence of the spiritual life. When we give insight too much prominence, it often ends up supporting a diseased introspection, actually impeding our spiritual life rather than contributing to it. An outcome of a diseased introspection might include a preoccupation with our choices and their consequences. Then a person becomes focused on behavior choices and the law rather than on God's grace and his provision.

The Faith Model

In some circles this has been a popular model, which really says that all spiritual growth stems from surrender to God. Certainly, submission and growth in faith are important aspects of our ongoing relationship with God. However, through practicing a variety of spiritual disciplines, we often come to see areas where we need to surrender, issues we might never recognize if we simply focus exclusively on pondering areas where we lack faith. This model often is overly confident about our ability, while sitting in a protracted worship service, to identify the parts of our lives where we lack faith and trust. Additionally, when we have correctly identified areas where we lack faith, surrender does not mean that God does all the work; we have to do our part as well. Surrendering to God and working on our relationship with him in no way decreases our need to cultivate healthy human relationships. Surrender is vital, but it is usually a by-product of our faithfully living before God and seeking to carry out his great invitations. In the process of seeking to follow Christ, we become more aware of the things that we must give up.

These six myths seem so attractive because we make them fit right into our consumer view of religion. They are very appealing to those who think their growth is dependent simply on consuming the "right thing." The deep longing for Christlikeness is a longing for God himself and the primary motivator for deep spiritual transformation. Seeking Christlikeness is a lifelong endeavor that requires personal and corporate commitment to both active and passive stances. To explore a curriculum of Christlikeness in a more detailed fashion, the four dimensions of *receiving*, *remembering*, *responding*, and *relating* have been introduced here and will be developed carefully in the following chapters.

For Further Reading

De Sales, Francis. *Introduction to the Devout Life*. Vintage Spiritual Classics. New York: Vintage Books, 2002. Detailed late-sixteenth-century classic thesis on spiritual well-being for the ordinary life, both then and now.

Foster, Richard J. *Celebration of Discipline: The Path to Spiritual Growth*. rev. ed. San Francisco: Harper & Row, 1988. Contemporary spiritual classic provides an excellent introduction to the spiritual disciplines.

Law, William. *A Serious Call to a Devout and Holy Life; The Spirit of Love*. Edited by P. G. Stanwood. Classics of Western Spirituality. New York: Paulist Press, 1978. Written by a man of great piety and social concerns, this is a call to live entirely by the will of God.

Mulholland, M. Robert. *Invitation to a Journey: A Road Map for Spiritual Formation*. Downers Grove, IL: InterVarsity, 1993. Defines formation as "the process of being conformed to the image of Christ for the sake of others" and provides sensible guidance on personal formation.

Sande, Ken. *The Peacemaker: A Biblical Guide to Resolving Personal Conflict*. 3rd ed. Grand Rapids: Baker Books, 2004. A biblically grounded treatment of how to handle conflict in a Christ-honoring way.

Thomas à Kempis. *The Imitation of Christ*. Translated and edited by William Creasy. Notre Dame, IN: Ave Maria, 2004. An immensely popular book on imitating Christ; filled with remarkable wisdom about the human spirit.

Willard, Dallas. *The Divine Conspiracy: Rediscovering Our Hidden Life in God*. San Francisco: HarperSanFrancisco, 1998. An emphasis on learning from Jesus, with a dense and comprehensive treatment of life in the kingdom of God. The author writes, "The really good news for Christians is that Jesus is now taking students in the master class of life."

———. *The Spirit of the Disciplines: Understanding How God Changes Lives*. San Francisco: Harper & Row, 1988. A remarkable exploration of how the spiritual disciplines work in our spiritual transformation.

3

Foundations of Receiving

Formation by Grace for the Broken and Thirsty

What are we to receive?

> We are to imbibe the healing, vitalizing, sustaining, and strengthening grace of God that we need for sustaining and growing our spiritual lives and healing our souls.

How do we do this?

> By learning in community to feast on God's grace, by learning to listen and be open before God, and by having a vision for the changed life we are being called to.

What stance does this require?

> Openness/brokenness: a disciplined "showing up" to meet God and a commitment to the indirect path of spiritual training.

Most of us are blessed by experiences in which the love of God is made real for us. Our problem is that we are not paying attention, and therefore miss the blessing of discovering the intimate presence of God in our everyday lives.[1]

Howard L. Rice

The problem of humanity is that there is a structural brokenness that
pervades the whole of the human experience.[2]

J. Harold Ellens

Attending to our restlessness, of course, can be hard work, for it assumes
continuous growth and change.[3]

John H. Westerhoff III

Understanding our pervasive brokenness is at the heart of true community formation. Unless brokenness is a prominent orientation, we
will not catch the truth that "the church is not a museum for saints, but
a hospital for sinners." A basic premise in medical care is that you will
be honest in describing your symptoms to the examining physician; a
basic tenet in spiritual care is that honesty before God precedes healing.
American folk wisdom declares, "If it ain't broke, don't fix it." Unless
people see that they have a deep spiritual need that goes beyond a simple
trying-harder cure, there will be little interest in spiritual formation.
Creating a climate of formation requires that people use their brokenness (contrition over self-protective strategies, brokenness of heart, the
pain of letting yourself down) and their thirst (deep longings of their
soul so eloquently cataloged in the Psalms) to drive them to God in and
through his community. A culture of pretending and simply trying to
look good works against true formation.

Three lived perspectives are necessary for the kind of spiritual openness that promotes true receiving:

- A deep sense of our sin (both personal and corporate) and knowing
  what the cross says about our sin.
- An awareness of the reality of our yearnings and how the embrace
  of God helps us live with these.
- A deep-seated conviction that all growth comes from grace.

Depth of Our Sin

The Christian life is not a short sprint, but a long marathon. We cannot survive the drain and ordeals of such a long spiritual journey simply
by summoning our willpower to do what is right. To win the race, we
have to be motivated from the inside out so that we actually yearn to
keep on going and reach our home. Eagerness to do right is a far better
state, and a more satisfying one, than simply willing and forcing oneself
to do right. Furthermore, God is not satisfied with mere conformity. He

Sin or Sickness

For many Christians, being a sinner is little more than a demographic fact—like height, sex, race, or hair color. When sin is described as a disease or malady, rather than as a theological abstraction, people are more likely to understand. In a number of his writings, the psychologist J. Harold Ellens goes to some length to show the debilitating effects of sin:

> The metaphor of sickness contributes a dynamically constructive dimension to the notion of sin. It sets human disorder in the context of grace. It also holds up the seriousness of that disorder in a manner that cannot readily be rationalized into superficial notions of legalistic transgressions. Moreover, the metaphor of sickness invites a realistic remedy, a formula of cooperation with God who embraces us unconditionally. It moves toward the notion of redemptive growth and healing as a divinely ordered process for our lives in Christ. It frees us to see our redemptive possibilities, as we mature through instruction and guidance, and grow from the pain of acknowledging the inevitable consequences of our orphaned condition and sinful behavior.
>
> A superficial concept of sin is too optimistic about the human condition and too pessimistic about the redeeming intent and function of God's grace. God intends not merely judgment and forgiveness but the healing of our generic disease and craziness. He invites us to grow, not merely to shape up. The biblical concept of sickness can help us to appropriate these truths, making our concept of human sin and our understanding of God's grace more profoundly adequate to the healing of human failure.
>
> *Adapted from "Sin and Sickness" by J. Harold Ellens,*
> *in* Counseling and the Human Predicament.[4]

Ellens also suggests that when we view salvation simply in legal terms, we often miss the deeply healing and restorative dimensions of salvation. He contrasts two ways that people often think of salvation. One is judicial and true, as far as it goes. The other is more holistic and sees the end of salvation as not just "taking the punishment," but as wholeness as well.

Blame-Justification Equation

(anxiety/shame/guilt/blame) + (justice/penalty/punishment/expiation) = (justification/forgiveness/restoration/equilibrium)

Grace-Wholeness Equation

(pain, shame, guilt, anxiety) + (passion, compassion, mercy, grace) = (forgiveness and other restorative actions/affirmation/healing/realizing potential)

The second equation is far more holistic. In it redemption touches all aspects of life. Too often redemption is limited to a narrowly defined "religious dimension." The disease of sin touches all our being, and Christ's redemption and lordship likewise touch all of life.

Adapted from "Sin or Sickness" by J. Harold Ellens,
in Seeking Understanding. *Used by permission.*[5]

wants us to love him with all our heart, soul, mind, and strength (Mark 12:30). God is no more pleased with grudging obedience than a parent is with a child who is outwardly compliant but inwardly hostile.

Many unexpected events as well as developed thought patterns contribute to our growth in joyful obedience. This combination produces, for example, a proper view of sin. Spontaneous moments of depravity mix with a growing awareness of our capacity for wrongdoing. When we see the depth, persistence, and hideousness of our sin, there arise sharp concerns over the possibility of true transformation. Seeing our sin for what it is need not lead to despair; it can lead to spiritual liberation. When we perceive the true depth of our sin instead of merely being embarrassed over individual sins, we are prompted to seek the grace that can heal. On the other hand, when we respond to our sin problem by saying, "I'm all right," or "I'm really doing better; it's been a long time since I . . . ," or "What can I expect? I'm so messed up," we are not open to significant transformation. It is our sin, not just our individual sins, that must be dealt with. Within us is a contradictory cauldron of self-destructive, egocentric, self-protective, sensual, control-seeking lusts that breed the sins we hate. It is right to attack sin from the outside by ceasing our destructive behaviors, but it is far more important to work from the inside out (what Paul called our flesh; Gal. 5) to reduce the pull sin has on our life.

When we regret our sins of omission (good things left undone) as keenly as our sins of commission (bad things done), we have begun to understand sin. And when we, like Daniel in his great prayer (Dan. 9), acknowledge that we have participated in the sins of our nation and grieve over these wrongs, we have opened one of the windows to true inner transformation. Furthermore, it is often through our dealings with the unlovely that we catch a glimpse of the sin that pulls us into self-centered and hurtful acts.

Our view of sin has immense implications for spiritual formation. Our view of sin can exist at a variety of levels: there will be a community understanding reflected in the worship and preaching of the church, a personal theological position (i.e., what you would say if asked about sin), and the personal lived reality (i.e., how you act and feel about the sin in your own life and the world). Place yourself on the continuum below by indicating how you view sin. The left side of the continuum represents a view that places its emphasis primarily on observable "bad things." If you tend to think about sin in your life in terms of lists of bad things you do or have done, you fall more on the left side of the continuum. The right end of the continuum places its emphasis on sin as an outflow of a bent will and sin-sick heart. For example, you are as repulsed by the awareness that you are the kind of person who would seek to get ahead by lying as you are by the actual lie you told.

View of Sin

External (sins)   Internal orientation (sin)

Figure 6. Sin-sins continuum

Our Yearnings

> But there are many kinds of idols, and the most dangerous ones are not
> those we fashion with our hands, but those we unconsciously carry with
> us in our heads.[6]

André Louf

Our view of our yearnings also affects our spiritual life. Do we as a
people sense our longings as deep thirsts that only God can begin to satisfy? Or do we think these desires for holiness should have disappeared
for the Christian, or that we can take care of them by our own efforts?
Again, take a moment to place yourself on the continuum below. The
left side describes the sense that spiritual longings persist, even for the
maturing Christian (e.g., a longing for a world of justice, a desire to make
a meaningful contribution, a desire for intimacy and companionship).
The position denoted by the right side sees our thirsts as being fully met.
In general, this perspective is optimistic about grace overcoming our
inner disquiet. Here, the yearnings that persist are seen to be the result
of compromised discipleship.

View of Yearnings

Redirected and persisting   Fully met in Christ

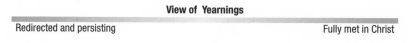

Figure 7. View of yearnings

We can take these two continua and form a matrix of four squares.
There are four basic combinations of responses to these questions about
sin and yearnings. The matrix then helps us visualize how our view of
sin and our yearnings affect our basic approach to discipleship. Communities of faith set their foundations through their teaching and faith
mentoring. It is a great gift when a community helps a believer live from
a position of optimistic brokenness.

Sin management. Here there is a focus on external sin and a perception that thirsts are met. Often a person in this category will be quick
to tell you what they have done wrong. The focus is on sins of commission (sins of action) rather than on sins of omission (sins of not doing).
There is a strong tendency to believe that one can overcome these sins
by just trying harder to stop doing them. There is also an embarrassment

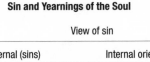

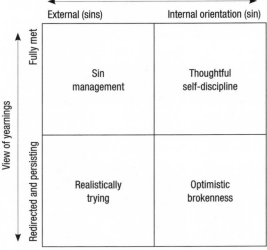

Figure 8. Sin and yearnings matrix

about the aches of the heart, a sense that they really should not be there. These aches seem to be evidence that a person is not living as faithfully as one should. The spiritual life in this quadrant is marked by striving and denial. The Pharisees were adept sin managers, highly skilled in denying glaring omissions and heaping rules on the backs of others in a strategy of painstaking prevention of sins.

Thoughtful self-discipline. In this quadrant sin is seen as heart orientation and thirsts are unacknowledged. These people have come to see the internal nature of their sin. They are not optimistic about just willing their sin away and recognize the need to change from the inside out. Often their sense of brokenness focuses on their sin and not as much on the yearnings from aches and disappointments of life. These people see the need to take their sin seriously and know that they have a problem they cannot fix on their own. They also are still optimistic that on this side of heaven their yearnings will vanish when their discipleship increases and the pervasive hold sin had on them decreases.

Realistically trying. Here there is an external sin focus and a deep sense that one's thirst persists. At some level these are people whose dreams have been shattered. They have come face-to-face with disappointments in life, and they realize that these are not an anomaly but that life is hard, potentially filled with joy, but nonetheless hard. At the same time the depth of their sin has not yet struck them. In this quadrant of brokenness, there is still a sense, as marked by the "great disappointment," of a moment when they see that they are climbing a ladder leaning against the wrong wall. Many spiritual writers tell of the "great disappointment" (terminology varies) that often occurs in adulthood when persons come to see reality of the tragic and brokenness in a new way. This often involves some level of awareness that our favorite projects are not all that we thought they were or we find that a relationship cannot bear all that we are demanding of it. This great disappointment can be a blessed brokenness in which we turn to God or become cynical and self-protective. Here we sense the presence of the tragic more than the presence of an idolatrous heart bent away from God. Cynicism often marks people in this quadrant.

Optimistic brokenness. The one who is here sees sin as a bent-heart condition. Thirsts persist, but their power is changed for the redeemed. This is the quadrant that is most open to true spiritual formation. The fields have been plowed and prepared in the hearts of these Christians. There is a willingness to see sin as a grievous problem that we cannot simply will away and to recognize that the tragic is present in life and that this side of heaven we will always feel ill at ease. The orientation here is optimistically labeled "broken" because there is a deep optimism about the power of grace to set things right. In biblical language, optimistic brokenness is hope. We can trace much of the spiritual success in the biblical psalms to this view. Psalm 51 offers a compelling model of painful self-disclosure before God combined with a relief and optimism that rise even as pride and self-protection diminish.

In the next sections we explore the nature of our thirsts and our brokenness. It is helpful to think of formation having two sides. One side is the formative work of teaching the Word, administering the sacraments, and using the gifts of the people of God in grace-saturated ministries. The other side is creating a receptive spirit on the part of the people. Without a receptive spirit, born through brokenness, there is no interest in formation.

COMMUNITY SPIRITUAL FORMATION COROLLARY 5

The fertile field for formation is a community genuinely aware of the depth of their sin and the reality of their spiritual thirst. True formation requires that the community deeply understands that they cannot cure the sickness of their souls through willpower alone.

Longing for Home

It was the Unicorn who summed up what everyone was feeling. He stamped his right fore-hoof on the ground and then cried: "I have come home at last! This is my real country! I belong here. This is the land I have been looking for all my life, though I never knew it till now. The reason why we loved old Narnia is that it sometimes looked a little like this. Bree-hee-hee! Come further up, come further in."[7]

C. S. Lewis

There have been times when I think we do not desire heaven but more often I find myself wondering whether, in our heart of hearts, we have ever desired anything else.[8]

C. S. Lewis

You stir man to take pleasure in praising you, because you have made us for yourself, and our heart is restless until it rests in you.[9]

Augustine of Hippo

If we are centered in ourselves, we experience the strangeness and restlessness of the homeless human spirit that yearns for God. Even if we are centered in God, we groan at the brokenness of creation and yearn for redemption. That is why we see everywhere the use of the metaphors of pilgrimage and sojourn to describe human life.[10]

Carol Lakey Hess

We are born homesick—longing for a land and a way of life we have never directly experienced, but which we know is somewhere, or at least ought to exist. We live in a lifelong culture shock. God designed us to live in a perfect environment—free of disease, with affirming, open, and caring relationships, meaningful work, and a perfect face-to-face relationship with God. But as a result of sin, we live in a far less than ideal world, and we find ourselves aliens here, never entirely at home. We are somewhat like a piece of highly sophisticated electronic equipment designed to operate in a temperature- and humidity-controlled environment, because its use in anything other than that proper atmosphere means it is subject to ongoing maintenance problems. We are searching for that perfect environment that will free us from our maintenance issues. We are like émigrés who have settled in a new land and raised a family but still yearn to return to the homeland forever closed to us. The apostle Paul described this unsettledness so forcefully when he said that it is as if all of us have been "groaning in labor pains" (Rom. 8:22).

Exiled from Eden

God designed humankind to live in the Garden of Eden. This garden is the Bible's picture of how God intended people to live. The Bible describes

The Cry of the Soul

Emotions are the language of the soul. They tell us if we are moving toward God or away from him. Emotions are like messengers from the front lines of the battle zone. Our tendency is to kill the messenger.

Our emotional struggles reflect far more than our battle with people and events; they reveal our deepest questions about God. Anger asks: Is God just, or will he let the wicked win? Will God protect me? Fear asks: Can I trust God to protect me from harm? Jealousy asks: Is God good, or will he leave me empty and bless others? Despair asks: Will God leave me isolated and alone? Contempt asks: Does God love me, or will he turn away in disgust? Shame asks: Does God love me, or will he hate me if he sees me as I really am?

God's mysterious method of persuasion is the path of pain. Affliction opens the heart to a change in direction. Doubt, confusion, even radical struggle are required before we are inclined to surrender to his goodness. Surrender is not possible without a fight. Although we should not glorify the struggle, it is apparently provoked by God and is therefore part of the process of transformation.

Adapted from The Cry of the Soul *by Dan B. Allender and Tremper Longman III. Used by permission.*[11]

Eden with evocative language. It images God's provision in the rivers that water the land, the lush vegetation, the animals, the garden's beauty, and the companionship of another. It is also called "the garden of God" (Ezek. 31:8–9), and we are told that God walked in the garden and communed with Adam and Eve (Gen. 3:8). While there was work to do in the garden, it was not toilsome. It was not a life of unchanging ease, but a time of creativity and work that used all of one's strength and imagination, and all this took place in an unspoiled land marked by beauty and true companionship. A beauty, symmetry, and simplicity marked life in the garden, and that was lost after the fall.

Sin entered the garden, and the human experience changed forever. Upon eating the forbidden fruit, Adam and Eve's "eyes were opened, and they suddenly felt shame at their nakedness" (3:7 NLT) and were fearful when they heard God walking in the garden (3:8). "The impulse to cover themselves and to hide from God embodies the essential change that has occurred, encompassing shame, self-consciousness, and the experience of loss and the awareness of separation from God."[12]

The groaning we all experience living this side of Eden shows itself painfully in relationships. So often domination, distance, and self-interest have replaced the trust, true partnership, and intimacy of Eden. We catch glimpses of how things are supposed to be in healthy marriages, committed friendships, healthy churches, and good work groups. But we also see much pain and ugliness in relationships as well.

Part of our yearning for Eden is the desire for a whole and open relationship in which we are fully known and understood. When things are set right at the end of this age, we will stand before God and, for the first time, be fully known by someone and yet not afraid because "perfect love expels all fear" (1 John 4:18 NLT). When another person learns something about our deepest thoughts and fears, they hold a certain power over us. We are very careful to whom we open up for fear that we might be rejected when our true selves are revealed. So imagine standing before God, being fully known and yet feeling more completely loved than ever before. When Eden is restored, when we come home to heaven, the children of God will know the reality of being fully known and having no fear. Only then will we have a deep sense of finally being home and fully understood. This sense of being deeply known is conveyed in an image from the book of Revelation. Jesus encourages those who remain faithful in Smyrna by telling them, "I will give to each one a white stone, and on the stone will be engraved a new name that no one knows except the one who receives it" (Rev. 2:17 NLT). George MacDonald used this verse as a basis for a meditation in which he pondered the wonder of being known by God and having that deep knowledge congealed into a worthy name.

> The true name is one which expresses the character, the nature, the being, the *meaning* of the person who bears it. It is the man's own symbol,—his soul's picture, in a word,—the sign which belongs to him and to no one else. Who can give a man this, his own name? God alone. For no one but God sees what the man is, or even, seeing what he is, could express in a name-word the sum and harmony of what he sees.[13]

An essential discovery in the spiritual life is the recognition that life, this side of Eden, is difficult, that it never measures up to our expectations, and that our attempts to fix this disquiet simply do not work. Until we come to this recognition, we will live under the illusion that our restlessness is situational. Our natural inclination is to blame our spiritual ennui on the stresses and depravation of the moment. It takes courage and grace to see it for what it is: a chronic ache at the core of our being. If we do not see the longing as a given, we will tend to treat it with the if-only cure. This strategy assumes that our spiritual restlessness can be placated by a change of circumstances: "If only I had a new job." "If only I had her as a friend." "If only I found the right church." The list of if-onlys is limitless, and sadly, many Christians have lists as long as their secular neighbors, but their lists are "spiritual."

We Are Thirsty and Broken

Brokenness eliminates the need for a self-preserving agenda.[14]

Julie A. Gorman

Brokenness forces us to find a source of love outside ourselves. That source is God.[15]

Jerry Sittser

A biblical image for the restless homesickness of Eden is thirst, a persistent, life-directing soul thirst. The Bible sees humans as thirsty people who will do almost anything to satiate this need. Everyone is thirsty for God, but not all learn to declare, "My soul thirsts for you; my whole body longs for you in this parched and weary land where there is no water" (Ps. 63:1 NLT). The story told over and over in the Bible is of those who seek to satiate their thirst in their own way (through power, idolatry, pleasure, money). Yet for those who take their thirst to God, Jesus gave a promise: "Blessed are those who hunger and thirst for righteousness, for they will be filled" (Matt. 5:6). The Bible openly acknowledges thirst and unsettledness and invites everyone:

> Come, all you who are thirsty, come to the waters; and you who have no money, come, buy and eat! Come, buy wine and milk without money and without cost. Why spend money on what is not bread, and your labor on what does not satisfy? Listen, listen to me, and eat what is good, and your soul will delight in the richest of fare. (Isa. 55:1–2 NIV)

God invites the thirsty: "Come, all you who are thirsty, come to the waters." The language of the invitation is wonderful. In a single verse, God invites us four times to "come." The invitation is not given to a select few, but is extended to "all" who thirst, and that is everyone. It is a remarkable invitation; it acknowledges our need and yet preserves our dignity. We are invited to come and buy. It is the image of the marketplace, where goods are procured, not by groveling or begging, but by the exchange of money. And here is the irony, for we come to "buy wine and milk without money and without cost." God acknowledges our thirst and invites us to come to a market where we can receive the water, milk, wine, and bread we need, and yet the money of exchange is not our own but is a currency of his grace.

Verse 2 addresses the foolishness of denying our thirst or trying to satisfy it ourselves. Isaiah simply asks, "Why are you wasting your money on food that does not satisfy?" The implied answer is, "For no good reason." The prophet Jeremiah used a compelling image drawn from

A Deep Longing for Purity

It is usually not so much the sex drive that overwhelms the sexually broken—and this means all of us, to some extent—as that sex seems to relieve our deeper longings and deep woundedness. Most of the time we sin sexually not just to give ourselves pleasure, but in a doomed attempt to protect ourselves from pain.

In other words, sexual immorality often develops as a means of finding relief from or avoiding certain pains, especially pains associated with a low opinion of ourselves. Our lives become structured around avoiding pain, and these habits block what the Lord wants to do in our lives.

Even after conversion our longing for a deeper relationship with the Lord will find itself competing with desires to satisfy other unmet needs. When we struggle with sin, almost always we are facing the conflict between two longings: a longing for an immediate release from pain (from loneliness, feelings of self-hatred, hunger, and so forth) and a longing for intimacy with our Lord. The latter may seem more distant and the rewards less direct, so we often opt for sin.

If we long for a relationship with the Lord, and if we desire purity and righteousness, why is the battle against sexual lust so difficult for some people, perhaps most people, in this heavily sexualized culture of ours?

The answer is simple: lust works every time. It delivers what we are looking for: immediate relief from pain or discomfort. Lust is more readily available than any other source we have to relieve pain. All we need is right there in our mind. For some of us, our minds are like a video store of almost unlimited stimulating resources: it's open twenty-four hours a day, and it does not charge rental fees.

Lust acts more quickly than any pain reliever on the market. It can instantly relieve us of any consciousness of pain. Feeling lonely or weak or inadequate? Feeling angry? Tired, but you can't sleep? Can't stand who you are? Take a little lust, and you'll feel better immediately.

Why do we sexualize our needs—or the solution to them? First, I believe we do this because sex is one of the most intense experiences most people have, and whatever sex touches becomes more alive. Just as salt enhances the flavor of food, sex intensifies the power of any experience. Sex empowers feelings.

Second, we use sex because our needs are fundamentally relational, and sex is a relational experience. Some people use food or drugs as a means of dulling the pains that arise out of unmet needs, but the numbing quality they offer is much less satisfying than the vicarious relationships that sex or sexual fantasy offer to those whose needs are primarily relational.

continued ➤

Third, sex has a power because it so profoundly symbolizes intimacy and connection. There is a tremendous symbolic power in coming together with another person, when they enter my body, or I theirs. Being enfolded in the arms of another offers feelings of security, nurturing, desirability. Sex can make me feel worthy (for a while), even if the other person is only using me.

Adapted from "A Deep Longing for Purity" by Alan Medinger. Used by permission.[16]

everyday life in ancient Israel. A major challenge of living in the land of Israel is the struggle for good sources of water. In Jeremiah's day, water was available from several sources. The first were streams, commonly referred to as "living water" because of their movement and good quality. People considered streams to be the best source of water a village could have because they were easy to draw from and were fresh. The second source of water was the well. Wells were difficult to dig, and it required a great deal of labor to shore up the walls and maintain the equipment for getting the water out. Drawing from a well involved lowering a bucket and bringing the water up. Though the water was of varying quality, people considered well water to be far better than cisterns.

Cisterns were plastered holding tanks for rain water and were the least desirable source of community water. The ancient equivalent of a rain barrel was easy to construct and could supplement a household's water needs, but cisterns had real limitations. They could crack, and the water could become stale and contaminated. With these sources of water in mind, consider Jeremiah's indictment: "For my people have done two evil things: They have forsaken me—the fountain of living water. And they have dug for themselves cracked cisterns that can hold no water at all!" (Jer. 2:13 NLT).

That is how God understands our failure to take our thirst to him. We are like a village that says, "Let's not use the stream for a source of water, but let's go out and dig cisterns in the sand (does sand hold water?) and rely on them instead." This would never happen. However, to enter the marketplace of grace and to buy the bread, water, wine, and milk without cost, we need to acknowledge that we cannot provide these necessities on our own. We must see that we often operate out of the conviction that we know how to meet our needs far better than God. We must constantly remind ourselves that obedience to God's plan may cost us convenience but never joy. Obedience really amounts to accepting the gracious invitation of God to a more sensible way of living—the path of joy, the path of sanity.

To be broken means we recognize we are personally powerless to manage our life in a way that will bring the kind of pleasure we most deeply long for. To be broken is recognizing that we face problems we cannot overcome by willpower alone. Brokenness was the experience of many Bible heroes: Abraham, Moses, Hannah, David, and Paul.

The Bible most commonly employs brokenness as an image for people overwhelmed by troubles that change them. Old Testament writers commonly express this by saying that the "heart" or "spirit" is "broken." The image represents feelings of anguish and despair and a loss of hope or sense of well-being. In the Bible, as in life, brokenness comes in two basic forms. It is the outcome of the experience of brokenness that differentiates these two. Some leave the experience wounded, despairing, and not fully functional. Others leave it humbled and changed, but even more effective. Paul captures the difference when he writes to the Corinthians:

> Now I rejoice, not that you were grieved, but that your grief led to repentance; for you were grieved in the way God intended, in order that you might not suffer loss in anything through us. For godly brokenness produces a repentance leading to salvation, without regret, but the sorrow of the world produces death. (2 Cor. 7:9–10, author's trans.)

In the Bible, truly broken people turn to God for help. Confessions of brokenness regularly occur in the immediate context of petitions for God's rescue or confessions of faith in God (Ps. 34:17–18). Openness to God awakens his compassion and moves him to bind up the brokenhearted (Isa. 61:1). In Psalm 147:2–3, the psalmist employs the language of healing the brokenhearted to celebrate God's saving actions toward the postexilic community in their struggle against political opposition and economic adversity.

At the outset of his public ministry, Jesus quotes Isaiah 61:1 to explain his own mission (Luke 4:18–19). Subsequently, he displays great concern for binding up the brokenhearted in his focus on the spiritually "sick" (Matt. 9:12; Mark 2:17; Luke 5:31), his frequent calls for repentance (Matt. 4:17; Mark 1:15; Luke 13:3), his gentle dealings with sinful people (Luke 7:36–50; 19:1–10), and his parables of acceptance for the repentant (15:11–32; 18:9–14).[17]

Every Christian must be a broken person. To enter the kingdom we must acknowledge that the inner peace we yearn for can never come by our own efforts but only as we admit our powerlessness to conquer our self-centeredness and then turn the rule of our life to Christ. We need to live the Christian life as broken people. The grace of God—the grace we need for healing, for the freedom to be good, and for the deep joy we long for—only flows downhill. It is available to the humble: "God opposes the proud, but gives grace to the humble" (1 Pet. 5:5).

Brokenness

Godly sorrow Broken/humbled/softened	Worldly sorrow Wounded/hardened/cynical
Synonyms: contrite, humble, softened, stripped of [some negative characteristic], broken in the right place	*Synonyms*: devastated, immobilized, crushed, hardened, nonfunctional, broken in the wrong place
Truly broken persons approach life with a humble spirit born from encountering the tragic with wisdom, appropriate acceptance, and deep reliance on God.	Wounded persons have a primary self-understanding of being wounded and hurt, with a hardening and bitter spirit marked by making excuses, defending self, and blaming others.
The experience is painful, but God supports and provides the strength needed.	The experience may be painful. Often a first response is to escape the pain or to blame others for it.
The amount of pain experienced through brokenness depends (1) on what is being broken (jealousy, pride, greed, lustful thoughts, etc.), (2) how deeply this has become a central part of your life, and (3) how responsive one is to the discipline.	The spiritually hardened have adopted elaborate self-protective measures. The experience of "good pain," that which teaches us about God and ourselves, is often missed.
The truly broken feast on truth and have an awareness of their limitations.	The wounded dwell on darkness often through worry, diseased introspection, self-hatred, and blaming others.

Unfortunately, the longer we spend around churches, the more we tend to see ourselves less as sinners and more as "people who are getting it together." The gospel promises deep transformation for those who follow Christ. However, there will always be points of brokenness, sin, and rebellion in our lives. I now am less inclined to think of charting our sanctification as it is often pictured (see the chart below). While indicating progress in our sanctification, this kind of "straight-line thinking" does not take into account the dynamic nature of our relationship with God. Where does the dark night of the soul fit on this linear path? What about times of brokenness as we see new areas of sin?

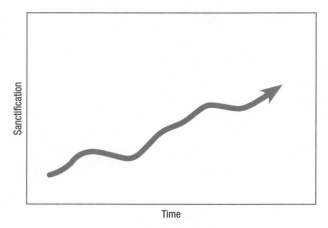

Figure 9. Progress in sanctification

Yearning and Idolatry

Do you want to be made well?

Jesus, in John 5:6

What do you want me to do for you?

Jesus, in Matthew 20:32

Whenever we wanted comfort, confidence, consolation, or celebration, we turned to a substitute for God. Substitutes for God are actually idols.[18]

Victor Mihailoff

The Scriptures consistently expose people as both thirsty and foolish. We long for the satisfaction we were built to enjoy, but we all move away from God to find it.[19]

Larry Crabb

Our thirsts and foolish strategies reveal what Pascal saw as the great tension of the human condition: our grandeur as bearers of the divine image and our misery as sinners who inhabit a world racked by sin.[20] We are people with an eternal destiny who were designed to rule with

God, and hence our longings reflect the grandeur of the *imago Dei* and the genetically remembered joys of Eden. Yet, in our foolishness we adopt self-defeating strategies for meeting these needs. New Testament writers count lusts—inordinate desires for things rooted in the world and not God—as a major impediment to our life with God. When Peter urges Christians "to abstain from fleshly lusts, which wage war against the soul" (1 Pet. 2:11 NASB), he is writing not about our homesickness, but about those "original longings" that have become, through practice, so strongly linked to wrong objects. Classically these deformed yearnings are referred to as our passions. Since we think we need the objects of our lusts (material goods, certain experiences, pleasant escapes) for life to be full, we may use whatever resources we can to get them, and hence, idolatry comes into play.

Our soul-thirst is powerful, and it makes all of us idolaters. To be sure, not many of my contemporaries bow before actual pagan altars. Nevertheless, the Bible sees idolatry as a universal problem. To be alive is to be an idolater. One of the most basic questions in spiritual formation must be "What am I doing about my idols?" not "Do I have any idols?" This is not just a rhetorical overstatement. Consider Paul's appeals to early Christians: "Therefore consider the members of your earthly body as dead to immorality, impurity, passion, evil desire, and greed, which amounts to idolatry" (Col. 3:5 NASB). "For a greedy person is really an idolater who worships the things of this world" (Eph. 5:5 NLT). In the Bible our communities have a unique ability to keep us away from idolatry or to promote idolatry.

I have found that telling people of their idolatry, naming it clearly, is often welcome news to broken people. When I listen to the stories of distress by those caught in patterns of sinning, they often seem so perplexed at what could have brought them to the place of sin they now routinely experience. Many want to attribute it to simply "being weak and sinful" or to "patterns learned in childhood." I have come to realize that when we allow people to blame their sinning simply on "being weak and sinful," we can create spiritual victims rather than disciples. The word we need to hear is that all sin flows out of breaking the first two commandments, to have "no other gods" and no "idol" (Exod. 20:3–5). Why do I lie? At the level of my soul, it is because I think that something other than God is a quicker way to the happiness I crave. Why do I constantly defend myself and protect my reputation? I do this because I am insecure in my belief that God is for me, and I find a sterling reputation to be an idol I can lean on.

Christians often are unwilling to admit the allure of sin. I remember sitting with a young woman who was tormented by shame and guilt over her sexual adventures and relational dishonesty. She kept wondering aloud why she fell into these defeating patterns, which "are so dumb." She was shocked when I suggested that "sex works." It provided her an immediate and tangible, gratifying interlude and gave a short-term answer to her longing for intimacy and being needed. We can begin to get some leverage in dealing with sin when we see that we do it for "positive reasons." We sin because our longings are so strong that at the operational level—not at the verbal level, where we confess "Jesus is Lord"—we feel that something in addition to Jesus is necessary for our happiness and well-being. We will never find the full freedom promised in the gospel if all we want from Jesus is relief.

Part of the amazing power of idols in our lives comes from their creation of a whole way of looking at the world. This is especially true in the context of community. We come to really believe, at the level of our souls, that "that new car," "that new job," or my current flirtation will bring the happiness I need and deserve, happiness that God will probably fail to give me. All religions come, in the phrase of Peter Berger, with a "plausibility structure,"[21] a kind of overall explanation for how the world operates that is so pervasive it is almost invisible to us. When we exhort someone to "stop daydreaming and get realistic," we reveal that our plausibility structure has no room for their approach: it just does not make sense to us. What is particularly pernicious about idolatry is that it creates delusional structures blinding us to the fact that we are pursuing (for example) career advancement above everything else. Look at how Isaiah describes the delusional effect of actual idolatry in speaking to a people mired in idolatry. The prophet describes idols: "Their eyes are closed, and they cannot see" (Isa. 44:18 NLT). He is aware of the power of the idol's plausibility structure when he asserts, "The person who made the idol never stops to reflect" (44:19 NLT). His summary of the idolater's condition is quite graphic: "The poor, deluded fool feeds on ashes" (44:20 NLT). Idolaters feed on ashes even though they think they are getting the best that is available. Yet God offers, "I would feed you with the finest of the wheat; and with honey from the rock I would satisfy you" (Ps. 81:16 NASB).

Wineskins, Idols, and Formation

> Then Jesus gave them this illustration: "No one tears a piece of cloth from a new garment and uses it to patch an old garment. For then the new garment would be torn, and the patch wouldn't even match the old garment. And no one puts new wine into old wineskins. The new wine would burst the old skins, spilling the wine and ruining the skins. New wine must be put into new wineskins."
>
> Jesus, in Luke 5:36–38 NLT

Feeding on Ashes

The wood-carver measures and marks out a block of wood, takes the tool, and carves the figure of a man. Now he has a wonderful idol that cannot even move from where it is placed! He cuts down cedars; he selects the cypress and the oak; he plants the cedar in the forest to be nourished by the rain. And after his care, he uses part of the wood to make a fire to warm himself and bake his bread. Then—yes, it's true—he takes the rest of it and makes himself a god for people to worship! He makes an idol and bows down and praises it! He burns part of the tree to roast his meat and to keep himself warm. Then he takes what's left and makes his god: a carved idol! He falls down in front of it, worshiping and praying to it. "Rescue me!" he says. "You are my god!"

Such stupidity and ignorance! Their eyes are closed, and they cannot see. Their minds are shut, and they cannot think. The person who made the idol never stops to reflect, "Why, it's just a block of wood! I burned half of it for heat and used it to bake my bread and roast my meat. How can the rest of it be a god? Should I bow down to worship a chunk of wood?" The poor, deluded fool feeds on ashes. He is trusting something that can give him no help at all. Yet he cannot bring himself to ask, "Is this thing, this idol that I'm holding in my hand, a lie?" (Isa. 44:13–20 NLT).

Ashes are a biblical image for complete destruction and wastedness. Ashes are the end result of battle and devastation as seen in Jeremiah's picture of a "whole valley of the dead bodies and the ashes" (Jer. 31:40), and the references to the complete destruction of Sodom and Gomorrah picture them as turned "to ashes" (2 Pet. 2:6 NIV). Ashes come to symbolize things weak, fleeting, and empty, as in "Your maxims are proverbs of ashes" (Job 13:12).[22] To feed on idols symbolizes our settling for what is worthless and far less than what the Father has for us. This passage in Isaiah 44 shows that when we settle for idols, our discernment becomes dulled, and we miss what should be obvious.

Little children, keep yourselves from idols.

1 John 5:21

Man's nature is a perpetual factory of idols.[23]

John Calvin

Christian spiritual formation is not primarily about programs or techniques, but it is first and foremost about an approach to life. I have seen this clearly in my teaching ministry. After I became more interested in the spiritual life, I began to teach courses concerning spiritual practices like solitude, prayer, and fasting. I observed that some students took the material and used these classical spiritual disciplines as a space to meet God and be refreshed and healed by his grace. Others used this material to become far more accomplished legalists. What became clear is that our deep theology, our life maps, may make a train wreck of any intentional spiritual formation. Unless challenged, legalistic souls will turn spiritual formation to a more finely honed legalism, and spiritual narcissists will use it for their own ends; yet the broken and spiritually hungry souls will grow and be healed and formed rightly.

COMMUNITY SPIRITUAL FORMATION COROLLARY 6

Our soul-thirst is powerful, and it makes all of us idolaters. The Bible sees idolatry as a universal problem. Communities have a unique way of embodying a corporate pride that blinds us to forms of idolatry. Also, faith communities can challenge idolatrous practices like racism in ways an isolated Christian seldom will.

Spiritual formation must continually return to the truths of sin, cross, redemption, grace, and true holiness because the prevailing plausibility structures of our culture push us in the direction of idolatry and false gospels. American religion has a deep moralistic flavor, which gives us the impression that we can earn God's favor by doing good. Jim Smith writes of God's love: "We did not earn it, we cannot lose it."[24] The message of God's love must be proclaimed over and over. Many Christians find themselves in Smith's position: "For years I related to God as if he sat in a swivel chair. When I did something bad, God would turn his back to me until I made amends, when he would swivel back and accept me again. I kept God constantly on the move."[25] We must reject the false dichotomy that would have us choose either proclaiming God's love or "getting serious about discipleship."

Acting as if what the Bible says of God's transforming love is true requires stepping out in faith. Sadly, few formation programs are done in faith and by faith. We often do them in the flesh, thinking we can orchestrate spiritual growth through our own means. We are fundamentally fearful of trusting God for spiritual growth in the lives of those we minister to, as witnessed by our lack of emphasis on prayer for their growth compared with our striving after it.

Feasting on God's Grace

We must be on our guard not to try to build up again what grace has broken down.[26]

André Louf

Formation in Faith and through Faith

When I wrote *A Long Obedience* twenty years ago, I was a parish pastor writing for my parishioners, the people I knew best in the place I knew best. Two convictions under-girded my pastoral work. The first conviction was that everything in the Gospel is livable and that my pastoral task was to get it lived. It was not enough that I announce the Gospel, explain it or whip up enthusiasm for it. I want it lived—lived in detail, lived on the streets and on the job, lived in the bedrooms and kitchens, lived through cancer and divorce, lived with children and in marriage. The second conviction was that my primary pastoral work had to do with Scripture and prayer. I was neither capable nor competent to form Christ in another person, to shape a life of discipleship in man, woman or child. That is supernatural work, and I am not supernatural. Mine was the more modest work of Scripture and prayer—helping people listen to God speak to them from the Scriptures and then joining them in answering God as personally and honestly as we could in lives of prayer. This turned out to be slow work. From time to time, impatient with the slowness, I would try out ways of going about my work that promised quicker results. But after a while it always seemed to be more like meddling in these people's lives than helping them attend to God.

More often than not I found myself getting in the way of what the Holy Spirit had been doing long before I arrived on the scene, so I would go back, feeling a bit chastised, to my proper work: Scripture and prayer; prayer and Scripture. But the *and* is misleading. Scripture and prayer are not two separate entities. My pastoral work was to fuse them into a single act: Scriptureprayer, or prayer-Scripture. It is this fusion of God speaking to us (Scripture) and our speaking to him (prayer) that the Holy Spirit uses to form the life of Christ in us.

Taken from A Long Obedience in the Same Direction *by Eugene H. Peterson. Used with permission of InterVarsity Press.*[27]

Grace is God's free gift, with repentance the way to access it.[28]

Philip Yancey

We must stop using the fact that we cannot *earn* grace (whether for justification or for sanctification) as an excuse for not energetically seeking to *receive* grace.[29]

Dallas Willard

Christian spiritual formation requires that we actively and continually receive from God. We need to be extraordinary consumers of his grace; we need to receive his words of love and correction, his forgiveness, his affirmation, his life, and the list goes on. Without receiving from God, there is no true formation.

Some years ago I was reading Ole Hallesby's classic *Prayer*, which gave me a powerful image of what grace is for the Christian. Hallesby wrote his book in his native Norway during the early twentieth century, and it is steeped in a warm piety that shows his firsthand experience of prayer. He wrote it from the perspective of a caring pastor who knew his congregants well. An initial picture of prayer comes from the early twentieth-century treatment for tuberculosis, before the arrival of the modern miracle drugs.

> Let us think of patients who are ill with tuberculosis.
>
> The physician puts them out in the sunlight and fresh air, both in summer and in winter. There they lie until a cure is gradually effected by the rays of the sun. . . . The treatment is most successful if the patients lie very quietly and are passive, exerting neither their intellects nor their wills. It is the sun which effects the cure. All the patients need to do is to be in the sun.
>
> Prayer is just as simple.
>
> We are all saturated with the pernicious virus of sin; every one of us is a tubercular patient doomed to die! But "the sun of righteousness with heal-ing in its wings has arisen" [Mal. 4:2]. All that is required of us, if we desire to be healed both for time and for eternity, is to let the Son of righteousness reach us, and then to abide in the sunlight of His righteousness.
>
> To pray is nothing more involved than to lie in the sunshine of His grace, to expose our distress of body and soul to those healing rays which can in a wonderful way counteract and render ineffective the bacteria of sin.[30]

Shortly after reading and pondering these words, my second daughter was born, and I was privileged to be given a vivid picture of sun-born healing. When we brought her home, she was jaundiced. This is a fairly common condition in newborn infants, the most observable symptom being a yellowing of the skin and the whites of the eyes brought about by too much bilirubin in the newborn's red blood cells and the tiny liver not functioning at full capacity. Light helps break down the bilirubin into waste products that the kidneys can eliminate, and in severe cases care-fully measured phototherapy under special lights is used. Our daughter had mild jaundice, so the doctor told us to use sunlight. We brought her home, placed her on a blanket spread out in front of a window, and let the sunlight effect the cure. In just a diaper she lay on a blanket, and as she slept the sunlight helped break down the toxins that her tiny liver was not able to process.

What a picture of sun-born healing! Our daughter was completely passive before the cure. She was completely passive in the sunlight. We carried her there and moved her as the sunlight shifted and the day passed; the cure did not depend on her but on her being kept in the light. At the time I juxtaposed the image of our dear one, sleeping essentially naked in the sun, with the image of a neighbor's child. A year and a half earlier while out for a walk, we had stopped to talk with parents who were also strolling with their firstborn daughter. It was a sunny but cool March day, and our neighbor's child was in a baby bunting with just a wee bit of her face showing and lying in a stroller covered by a canopy. Her parents explained that her physician had told them that she had jaundice and should be out in the sun! As I thought of her outdoors, but not in the sunlight, and looked at our newborn lying in the sun, I thought of my own life before God. I remembered Richard Foster's words: "How often we fashion cloaks of evasion—beam-proof shelters—in order to elude our Eternal Lover. But when we pray, God slowly and graciously reveals to us our evasive actions and sets us free from them."[31]

I stand in need of divine healing. Yet I realize that so often I come to God only revealing the tiniest patch of skin for his healing light. We need to actually seek cleansing and renewal. For me, the clothing that blocks the healing light of Jesus most often is my pride, seen in the form of denial—I deny that I need cleansing. I think I can take care of my problems by myself. Yet Isaiah reminds us that those who seek to heal themselves spiritually are unable to do so because they are "like the tossing sea that cannot keep still; its waters toss up mire and mud" (Isa. 57:20).

One of the tragic misunderstandings in our present religious milieu is the popular notion that grace is merely a description of God's kindness toward us. Grace is often limited to justification. While grace is God's free and unmerited favor, it is also his regenerating and strengthening power. There are over one hundred references to grace in the English New Testament, and fewer than 10 percent of these refer principally to justification. Grace has much to do with how we live. For too many people, grace is about how we are "saved," and work is about how we "grow." Yet the New Testament is clear that grace is God's merciful and restoring power as well.

The way of grace is a pathway of change. It is a pathway of change that leads us to depths of character, integrity, joy, and true friendship with God. The truly good news of the gospel is that God wants us to be his friends and invites us to live in relationship with him. When we really see the outstretched hand of God, our whole view of the spiritual life changes. Instead of being just something else to do for a God who is distant, we see it for what it really is: an offer for us to spend time with the Savior, who draws near every day and in every moment. Receiving is more than avoiding the harmful; it is cultivating openness to the spiritually helpful.

In Jesus' day many people believed that spiritual danger came primarily from certain outward actions or events, but Jesus reminded them

that we are most harmed by what comes from within. He said, "For out
of the heart come evil thoughts, murder, adultery, sexual immorality,
theft, false testimony, slander. These are what make a man 'unclean'"
(Matt. 15:19–20 NIV). We are also affected by the culture in which we
live, which bombards us with subtle messages and false images that
have a deadening effect on our spirits. The world seeks to "squeeze you
into its own mould" (Rom. 12:2 Phillips). This imperceptible but ever
so effective pressure leaves our souls deformed and encrusted with the
dust that blinds us to the ultimate reality of God. Remember that *grace*
is also a verb, powerful and active, and not just a noun.

For Further Reading

Allen, Diogenes. *Spiritual Theology: The Theology of Yesterday for Spiritual
    Help Today*. Cambridge, MA: Cowley Publications, 1997. A compre-
    hensive spiritual theology grounded in historical sources.
Allender, Dan B., and Tremper Longman III. *The Cry of the Soul: How Our
    Emotions Reveal Our Deepest Questions about God*. Colorado Springs:
    NavPress, 1994. Using the psalms, the authors intently study anger,
    fear, envy, jealousy, abandonment, despair, contempt, and shame in
    order to better understand the heart of a person, the heart of God,
    and their relationship.
Augustine. *The Confessions*. Translated by Maria Boulding. Vintage Spiri-
    tual Classics. New York: Vintage Books, 1998. The first and most
    influential Christian spiritual autobiography, told with an eye on the
    longings of the heart and a celebration of grace poured out on the
    repentant.
Hausherr, Irénée. *Penthos: The Doctrine of Compunction in the Christian
    East*. Cistercian Studies Series 53. Kalamazoo, MI: Cistercian Publica-
    tions, 1982. A classic study of the role of brokenness (compunction)
    in the Eastern church.
May, Gerald G. *Care of Mind, Care of Spirit: A Psychiatrist Explores Spiri-
    tual Direction*. HarperCollins paperback ed. San Francisco: Harper-
    SanFrancisco, 1992. A wise discussion on the nature of spiritual guid-
    ance and its relationship to counseling and psychiatry.
———. *Will and Spirit: A Contemplative Psychology*. San Francisco: Harper
    & Row, 1982. An integration of insights by a psychiatrist on spiritual
    growth and change.
Smith, James Bryan. *Embracing the Love of God: The Path and Promise of
    Christian Life*. San Francisco: HarperSanFrancisco, 1995. A brief yet
    immensely practical guide to opening oneself to the love of God.

4

To Foster Receiving in Community

Ours should be a stance of waiting in patience, ready to receive the imprint of the word in the depth of our soul, yet also ready to bear with the absence of any consolation.[1]

Susan Muto and Adrian van Kaam

Without receiving love, we cannot love others, no matter how hard we try.[2]

Howard L. Rice

A sense of humble receptiveness on the part of the Christian community is so essential to true spiritual formation. A receptive stance requires both corporate and individual humility and spiritual provision, which is available for those who humbly seek. We must seek to promote an appropriate humility and brokenness on the part of God's people, so that they are receptive to the Spirit's work of formation and reformation in our lives. Earlier I referred to the desired quality of this brokenness by using the term *optimistic brokenness*. I use the qualifier *optimistic* because we are not content simply to give the message of how hard life is and to catalog our moral failures; but all of this must have the purpose of making us more reliant upon God, admitting God's claim on our life and receiving the hope and healing he has to offer.

With some tentativeness I begin to explore how one might cultivate a pervasive sense of optimistic brokenness in a congregation. The churches and Christian communities where I have seen and experienced this per-vasive sense of brokenness did not explicitly set out to engender it. They discovered it in the midst of their life. However, leaders in these churches did reflect on things that fostered the presence of this divine, humble dependence. Here are a few suggestions of what we can do, and I begin these by talking about what the leadership of a church must do.

Creating a Culture of Openness

Hope emerges when the broken edge of life becomes the growing edge of faith: growth begins with openness to the Spirit as the source of change.[3]

Ray S. Anderson

Through pain, we often develop a hunger for change.[4]

Peter Scazzero

A vision without a task is but a dream;
a task without a vision is drudgery;
a vision with a task is the hope of the world.[5]

Inscription in a church in Sussex,
England, 1730

Seeing a vision acted out demonstrates that it is more than abstraction. . . .
As a vision is lived out, it can also become harder to recant under threat.[6]

Charles F. Melchert

A true spiritual openness has at its core a personal brokenness that results in humility and a tender openness to God's work in us. As a small child I witnessed the adventures of my family and a passive-aggressive mule we named Speedy Mule. The mistreatment of a previous owner had reduced this animal to a passive and pathetic life. He was a "broken" and untrusting animal, but not "broken" in a true spiritual sense; spiritual brokenness does not result in "bitterness, cynicism, or low self-esteem"[7] but rather in a realistic assessment of our abilities, in an acknowledg-ment of our utter dependence on God, and in a shocking sense of how easily we can be deceived about our motives.

In the story of the prodigal son (Luke 15:11–32), Jesus pictures two young men who have made choices that keep them, at first, from expe-riencing the father's embrace. I find myself returning to this story again and again. As a child I learned this redemption story of the waiting father who welcomes back his estranged son. I learned it in a largely sentimen-talized version, with no hint of the cross, but I came to delight in the picture of God welcoming the rebellious sinner back. I could identify with the rebellion of the younger son and with his desire to return when he hit rock bottom.

Some time ago I found myself reading the story from the perspective of the older son. For years he had just been a stage prop for me. He was not a full-fledged character, merely a foil to show off the father's great love. But then I strangely began to wonder: Could I be the elder brother? Could I be that overly socialized, highly compliant one, envious of the sins of others? Yes! Like the older brother, I thought God was lucky to have me on his team. I was compliant and deserving of good treatment—just like the Pharisees for whom the story was first given. What was most shocking was to find that the eldest son, in his pride, also missed the father's embrace. Henri Nouwen writes about his own realization that he too was an eldest son:

> For my entire life I had been quite responsible, traditional, and homebound. . . . I suddenly saw myself in a completely new way. I saw my jealousy, my anger, my touchiness, doggedness and sullenness, and most of all, my stubborn self-righteousness. I saw how much of a complainer I was and how much of my thinking and feeling was ridden with resentments. For a time it became impossible to see how I could ever have thought of myself as the younger son. . . . I had been working very hard on my father's farm, but had never fully tasted the joy of being at home.[8]

We desperately need to see that intimacy with God and the transformation it brings can easily be blocked by the bitterness and pride exemplified in the older son. That rebellion keeps us away from God is a truism, but that the pride of compliance and competence could keep us away is shocking. Sadly, the story of the prodigal ends without resolution. The older son resists and misses the embrace. I fear, at times, that so many false spiritualities simply turn younger sons into older brothers.

Christian spiritual formation requires that we cultivate openness to God. We should be intellectually open like the Bereans, who "were more open-minded than those in Thessalonica, and they listened eagerly to Paul's message" (Acts 17:11 NLT). We should pray for openness to Scripture as the psalmist did: "Open my eyes to see the wonderful truths in your law" (Ps. 119:18 NLT); thus we would come to treasure and obey it. We must seek to discern God's voice in the everyday events and in his call to us. We think of Elisha's servant, who missed seeing God's provision until "Elisha prayed, 'O LORD, open his eyes so he may see!' The LORD opened his servant's eyes, and when he looked up, he saw that the hillside around Elisha was filled with horses and chariots of fire" (2 Kings 6:17 NLT). It is so easy for us to go about our days and miss what God is seeking to communicate: "You have seen many things, but have paid no attention; your ears are open, but you hear nothing" (Isa. 42:20 NIV). A humble openness to listen and be taught is the rich, fertile soil God delights to use to grow his good fruit.

As a speaker in various churches, I confess how precious an open and teachable spirit is to a speaker. Its presence is almost palpable—it affects the teaching space and generates a bond of trust between teacher and student. There is a receptivity on the part of the learners that calls forth the teacher's best effort, a deep respect, and a holy caution, lest this trust be violated. A listening and receptive spirit is not a spiritual luxury. Jesus asserts that hearing his voice is basic to being a true disciple: "My sheep hear my voice. I know them, and they follow me" (John 10:27). A stance of openness must be cultivated to hear God's Word. The refusal or inability to hear spiritually is one of the most stinging indictments given by God: "Thus says the LORD, Stand by the ways and see and ask for the ancient paths, where the good way is, and walk in it; and you will find rest for your souls. But they said, 'We will not walk in it.' And I set watchmen over you, saying, 'Listen to the sound of the trumpet!' But they said, 'We will not listen'" (Jer. 6:16–17 NASB).

There is great need for wise and godly persuasion in our church education and formation programs. All of us are closed on some issues and must be persuaded if we are to move to a better position. Consider the negative effects of racism, which Christians must see as a false gospel offering a "sense of righteousness" through perceived superiority. Many of us who have grown and repented in this area did so because of persuasive messages that confronted our sinful blindness.

When I speak of persuasion, I am endorsing the subtle and subversive teaching of Jesus and the prophets. Persuasion for them was not just cranking up the volume and intensity of the message, but the skilled and artful confrontation of their audiences' errant ways and beliefs. Through drama, parable, and questions, these teachers actively sought to affect their hearers.

A Vision for Change

> But a vision is not only a way of seeing; it is also a way of going. The vision comes with a task wrapped up in it.[9]
>
> Gloria Goris Stronks and Doug Blomberg

The conviction that change and growth are possible and worth the effort is essential to spiritual formation. Vision is part of what provides the hope that transformation is a real possibility. This is a moral and spiritual vision, more than simply a vision that moves us emotionally. This idea of vision is reflected in Paul's urging that we should have "a view of things" that would cause us to press forward spiritually (Phil. 3:12–15 NIV). Vision is what a friend of mine found when he went to his first AA meeting, where he was offered "hope, the possibility of sobriety." It is what a former student found when, through teaching, prayer, and therapy, she realized that she could step free from the generational patterns of anger and abuse in her family. She found "a picture of another way of living," and that picture has guided her life. With the same perspective, Ray Anderson has written that "spiritual healing begins with the recovery of hope."[10]

In a pluralistic society like ours, there are competing visions—visions that would lead toward hedonism, toward seeking fulfillment through work, toward environmental consciousness, and toward creating a family-centered life. The vision I am speaking of is not grandiose, but it has the power to remind us that hope and healing are possible through Jesus. It offers encouraging words that in Christ we no longer are enslaved to doing merely what we "want to do." It also shows a realistic process that we can follow to become apprentices of Jesus.

Vision is the wild card of spiritual formation. There are churches that one would expect to be rather marginal in terms of formation (large and impersonal, relatively poor educational programs, little to no soul care), but they consistently produce dedicated followers of Christ. One reason for this is vision. The ability to cast a vision of change and discipleship is a powerful means of grace. I know of many people whose spiritual lives have been forever transformed through a vision-communicating speaker, who was able to call them to a different way of life by giving them a moral/spiritual vision.

This transforming vision serves as a map and a source of empowerment, as persons come to see that they can live differently. One person likened receiving this vision to Christ calling Lazarus from the grave. In essence, he said, I was trapped in anger and lust; I could not maintain any long-term relationships. Then a speaker-counselor "called me out of my tomb; realizing I could change was half the battle, but I still had to get the grave clothes off."

Worship, Confession, and Formation

Worship plays a crucial role in shaping a formative vision for Christians. This formation can only come when the worship is truly centered on God and not simply done as a means toward the end of formation. One of the great obstacles to growth that many people experience is their limited or distorted view of God. It is in truly creative and engaging worship that we not only confess what is true about God but also experience God and learn firsthand of his character. Another aspect of worship so crucial to spiritual formation is that of confession and repentance. The Greek word for confession is *homolegeō*, and it literally means "to say the same thing." When we speak of confessing our faith or confessing sins, we are acknowledging that, to the degree possible, both we and God are saying the same thing. To confess our sins means that we stop calling our actions "a necessary evil" or saying "I had no other choice" or "Everyone else is doing it," but instead we acknowledge, as God already has, that it is a sin, and it is wrong. Confession is an extremely powerful spiritual action, and through it we avail ourselves and open ourselves to the process of growth and spiritual repair at deep levels. Lauren Winner shares candidly of her experiences with confession during her struggle with chastity:

> The rite of confession is, to my mind, the most mysterious and inexplicable of the Christian disciplines. In fact, many Christians do not observe a formal order of confession at all. I have never really understood intellectually what happens at confession; rather, I have taken on faith that in the confessional God's grace is uniquely present, regardless of my ability to articulate why or how. So it is fitting that in that moment full of grace I made a real beginning of chastity, because it is only God's grace—and not my intellectual apprehension of the whys and wherefores of Christian sexual ethics—that has tutored me in chastity.[11]

Repentance follows confession, for it speaks not only of our acknowledging our sin, but also of a commitment to respond to grace and act differently in the future.

COMMUNITY SPIRITUAL FORMATION COROLLARY 7

Worship filled with prayer and praise and opportunities for confession, repentance, receiving the sacraments, hearing and giving testimonies of God's activity, and learning/challenge is the most important context of community formation.

A number of years ago I talked with a friend who told me that he was spiritually stuck. Part of his problem was wondering where to go next spiritually, since he had "taken care of the big sins in my life." I do not know if my friend simply didn't understand or if this was a symptom of his church. But here was a man who, after several decades in the church, had not learned to make repentance and confession a true part of his life. We must always recognize that, while we hold forth a vision of deep and substantial change, our task is the spiritual formation of broken and imperfect people; therefore, one of our main treatment options is that of humble confession and repentance.

Finally, in terms of worship, we need to make certain that the message of God's amazing love is continually and creatively taught. Revelation 12 tells us that Satan's full-time occupation is that of accusing Christians. Our adversary is not so much lurking to tempt us into new sins, but to defeat us through our doubting God's love and goodness, which then takes us to the narcissism that comes from such self-loathing. Part of the teaching on God's love must be the reality of God's grace. In simple terms, we need to always remember that God's grace has two aspects, that of pardon and that of power; we must present both of these and teach people how to avail themselves of both.

If You Want Brokenness, You've Got to Be Broken

In emotionally healthy churches, people live and lead out of brokenness and vulnerability. . . . It is leading out of failure and pain, questions and struggles—a serving that lets go.[12]

Peter Scazzero

Communities marked by a constructive and pervasive sense of brokenness all have leaders who are broken and open people. Some of these leaders are people who have genuinely been broken and seen the bottom through their own experiences. These are people who have known the betrayal of a spouse, their own indiscretions, or struggles with drugs and alcohol and have come to trust Christ more deeply as a result. Other congregations are headed by people whose stories are not as dramatic, but, through deep empathy for others and a heightened sense of their own sinfulness, they own the brokenness of humanity and their own need for healing.

A subtle myth pervading much of ministry holds that we minister most effectively when we are at "the top of our game." I remember a speaker who urged young seminarians to be secure in their faith because they are to stand on the dock and throw out the lifesaving ring to those who are drowning. There is a degree of wisdom in the picture, but it gives the idea that we minister out of our competence to those who are spiritually incompetent. The metamessage we send out is this: Once I was messed up just like you, and now, since I've gotten my life squared away, wouldn't you like to become like me? Over time, that puts intense pressure on the minister to keep looking good so that people will want to be like the minister. And we miss the joy and power of ministering out of our weakness: "Therefore I am content with weaknesses, . . . for whenever I am weak, then I am strong" (2 Cor. 12:10).

Our message needs to have far more emphasis on the fact that we are all in this together. We all suffer from the same deadly disease of sin, and we are all in the same treatment facility. While there is progress, and while there is hope, there are also relapses, and there is an ongoing struggle. Leaders in their teaching, preaching, and pastoral ministry need to be open about the reality of struggle and awareness of brokenness in their own life if they want to create a climate that supports authentic recognition of our brokenness.

To Foster Receiving, Provide Places for Broken People

One of the clearest ways we minister to people who have aches and hurts in their lives is by putting in place programs, services, and people aimed at helping them deal with the struggles of life. To the extent that we see our problems named clearly, there will be a recognition that all Christians struggle with sin and brokenness and that we need to seek help rather than simply try to look good.

In actuality, Scripture addresses all human problems. However, it takes a deeply thoughtful approach to Scripture to make the deep life connections that open us to healing. An illustration of this comes from teaching Galatians. When I was in college, I led a Bible study based on Galatians. My approach was to expose the spiritual stupidity of the Galatian Christians and warn my group members to avoid the spiritual legalism seen in their reliance on circumcision. As I led the study, I made it clear that the problem facing the Galatians was definitely not "my issue." However, I have since come to realize that Galatians demonstrates that all of us rely upon false gospels to help bolster our fragile sense of righteousness. Whoever teaches that letter wisely will help us understand how we by nature are legalists who doubt God's grace and seek to justify ourselves. Such wise and well-studied pastoral teaching can do wonders in opening a Christian's eyes to the pervasive problem of Christian self-reliance. Likewise, the psalms explore human experience, and when taught appropriately, they help us become aware of the depth of our sin and our neediness. We can learn to lay our experiences alongside those of the psalmists, who saw themselves as broken and yet recognized that they were broken before a God of immense love and grace.

The Bible contains many stories of dysfunctional heroes because its purpose is to show us our exceptional God, a God of love and grace and power, who works through people who have limitations—just like we do. These stories help us develop a vocabulary to identify and describe the reality of brokenness in our own lives. It is essential for us all to realize that admitting to brokenness is not to doubt the healing and restoring grace of God. Rather, the brokenness needs to call us to a dynamic discipleship, which grows through faith beyond the mere acknowledgment that brokenness is all that we can expect from life.

Receiving Requires a Discipleship That Emphasizes Our Growth and Our Brokenness

One of the confusing messages that many people receive about brokenness is the sense that broken persons are welcomed at the front door of the church, but once you have entered, brokenness is no longer acceptable. Nevertheless, even if we escape the life that was increasing our brokenness by allowing the body of Christ to enfold us, we still bring our memories, wounds, and nightmares with us. The message that broken people need to hear is that we all struggle with issues from our past, and that our characters are in formation. Jesus claimed that he came for the sick, not the healthy (Luke 5:31). With such a physician to help us, who would want to pretend to be well? The question of discipleship is not "Are you struggling?" but "What are you doing with these struggles?" "Where is God in the midst of these struggles?" "What plans are you making to grow into a more whole life in the face of these struggles?" We need to emphasize that the existence of struggle is not a mark of nondiscipleship.

Another way that we cultivate brokenness is by instruction concerning the nature of sin and its effects on our life. Sin is often taught as nothing more than a theological construct, so that even Christians who have been taken through the Bible several times in careful expository teaching may not have seen that they suffer from the effects of this spiritually chronic disease. It is essential to our proper formation that we emphasize the lived reality of sin. It is not a mere demographic fact.

In this section we revisit the great invitations of Jesus found in the Gospels and summarized in chapter 2, "Curriculum for Christlikeness," which details the two great invitations of Jesus and invitations that flow from them. The four formation pillars (the four *R*'s: *receiving, remembering, relating,* and *responding*) provide the framework for a curriculum for Christlikeness. Here we pause and look again at the invitations of Jesus to see in his own words how he invites us to develop a stance of receiving. Remember that accepting the invitations of Jesus involves both our active imitation of Christ and our intentional openness to the Holy Spirit's work of conforming us into Christlikeness.

The Two Great Invitations of Jesus

Jesus Invites Us to Love and Obey God

When we think we're waiting for God, He is usually waiting for us, waiting for us to get ready to receive what we need.[13]

Lois LeBar

Disciplines that engender a soft and submissive heart toward God are clear responses to this core invitation to love and obey God. The abuse of the discipline of submission does not minimize the need for the body to practice submission to one another and to the godly leadership in our midst. The lesson learned from this is that my life is not simply about me but that, in becoming a Christian, I have become part of a larger body, and it is the glory of Christ and the mission of his church that I must consider first. I listen with a stance of submission to Scripture and to the wise teaching and counsel of others. As I practice the corporate discipline of submission, I am in a position to receive God's grace and strength.

COMMUNITY SPIRITUAL FORMATION COROLLARY 8

"Be subject to one another out of reverence for Christ" (Eph. 5:20). Submission, restorative discipline, and accountable spiritual leadership are ancient formative practices that mark healthy formative churches.

Jesus Invites Us to Love One Another

The invitation to be a people of love contains an invitation to receive. The love we are to share is not the love of well-intentioned willpower, but a grace-saturated love infused by God's wisdom. This compassion is received through the Holy Spirit, since "God's love has been poured into our hearts through the Holy Spirit" (Rom. 5:5) and produces the tender, long-suffering love Christ invites us to share with one another.

These Invitations Flow out of the Call to Love God and Neighbor

Jesus Invites Us to Depend More and More on God and His Grace

We affirm Christian spirituality as a cultivation of openness to God, but we must add an important footnote. This cultivation of openness

Submission

Discipline of Submission

The primary purpose of submission is to place us under the lordship and sovereign guidance of Jesus Christ, where through the practicing of submission we are enabled to have the attitude of Christ. Submission relates to the three dimensions of God, oneself, and others. Upon closer examination there is an interactive dynamic between the submission to self and others that finds meaning and direction only under the prior and supreme subordination to God.

Reexamination of Submission

Submission begins with God, imitates Jesus' life of servanthood, and is empowered by the Holy Spirit. Acknowledging God's revelation through Scripture is one specific means of submitting to God. Jesus' life reflects a desire to discern and obey God's will. In taking the role of a humble servant, he lived his earthly life in joy and gratitude and not bitter resentment or forced compliance. The Holy Spirit guides us into all truth, searches our hearts to direct our intercessions, and functions in a protective role.

Developing Submission through Christian Community

The greatest aid to learning submission and obedience is participating in Christian community. Primary to any attempt at building Christian community is *honesty*. However, due to our many blind spots and defense tactics, at times we perceive the truth only as we hear it mediated to us through a small group of concerned friends. Honesty is fashioned on the anvil of *vulnerability*, the second factor that fosters community. To be vulnerable is to risk being real before God, ourselves, and others. *Acceptance* is the third feature of our community composite. Acceptance is ultimately living by grace. Acceptance asks two things of us: first, to realize and know deep within our hearts that we are the beloved of God; and second, to manifest (pass on) the approval we have received from God to others. After honesty, vulnerability, and acceptance, the fourth factor that enables the discipline of submission is *accountability*. Being accountable to another is the act of submitting to them for prayer, encouragement, and the periodic review of how we are progressing.

Adapted from "Pilgrim's Process" by Tom Schwanda. Used by permission.[14]

to God begins with God's initiative toward us. Because of the cross, the redemptive work of Christ, we can speak of having a friendship with God. Further, this cultivated openness is not a means to justification, but an aspect of "work[ing] out your salvation with fear and trembling, for it is God who works in you to will and to act according to his good purpose" (Phil. 2:12–13 NIV). The Westminster Larger Catechism speaks of "improving our baptism by growing up in assurance of pardon of sin, . . . by drawing strength from the death and resurrection of Christ."[15] Through faith, we open ourselves to God's grace and are justified. Through love and obedience, as we continue to open ourselves to his grace, we are sanctified.

We are to grow in grace: "Grow in the grace and knowledge of our Lord and Savior Jesus Christ" (2 Pet. 3:18). We are to be "rooted and grounded in love" (Eph. 3:17). We are to be "rooted and built up in him" (Col. 2:7). Peter's prayer should be ours: "May grace and peace be yours in abundance" (2 Pet. 1:2). Grace is essential to our growth, and we must cultivate a humble dependence on grace in ourselves and those to whom we minister. We may rely on the promise that "God is able to make all grace abound to you, so that in all things at all times, having all that you need, you will abound in every good work" (2 Cor. 9:8 NIV). Because reliance on God's grace generated evidence in the lives of the Corinthians, Paul gratefully wrote: "I always thank God for you because of his grace given you in Christ Jesus. For in him you have been enriched in every way—in all your speaking and in all your knowledge—because our testimony about Christ was confirmed in you" (1 Cor. 1:4–6 NIV). A curriculum for Christlikeness, which confirms Jesus Christ as Lord and Savior, must lead us to see our brokenness and wretchedness and teach us where and how to receive the sustaining grace that God freely offers.

Jesus Invites Us to the Joy and Freedom of Practicing Spiritual Disciplines

The disciplines of the faith are never ends in themselves but means to the end of knowing, loving, and trusting God.[16]

Kenneth Boa

Fight bravely, for habit overcomes habit.[17]

Thomas à Kempis

A practice is an ongoing, shared activity of a community of people that partly defines and partly makes them who they are.[18]

Craig Dykstra

The disciplines allow us to place ourselves before God in order to receive his grace and be transformed by it. God acknowledges our hunger and thirst and invites us to come. We saw this earlier in Isaiah's call to "come, all you who are thirsty, come to the waters" (Isa. 55:1 NIV). The language of this beckoning is profoundly inviting. In a single verse, God invites us four times to "come." The spiritual disciplines are one of the primary ways that we come and drink these life-giving waters. They are not primarily about easing the discomfort of our brokenness, but they do foster a process of mending the brokenness and quenching our thirst.

The consistent practice of spiritual disciplines marked Jesus' life. Prayer, solitude, fasting, meditation, worship, and service were part of the very fabric of his life. They are critical because they place us in God's healing and sustaining presence. Also, they contain physical, psychological, social, intellectual, and emotional dimensions and demonstrate that "spiritual growth and vitality stem from what we actually *do* with our lives, from the *habits* we form, and from the *character* that results."[19] The proper grace-oriented practice of these disciplines is an essential part of our formation, moving us from reliance on our own willpower to dependence on God's grace. Spiritual disciplines in themselves can do very little by way of spiritual change, but when we use them to place us in God's presence, God can do his loving, restorative work.

The disciplines are aimed at heart transformation and the growth of inner beauty. They do not take us out of our situations and away from trouble, but within the brokenness they place us in God's healing and sustaining presence. They are like the food and drink on the table described in Psalm 23:5, where David says: "You prepare a table before me in the presence of my enemies; you anoint my head with oil; my cup overflows." We need routines, rhythms, and structures in our lives that will bring us to the table and get us to sit still and take in the grace provided. Jesus was consistently taking time apart to pray and commune with his Father at a table set for him in a solitary place after a day of intense ministry. The disciplines provide the routines, rhythms, and structural habits that enable us to adopt Jesus' overall lifestyle. The corporate disciplines of receiving form a foundation of cultivated spiritual receptivity and provide a means of our receiving the strengthening grace, care, and knowledge needed for living the Christian life.

When spiritual disciplines are mentioned, we generally think of voluntary disciplines, disciplines like fasting or confession. These are important, but we must never forget that we always have the opportunity to practice involuntary/situational disciplines like suffering, conflict, persecution, and the dark night of the soul. True formation must teach, mentor, and guide Christians in both voluntary and involuntary discipline.

Criteria for Discernment

The history of the church is littered with the stories of people who have claimed guidance from the Spirit when the prejudices of self-deception reigned instead. From the earliest days of Judaism and Christianity, awareness of this danger has prompted faithful people to articulate criteria by which to judge the authenticity of claims regarding the Spirit.

- *Fidelity to Scripture and the tradition*. At the top of any list of criteria we can find the test of fidelity to the essential vision of the sacred writings and teachings that constitute the faith tradition. Applying this guideline is more complex than simply citing biblical passages, however. It requires us to know Scripture as a whole and to continue searching it with the guidance of the Spirit.
- *Fruit of the Spirit*. Another indication of the authenticity of spiritual discernment is the degree to which the outcomes nurture the fruit of the Spirit in a person or community (Gal. 5:22–23). We usually give priority to the virtue of love.
- *Inner authority and peace*. One indication of the work of the Spirit is a deep sense of peace and calm certainty about the prompting of the Spirit. Such inner authority is distinct from dogmatism because it is humble, serene, and open to correction.
- *Communal harmony*. The Spirit works toward reconciliation and harmony among people. The presence of this harmony is an indication of the Spirit's presence (John 17:23; Acts 4:32; 1 Cor. 3:1–3; Eph. 4:3). Again, however, there is no easy rule. Sometimes the Spirit's prophetic work

continued ➤

Jesus Invites Us to Practice Discernment

Devout conversation on spiritual matters greatly helps our progress, particularly where people of like mind and spirit are bound to each other in God.[20]

Thomas à Kempis

We all face decisions throughout life and find ourselves asking about God's will in a given situation. One of the tasks of spiritual leaders in the church is to meet and, through prayer and scriptural counsel, to offer wisdom and godly perspective on situations we face. As an elder and spiritual director, I often have done this when a crisis has emerged, when people are facing issues that have boxed them in. In such cases discipleship looks very costly, and the community can help us discern is divisive rather than unitive, at least for a time, as when it leads us to protest injustice. In addition, there are forms of superficial placidness that actually entail a "tyranny of the majority," violating true harmony.

- *Enhancement rather than extinction of life.* The Spirit is a Spirit of life and wholeness and health. Experiences and promptings of the Spirit should contribute to wholeness, personal empowerment, heightened selfhood, and positive relationships. Insights that disempower, diminish creativity, fragment persons, or contribute to relational dysfunction are suspect.

- *Integrity in the process of discernment.* A final indication that an experience or prompting is of the Spirit is the degree to which the person or community has engaged in a discernment process with integrity. To be sure, the Spirit blows where it will, and even the most diligent discernment does not yield any guarantee of the Spirit's presence. Nevertheless, a person or community's action is more suspect to the extent that it ignores or violates dimensions of the practice of discernment. When a group or individual has refused to consider various alternatives, failed to heed advice, avoided issues of faith, and suppressed deep emotions—then their decision is suspect.

None of these criteria is absolute; each of them is open to distortion and exception. In the end, spiritual discernment depends on faith. We do our best within the forms we have, but we ever depend on the mysterious emergence of the Spirit, who resonates and persuades and, always, comes as a gift.

Adapted from "Discernment" by Frank Rogers Jr. in Practicing Our Faith. *Reprinted with permission of John Wiley & Sons, Inc.*[21]

the best path in a realm of hard choices. Churches should seek to build into their culture encouragement to turn to others for discernment in times of decision making so that they can receive wisdom from the body of Christ. This model is a powerful message to people, as we learn the value of wise counsel.

Jesus Invites Us to Pray for and Bless Others

The life of the individual believer, his personal salvation, and personal Christian graces have their being, bloom, and fruitage in prayer.[22]

E. M. Bounds

Prayer is a way to express faith, a meditation about what one wants by reason of having faith.[23]

C. Ellis Nelson

Prayer is one of the most important acts of receiving. In prayer we have direct interaction with God and the opportunity of receiving his care and grace, and naturally we put ourselves in a posture of receiving. While we often think of prayer as primarily a personal spiritual discipline, the emphasis in the New Testament is on believers gathering to pray corporately (Acts 4:31; 8:15; 13:3; Eph. 6:18; James 5:14). A primary place where corporate prayer happens in the church is during our gatherings for worship. Here, through corporate prayers and through opportunities for quiet reflective prayers, people have the opportunity to pray and see prayer modeled for them. There are many other venues in which prayer can be a corporate activity of the church. When the disciples asked Jesus to teach them to pray, the first word in his sample prayer was a corporate word—*Our* Father. Jesus invited them (and us) not only into communication to the Father but also into intimacy with the Father.

My personal prayer life has been greatly enhanced by corporate experiences of prayer. My first sustained time of individual prayer was on a corporate prayer retreat, where we had prayed together as a group and then were given time to pray individually yet in close proximity to one another. The forty-five minutes I spent alone in prayer was the longest that I had ever prayed, and the experience initiated me into a pattern of extended personal times of prayer. Some of the ways churches can cultivate a receiving stance through prayer include the following:

- **Prayer meetings.** Christians can gather spontaneously or on a planned basis to pray for the needs of the church, the world, specific missions, social concerns, or individual needs. These meetings give Christians an opportunity to be informed in their praying and to experience the solidarity that comes as people join together in prayer.
- **Prayer ministries.** Much soul work occurs as people listen to sermons and worship God, and having a prayer team that can meet and pray with people following a service can be a valuable avenue of spiritual formation. Prayer teams can be part of an ongoing pastoral care program in a church.
- **Prayer retreats.** Some of my most memorable times of corporate prayer have occurred on half-day prayer retreats for church or a ministry. The focus of these gatherings should not be on teaching people to pray but on actually giving people an opportunity to experience solitude and prayer.
- **Special seasons of prayer.** During times of transition or discernment in a church, the leadership may want to call the church to

a season of twenty-four-hour prayer, with people coming to the church to pray through the issues at hand.

- **Prayer chains and email notification.** Letting people know the prayer needs in the congregation begins to build into the fabric of the church the priority of prayer. People learn that the first response to a crisis should be a call for prayer.
- **Prayer immersions.** Have sessions with those who long to develop intimacy with God but have never been in a corporate setting that encouraged spontaneous prayer. Use the hymnody of the church to pray out loud and then expand upon the lines of the hymns, giving folks a starting place. Martin Luther used the Lord's Prayer as a structure for long prayer times, going word by word or phrase by phrase, and speaking with God about the significance of the words in his life.
- **Opportunities for practicing prayer.** Provide simple exercises affirming God's willingness to hear the plain prayers of people as eloquent expressions of their hearts.

Now may the God of peace, who brought back from the dead our Lord Jesus, the great shepherd of the sheep, by the blood of the eternal covenant, make you complete in everything good so that you may do his will, working among us that which is pleasing in his sight, through Jesus Christ, to whom be the glory forever and ever. Amen.

Hebrews 13:20–21

Now may our Lord Jesus Christ himself and God our Father, who loved us and through grace gave us eternal comfort and good hope, comfort your hearts and strengthen them in every good work and word.

2 Thessalonians 2:16

Benediction can be formalized at the end of a worship service and be little more than the clergy's closing remark. However, benediction is a powerful means of providing grace to other believers. It is intended to be *bene* (good) words, not simply words for closing the service. Benediction offers an important way in which Christians who are trained in spiritual disciplines and seek to live in God's grace are able to distribute that grace and make it available to other people. Teaching on the role of blessing, particularly aimed at parents, families, and leaders, is a crucial teaching in the church. It is also important to train people to place themselves in a stance to receive the true benediction that Jesus offers through the church as we gather for worship.

Intercession for the needs of others is one of the most loving things a Christian can do. The secret time in prayer is an act of charity. Certainly one of the ways we "bear one another's burdens" (Gal. 6:2) is by specific prayer. We can encourage believers to foster genuine prayer for one another by offering simple instruction and resources on how to pray for those with various needs. Through intercessory prayer both the one who prays and the one who is being prayed for are placed in a position where they can receive evidence of God's grace to them.

In times of suffering we are oftentimes most open spiritually and we especially need the body of Christ to keep us open to God and his grace. In times of suffering we benefit greatly from the solidarity expressed by people praying for us and by the healing, restoration, and comfort made available through such prayers. When individual suffering comes, we can recognize the value of intentional solidarity already experienced in times of ease: from habit we still sense connection with the rest of the body of Christ. As we minister to others and as we receive the ministry of love and care by the body of Christ, we are put in a position that makes us more and more receptive. In times of war, natural disaster, and persecution, the church suffers together and witnesses to a watching world by showing the reality of Christ's love.

Jesus Invites Us to Worship and to Celebrate the Sacraments

To worship is to be fully occupied with the attributes of God—the majesty, beauty, and goodness of his person, powers, and perfections.[24]

Kenneth Boa

Worship is the first and most fundamental act of a congregation, an act that separates it from all other human groups. . . . Every part of the public worship of God goes counter to the prevailing culture.[25]

C. Ellis Nelson

Jesus observed the capacity of children to be wholehearted in faith and wonder. His maxim, "Whoever does not receive the kingdom of God as a little child will never enter it" (Luke 18:17), is rooted in the observation that awe, wonder, trust, and faith seem easy and natural for children. The so-called "sophistication" of adulthood stunts our formation when it diminishes our capacity to marvel and stand in awe before God, his Word, and creation. True spiritual formation can only be conducted in an atmosphere permeated by mystery, wonder, awe, reverence, and beauty.

Worship is the primary corporate spiritual discipline of the church. The discipline aspect of "worship" is to actually make it worship. Worship is not always easy: it is advanced intimacy. On a personal level, we may find barriers and distractions that would keep us away from a worship service or would distract us while we are there. On a corporate level, worship can also be very difficult. It is not wise to operate with an assumption that simply gathering people together results in worship. There needs to be instruction and a call to worship God with all that we have.

Worship cultivates a receptive attitude and fills us with God's grace. Confession in worship acknowledges weeds, and forgiveness removes them. Preaching and sharing in the sacraments plows the soil of our souls and plants seeds for future harvests. Praise is the harvest. Sometimes all of these facets of spiritual agriculture occur within the same time of worship. One of the basic gestures of worship is a call for us to look up and out to God, rather than down and in at our own problems and our own solutions, or around at what others are doing and how they regard us. The simple gesture of the posture of looking up and out to God can become a sign of cultivated receptivity. We have the pattern of Jesus' posture in the high priestly prayer of John 17:1, where "he looked up to heaven and said. . ." He did not close his eyes and bow his head; he raised his eyes in expected intimacy with the Father. This is not to say that the other posture is wrong or inappropriate but rather to say that our posture can contribute to the expression of our souls. In the ministry of the Word and sacraments, we learn to open ourselves and receive from God. We hear the truth of God proclaimed and receive the grace-filled words. We are built up as we receive the sacrament of communion and strengthened as we trust in Christ's work on our behalf.

Jesus Invites Us to Use Our Bodies in Prayer and Worship

The Scriptures tell us plainly that the body is a temple of the Holy Spirit, and a temple, after all, is a place of prayer and worship.[26]

Ruth Barton

Jesus lived a life of fully embodied spiritual practices. His life of devotion was not simply done in his head: he carried it out with his whole being. He began his public ministry with the very bodily act of being baptized in the Jordan (Matt. 3:13–17). He then went into the wilderness for a time of solitude, a bodily discipline in which we also can relocate ourselves in time and space for spiritual purposes and fasting. In this unusual fast, Jesus abstained from both food and water for spiritual purposes for forty days (Matt. 4:1–11; Luke 4:1–13). In his healing ministry, Jesus often touched the one being healed (Matt. 8:15; 9:29; 20:34; Luke 22:51). Jesus' sense of the connection between our body and spiritual activities comes through in his parable of the Pharisee and the tax collector (Luke 18:9–14). The Gospel describes the proud Pharisee as standing to pray, a common biblical prayer posture. "But the tax collector, standing some distance away, was even unwilling to lift up his eyes to heaven, but was beating his breast" (Luke 18:13 NASB). Jesus commends the repentant embodied prayer of the tax collector. When we neglect the incorporation of our bodies into our spiritual activities, we essentially shunt the spiritual life to the sidelines. Body and soul both must pray and praise.

Jesus Invites Us to Use Our Money Wisely

Our money is a symbol of ourselves. When we share our substance we are sharing our life with others.[27]

Howard L. Rice

The complexity of rushing to achieve and accumulate more and more frequently threatens to overwhelm us. . . . Christian simplicity frees us from this modern mania. . . . In one form or another, all the devotional masters have stressed its essential nature.[28]

Richard Foster

For many Christians, the bulk of their charitable giving occurs in the context of their local church and often in the worship service. Our giving can become a routine function, with little spiritual reflection. Thoughtful corporate generosity can be a quite moving and formative event. For example, perhaps a church adopts a funding goal to support a new mission project. Meeting this goal requires sacrificial giving across the congregation, and as people give sacrificially and tell stories of God's grace being poured out in the midst of this sacrifice, the congregation is built up and people receive more of God's strengthening grace. In the context of corporate generosity, people who might not have given on their own are drawn along to give as they see the fruits of giving to God and trust him to be their provision.

The example of others who practice greater freedom with their finances can validate the wisdom of Jesus' invitation to use our money wisely. Wealth and possessions often represent a negative spiritual stronghold where fear, doubt, greed, and self-worth dwell and hold us in bondage. In our culture there are few venues where gospel values toward money are even approximately exercised; thus it is vital for the church to help its people follow the invitations of Jesus here. The emphasis Jesus placed on money speaks of the power he believes money can have over our souls. He made the choice quite clear in his statement about the impossibility of serving two masters: God and mammon (the world's values). Whichever we treat as master will receive our sacrifice of the other.

Jesus Invites Us to Repentance and to Draw Close to God and Jesus

Confession in the presence of a brother is the profoundest kind of humiliation. . . . Confession is discipleship. Life with Jesus Christ and his community has begun.[29]

Dietrich Bonhoeffer

Genuine repentance is brought about, ultimately, neither by the fear of consequences nor by the fear of rejection, but as a ministry of the Holy Spirit, who gives to us a deep conviction of the mercy of God.[30]

Robert M. Norris

The gospel is an invitation to abundant life in the kingdom of God. The gospel is not simply the good news that begins the Christian life, but it should also provide a pattern for our living. We must be gospel-centric people, who recognize that "the Christian life is a process of renewing every dimension of our life—spiritual, psychological, corporate, social—by thinking, hoping, and living out the 'lines' or ramifications of the gospel."[31] Our heartbeats and breathing ought to keep to the rhythm of the kingdom.

Confession should be an important part of church life. I have seen public confession made very appropriately as a result of church discipline, when there was an offense grievous enough that it needed to be confessed and repented of before the body. In that moment of brokenness, Christians can then gather in prayer and love in a spirit of restoration around the person who makes confession. I have also experienced, in times of revival and renewal, confessions before the body of Christ where people told of how God was at work and what burdens they were laying aside. The power of such confessions to further revival is remarkable and beautiful.

The open perspective of a receiving attitude models the life of Jesus, who lived in dependence on God: "I do as the Father has commanded me, so that the world may know that I love the Father," Jesus said (John 14:31). This stance of openness reflects humility on our part as we learn that "apart from me [Jesus] you can do nothing" (15:5). True Christianity is a charisma, a gift of the Spirit. We cannot build community as one thinks of building a house or school. We can, however, foster a lifestyle of corporate receptivity, which is the rich fertile soil out of which a graced community springs.

These two chapters on receiving are the largest of the R sets. A thorough understanding of *receiving* is necessary to see *remembering, responding,* and *relating* in a grace-oriented manner. In our state of human brokenness and extreme need, the gospel brings grace to those who own their brokenness and seek repentance instead of building idols. Repentance includes a vision for a change brought by humbly acknowledging sin and devoting oneself to investing in a life driven by the invitations of Jesus. Jesus laid out a road map for those who could see that their idols were empty and who wanted to turn away to a different path. In the chapters that follow, we must remember the grace and vision received and then respond and relate to them. In receiving grace, we are enabled to remember who we are and to whom we belong, we are called to a response of service, and we find that the spiritual formation we are seeking happens best in and through community. Again, for each of these R's, there will be a chapter of foundational material and a chapter of application that includes Jesus' invitations.

For Further Reading

Banks, Robert J. *Paul's Idea of Community*. Rev. ed. Peabody, MA: Hendrickson, 1994. A clearly written examination of what the author sees as Paul's unique contribution on the Christian community.

Clapp, Rodney. *A Peculiar People: The Church as Culture in a Post-Christian Society*. Downers Grove, IL: InterVarsity, 1996. Clapp suggests that evangelicalism, often focusing on the individual to the exclusion of cultivating true community, has thus limited its impact on the broader culture.

Dawn, Marva. *Keeping the Sabbath Wholly*. Grand Rapids: Eerdmans, 1989. A first-person invitation to observe the Sabbath.

Melchert, Charles F. *Wise Teaching: Biblical Wisdom and Educational Ministry*. Harrisburg, PA: Trinity Press International, 1998. Highlights Jesus' use of wisdom literature and explores the interaction between pedagogical questions and the Wisdom literature.

Muto, Susan Annette, and Adrian van Kaam. *Commitment: Key to Christian Maturity*. Pittsburgh: Epiphany Association, 2002. Explores in depth what it means to experience commitment in the threefold path of spiritual deepening: listening, liberation, and love.

Vanier, Jean. *Community and Growth: Our Pilgrimage Together*. Toronto: Griffin House, 1979. Community offers forgiveness and celebration, growth and liberation for a mission of service and communication, through which we gain the strength to accept "our own essential solitude."

―――. *From Brokenness to Community*. The Wit Lectures. New York: Paulist Press, 1992. Vanier, the founder of the international L'Arche movement and spiritual friend to Henri Nouwen, lectures at Harvard Divinity School on the meaning of brokenness, communion, and community.

5

Foundations of Remembering

Letting the Cross Grow Larger

What are we to remember?

> We are to remember who we are (God's beloved children), how we came to this place/position, whose we are (I belong not to myself but to my faithful Savior Jesus Christ), what God intends for our lives, and where wisdom for living is found (in Scripture, "which are able to give you the wisdom that leads to salvation," 2 Tim. 3:15 NASB).

How do we remember?

> We do this as we hear people testify to the work of God in their lives, tracking God's work in our lives also; we do this as we read and hear the stories of God's faithfulness to his people through the centuries; we do this as we learn of God and his wisdom for us; we do this as we remember our baptism and its meaning; and we do this as we learn spiritual practices that keep our minds focused on God.

What stance/preparation does this require?

> A willing humility to learn.

Where does remembering occur?

> Though there are benefits to remembering in solitude and in solidarity, we seek to practice both, knowing that we are individual

members of a body. Personal history and corporate memory can both inform our remembering. We reflect alone so that we might serve by sharing our reflections with others; they in turn share their reflections and inform further times of solitude.

After that generation died, another generation grew up who did not acknowledge the LORD or remember the mighty things he had done for Israel.

Judges 2:10 NLT

Remember that you were a slave in Egypt, and diligently observe these statutes.

Deuteronomy 16:12

Remember your creator in the days of your youth.

Ecclesiastes 12:1a

Remember this and consider, recall it to mind, you transgressors, remember the former things of old; for I am God, and there is no other; I am God, and there is no one like me.

Isaiah 46:8–9

Spiritual remembering, on the other hand, involves gratefully recalling the past moments of epiphany or dramatic awakening in life so that we can muster the courage and perspective to continue seeking God and God's will.[1]

Robert Wicks

One of the chief goals of Hebrew education was to make sure the people would never forget and would, therefore, always fear God and obey his commandments. In Hebrew thought the chief spiritual malady was forgetfulness. Therefore, one of the chief ends of education was the remembrance of the mighty acts that God had performed on behalf of his people. We are indeed forgetful pilgrims, and we need to be reminded of the good things that God has done in our lives, in the lives of our brothers and sisters in Christ, and in salvation history. In an age in which we are bombarded with information and everything is recorded, we can just as easily forget to remember. Accordingly, in our teaching we must take time for testimony, reflection, and remembrance. We remember best when concrete examples of what God has done are brought to mind. Stories of God's work in individual lives reveal the personal nature of the interaction between God and a person or group. They remind us that our gracious God is a person to whom we can respond and with whom we can relate.

The God-Human Gap

Our first problem is that our attitude toward sin is more self-centered than God-centered.[2]

Jerry Bridges

A recovery of the old sense of sin is essential to Christianity. Christ takes it for granted that men are bad.[3]

C. S. Lewis

It would be helpful to return to the bridge diagram (in chap. 1 see "The Gospel and the Christian" and figs. 3–4) and consider how our perception of "the gap" relates to spiritual formation. The God-human gap always exists in two forms. First, there is the reality of an infinite moral, spiritual, and relational gap between God and humans, which reflects our need for God's limitless grace. Our sins, areas of healing, pain, and the needs of those around us require enormous amounts of grace. Second, we live as if the God-human gap is actually much smaller than it really is. We sometimes deliberately narrow this gap through boasting and impression management, but we are blind to much of this narrowing and do it through subtle patterns of denial, ignorance, and self-protection. Here enters a simple maxim of the spiritual life: the grace of God that affects us (grace as God's transforming and healing power) generally does not exceed our perceived need for grace. People with a very small God-human gap will conclude or assume that they need little grace and will receive little transforming grace.

A major task in spiritual formation involves increasing our awareness of our need for grace. One way of doing this is by letting the cross grow larger. This means facing up to the reality of sin and growing in awe of the majestic holiness of God. We are at our best spiritually when our sin drives us to the cross, when we cling to it and nothing else. The law, our sin, our failure, our ache for beauty, and our yearnings—all can drive us to the cross. We must resist our "natural" inclination to think that *we* can handle our sin (its guilt, shame, conviction, pain, enslaving power, and so on). The cross is the place where God most clearly tells us who he is and how he feels about sin. He is holy, hates sin, and weeps over the pain it causes his beloved. It is also the place where God most clearly tells us what he thinks of sinners: "I would rather die than live without you; I will die to provide you a way of escape." As our appreciation of our sin grows and our appreciation of God's holiness grows, so too must our understanding of the cross.

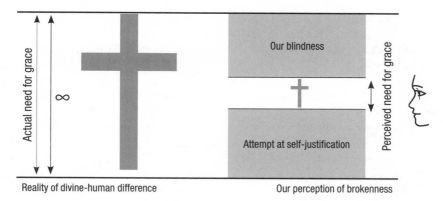

Figure 10. Need for grace
Because of our blindness and self-justifying behavior,
we can only perceive a small cross.

Letting the Cross Grow

Chesterton has a wonderful section in *Orthodoxy* where he compares the numbing limits of an Eastern mind-set, with its symbol of the snake chasing its own tail in an eternal circle, and Christianity with its cross: "For the circle is perfect and infinite in its nature; but it is fixed forever in its size; it can never be larger or smaller. But the cross, though it has at its heart a collision and a contradiction, can extend its four arms forever without altering its shape. Because it has a paradox in its center it can grow without changing. The circle returns upon itself and is bound. The cross opens its arms to the four winds; it is a signpost for free travelers."[4]

Jesus pointed out this principle when he spoke to Simon the Pharisee about the love of those who have received much forgiveness. Simon was quite appalled when the woman anointed Jesus' feet at Simon's party. Jesus first asked Simon about various degrees of appreciation after certain amounts of debt were forgiven, and then went on to explain that in this woman's case "her many sins have been forgiven—for she loved much. But he who has been forgiven little loves little" (Luke 7:47 NIV). To grow, one needs to see one's sin as clearly as this woman did. Dallas Willard advises that we seek out massive amounts of grace because we know our need:

To "grow in grace" means to utilize more and more grace to live by, until everything we do is assisted by grace. Then, whatever we do in word or deed will all be done in the name of the Lord Jesus (Colossians 3:17). The greatest saints are not those who need *less* grace, but those who consume the most grace, who indeed are most in need of grace—those who are saturated by grace in every dimension of their being. Grace to them is like breath.[5]

Saints, like the woman at Simon's party, know their need and God's provision of grace through a large, strong cross that covers their every sin, weakness, and concern. They do not delude themselves into thinking that they could ever get just enough grace to make it on their own. They are shamelessly, hopelessly, and relentlessly in pursuit of more of God's grace than they have right now.

Allow me to make this dynamic more concrete by sharing the stories of three individuals. When I first met Sam, I was struck by his energy and obvious love for his three children and his wife. He was the product of a happy, working-class, church-attending family. He was the first person in his family to go to college, and as the firstborn son he exceeded all expectations. In college his girlfriend urged him to attend a campus ministry, where he heard about personal faith in Christ as a present reality and power. Following Christ was more than simply trying to live a moral life—which seemed to him to summarize his church's teaching back home. Over the course of the year he attended the meetings, and he came to relate to Christ as his Savior and Guide. He graduated from college, married his sweetheart, and started what became a very successful home-building company. For the next twenty years he lived his life as a generous, moral, caring, and churchgoing guy. Prayer and Scripture reading marked his early days out of college, but they were less and less present. In fact, he confided to a friend that he thought personal devotional activities were a bit like a laxative: you take it when you need it, but as you try harder and get better, these "props" are less necessary. Unbeknownst to Sam, his cross was growing smaller and smaller.

Then the bottom dropped out. For Sam it was the 1–2–3 punch, all in six weeks' time. He discovered that his son-in-law, the heir apparent to the business, was having an affair with a member of his staff. In the midst of this awkward betrayal, he ended up in the hospital with a heart attack that required a protracted rehabilitation routine. Finally, the local paper did an exposé on the business practices of some local home builders. Nothing illegal was reported, but Sam was shocked. He was humbled to see his business lumped with everyone else. He had been proud of having been "ethical" and different from the other guys.

Sam was fortunate to have a wife whose deep faith had prepared them for this time. Through her counsel and the guidance of friends, he moved from angry and despairing inactivity to a place of growth and transformation. His humility grew and concomitantly so did the cross's reality in his life.[6]

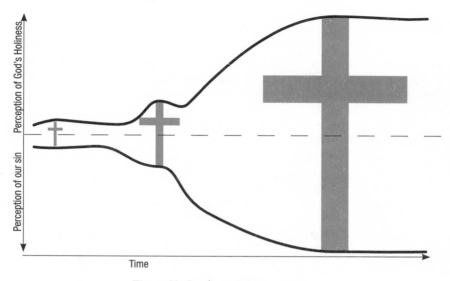

Figure 11. Sam's receiving more grace

I know Maria's story from hearing her tell it. She grew up in a Christian family to become what Bushnell describes as "growing up a Christian and never knowing a time when she was otherwise."[7] She went away to college and then on to seminary. She left seminary before completing a degree, and she and her physician husband immediately began a family. Through college, seminary, and early marriage the cross was gradually shrinking. She was competent at all she did, loved by her friends, commended for her parenting, and deeply needed by her shy and insecure husband.

She was active in her church, and one day her pastor spoke to her about how her "perfectionism hindered her ministry." To her, it was a weird conversation: "Perfectionism, how could that be a problem? Wasn't that next to or the same as godliness?" she wondered. Over the next few months she received more feedback about her "demands and expectations," "her touchiness when questioned by others," and "her put-downs of some people." This was hard to take; as she shared it with her parents and husband, they suggested that it was time to find another church where she would be appreciated. Yet the comments were consistent and came from people she respected, so she stayed. At this point she was at a critical spiritual stage. We might say the cross was smaller than the gap. The cross can only stay smaller than the gap for a short period of time. She was busily filling in the gap by listening to her loved ones' affirmation and making excuses, when all of a sudden she "got it." While her child was napping, she thought with anger at what her friends had said, and then suddenly, through tears, she realized that they were at least mostly right. She was broken. And the cross began to grow. Over time, she tossed aside the stuff that she had used to fill in the gap around her small cross. As Maria sat before God, more aware of her sin and far more aware of his grace than she had been in years, the cross towered over her life in an increasingly comforting way.

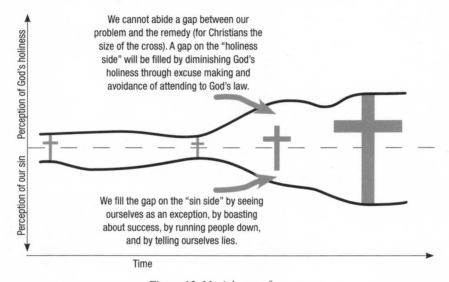

Figure 12. Maria's gap of grace

Susan's life changed immensely in college. Her goal of being a physician was set aside for the more immediate goal of fun. She did well in school, but she never let studying get in the way of a good party. One Saturday, like so many others, she was serving beer at a sorority party when she found herself outraged and disgusted by the self-centered and cruel behavior of a sorority sister. Too angry to confront her directly, she stepped aside for a minute to regain her composure, and in the quiet she looked into an ethical mirror. The image was familiar. *She* was that girl. She had put people down like that hundreds of times. She had acted as if the world revolved around her. She was appalled at herself and walked away from the party, never to return.

Over the next months she sought out Christian friends from high school, and by the end of the school year she had committed her life to following Christ. She spent the summer at a discipleship-training

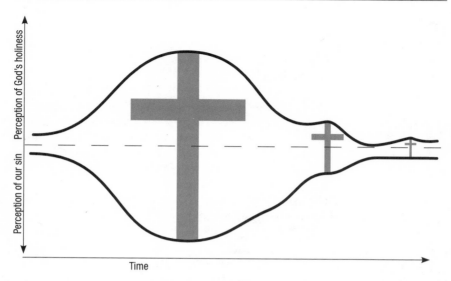

Figure 13. Susan's shrinking cross

program run by a campus ministry. She returned in the fall, full of
enthusiasm for Jesus. She spoke of her faith and touched the lives of
countless people, from janitors to professors, with her love and quick-
minded defense of the faith.

She entered law school and did well, despite an enormous amount
of time spent with a college ministry. She was affirmed for her teaching
ministry, but the compassion, fun, and witness were not as prominent
as they had been. In her adult life she has continued to be involved in
ministry, much of it pro bono legal work on certain social issues on which
she believes "a Christian must take a stand." All who meet her are struck
by her charisma, competence, and togetherness. Over the years, as she
succeeded in following a rigid pattern of discipleship, she has grown more
confident of her strengths and less accepting of those who are struggling.
After helping to mediate a dispute involving Susan and a ministry leader
at her church, a friend confronted her: "Susan, there is no grace in you."
As her perceived spiritual competence has grown, the cross has shrunk.

The cross never changes, but as Sam, Maria, and Susan moved through
different experiences, they came to see their need of the cross differently.
For Sam and Maria, the cross became larger and far more critical as
they owned their sin, need, and yearnings. As the gospel broke through
and they were able to get the logs out of their eyes, they could see their
own need and not be totally preoccupied with the shortcomings of others
or their unexpected circumstances (Matt. 7:3–5). Community relationships and the words of others helped Sam and Maria to appraise their
nearness to the cross. Susan's story is unfinished. We hope that she will

be open to listen to her friends and seek grace for deeper and renewed formation.

Jesus healed ten lepers and sent them to the priest to have their healing confirmed. One returned to give thanks for the grace he had received. He wanted to verbalize his gratitude personally, to worship, and to prolong his encounter with his Savior. Like the woman at Simon's party, he loved much because Jesus had noticed his great need and healed his sickness. His gratitude reflects both an awareness of a deep, desperate need and the joy of new hope and wholeness. Jesus responded to him with further instructions: "Get up and go on your way; your faith has made you well" (Luke 17:19).

How often did the grateful returning leper recall the day of his healing? How long did he remember the look of pleasure on Jesus' face when he returned and worshipped? How long do we remember the grace we have received? Those with a large cross perspective take time daily to reflect on grace received. They are determined to share with others their healing and their need to remember their healing. The community disciplines of worship, confession, and learning ought to remind us that we are needy people who require enormous amounts of grace from a large cross. We will not be able to respond to this truth or relate to God and others in light of this truth if we do not first remember it.

For Further Reading

Crysdale, Cynthia S. W. *Embracing Travail: Retrieving the Cross Today*. New York: Continuum Publishing, 1999. Theological exploration of Jesus' crucifixion that encourages Christians to see themselves both as "a victim and a perpetrator of sin." Other topics include sin, grace, evil, resistance, surrender, and "voice."

Griffin, Emilie. *Turning: Reflections on the Experience of Conversion*. Garden City, NY: Doubleday, 1980. Based partly on the author's personal experience of conversion to Christianity, this work traces successive stages in conversion and their psychological dimension.

Lovelace, Richard F. *Dynamics of Spiritual Life: An Evangelical Theology of Renewal*. Downers Grove, IL: InterVarsity, 1979. Comprehensive theological treatment of Christian growth with a strong community orientation.

Packer, J. I. *Knowing God*. Downers Grove, IL: InterVarsity, 1973. An invitation to pursue the knowledge of God and a demonstration of the power of theology in personal formation.

Tozer, A. W. *The Knowledge of the Holy: The Attributes of God; Their Meaning in the Christian Life*. HarperCollins gift ed. New York: Harper-SanFrancisco, 1992. A brief, compelling, and readable work on the attributes of God.

Tugwell, Simon. *Ways of Imperfection: An Exploration of Christian Spirituality*. London: Darton, Longman, & Todd, 1984. An accessible history of Christian spirituality.

6

To Foster Remembering in Community

If remembering the Story is a conserving activity, proposing the Vision is the liberating dimension of our ministry as Christian religious educators.[1]

Thomas H. Groome

Do this in remembrance of me.

Jesus, in 1 Corinthians 11:24

Faith can remember that the Spirit who made his home in your heart promised to stay—whether you feel him or not.[2]

Jack Haberer

Patterns of Community Learning

"We always give thanks to God for all of you and mention you in our prayers, constantly remembering before our God and Father your work of faith and labor of love in steadfastness of hope in our Lord Jesus Christ" (1 Thess. 1:2–3). Paul tells us that he was "constantly remembering" the Thessalonians. That is quite a testimony to his affection for them. He was always thinking about these believers. I use this verse at the outset of our section on seeking to enhance remembering in our churches because we are far more likely to remember enfleshed truth,

114

truth in the context of relationships, than mere abstract propositions. Paul's letters display a remarkable consistency, in that truth was never an abstract object but always a very personal subject. The truth of the gospel had set him free and was guiding his life by changing the lives of people who received it. Parker Palmer reminds us, "This distinction is crucial to knowing, teaching and learning: *A subject is available for relationship; an object is not.*"[3]

Creating a Space for Truth

Palmer calls us to put obedience to truth at the heart of our teaching: "To teach is to create a space in which obedience to truth is practiced."[4] Teaching is not simply laying out the truth before people as just one more item to appraise, but it is calling for obedience to the truth of Jesus Christ as we teach the truth we have come to understand. Within the body of Christ, we teach by the way we speak and listen, the way we make appropriate claims on one another, and the way we allow ourselves to be held accountable by this learning community. We must see that our learning environment is not just a place where we present truth as so many options on a great religious smorgasbord but rather as a part of the very fabric of our relationship with Christ.

Seeking Wisdom

> Wisdom is the conscious recognition that all we have and are come from God and that every aspect of our lives needs to be under his dominion.[5]
>
> Kenneth Boa

We commonly understand wisdom to mean having extensive applied knowledge or understanding and being able to use or apply that information in efficient or helpful ways. A. W. Tozer writes:

> Wisdom, among other things, is the ability to devise perfect ends and to achieve those ends by the most perfect means. It sees the end from the beginning, so there can be no need to guess or conjecture. Wisdom sees everything in focus, each in proper relation to all.[6]

The writer of Proverbs reminds us that human wisdom comes from deferring to divine wisdom. Our redemption illustrates the working of this divine wisdom, which demands a response of awe, for as John Piper says, "The wisdom of God has ordained a way for the love of God to deliver us from the wrath of God without compromising the justice of God."[7] We should honor such wisdom and embrace an understanding that God's ways are not our ways and be willing to live by the promise, "I will lead the blind by a road they do not know, by paths they have not known I will guide them. I will turn the darkness before them into light, the rough places into level ground. These are the things I will do, and I will not forsake them" (Isa. 42:16).

Wisdom is humble and seeks to learn by asking questions. Wisdom takes a long and eternal outlook on life and, in humility, knows that there is more to learn and more growing to pursue. Over time, the wise ones have gained a wealth of knowledge and understanding, but they are quiet listeners whose words, while challenging, are always inviting and generous. Wisdom respects God's timing and has a humble openness to God's leading, however mysterious and challenging, and to the concerns of others in a search for the long and eternal outcomes that honor God. Solomon says, "The fear of the LORD is the beginning of wisdom, and the knowledge of the Holy One is insight" (Prov. 9:10). David writes, "The fear of the LORD is the beginning of wisdom; all those who practice it have a good understanding. His praise endures forever" (Ps. 111:10). We cannot love or revere or follow a person that we do not know. Wisdom is to know the Lord and his commands and to live by a knowledge that stretches us beyond ourselves. Wisdom "transcends human intelligence and cleverness," and it is essentially the "skill of living within the moral order of Yahweh's world."[8]

Congruence/Integrity

Education in spiritual formation practices is always multidimensional. Congruence refers to how well the various dimensions of the spiritual formation process complement one another. For example, consider the social atmosphere of many youth groups. The message promotes respect for community and proclaims that spiritual giftings and passions are to be the bases of one's involvement in ministry. However, many students perceive that the social pecking order so common in their high schools carries over into the youth program; hence, "popular kids" are selected for leadership, and those who might have the spiritual passions and gifts to lead are not given prominence. To the extent that such a caricature is valid, it describes a lack of congruence in an important area of our churches' spiritual formation.

Lawrence Kohlberg, the moral educator, explored the connection between teaching justice and learning it in *The Just Community Approach to Corrections*. Kohlberg learned that everyone claimed to support moral education and justice education, but few principals and administrators were really willing to help create a just community in their schools that would be congruent with the moral education being offered. Kohlberg believed so strongly in this principle of congruence that he went on to establish an experimental school committed to creating an environment of justice.[9] Particularly in youth ministry and discipleship programs aimed at new believers, the issue of congruence must be front and center. Congruence should be a mark of all true spiritual formation, but in groups for youth and new believers, it needs to be carefully audited and intentionally cultivated.

My Story, Our Story

The present cannot be experienced as present if the past cannot be remembered as past. A man without a past cannot celebrate the present and accept his life as his own.[10]

Henri Nouwen

Spiritual formation always works the delicate balance between the personal appropriation of spiritual truth and the reality that our faith is a historically grounded community event. Both the individual aspects of our faith and its communal reality need to be part of our spiritual formation. It is necessary that the believer personally appropriate the benefits of Jesus' redemptive work on the cross to be spiritually well formed. At the same time, a deep assurance of the reality of this redemption will only come when one understands it through a historical and communal lens. A friend of mine in college struggled with the assurance of his salvation, and his well-intentioned spiritual mentor could only offer him the advice to go back to the night that he had made an emotionally grounded decision to "follow Christ." Over time my friend came to a deep assurance of God's love, and in part this grew as he developed more of a communal understanding of the reality of his faith and saw Christ's work as something that was more than just an emotional experience; it was something grounded in historical reality. An important moment in spiritual formation comes when we link "my story" with the "our story" of the church universal and understand that we are part of something far larger than ourselves.

Creatively Presenting

One of the perennial problems in spiritual formation is the gap between our profession of faith and our living out our faith. We may find ourselves cognitively knowing certain biblical and theological truths but not letting them guide our lives. For instance, one may know Jesus' warning about improper judging, "Do not judge, so that you may not be

The Joseph Paradigm

The Christmas story is the fullest, grandest story ever told. It discloses the miracle of the incarnation and includes many characters, drama, and mystery. Enfolded within the larger narrative is the story of Joseph, the husband of Mary. We may see his transformation as moving through four phases: *tradition phase*, *crisis phase*, *awareness phase*, and *obedience phase*.

Joseph has been raised within the *Jewish tradition* and has a firm understanding of its history, expectations, and ground rules. The tradition had impacted his formation, and he was a representative product of its cultural and spiritual past. Therefore, as he becomes aware that Mary is pregnant with a child that he knows is not his, the news generates a particular crisis and challenge for him.

The *crisis phase* requires that Joseph evaluate and reexamine what he is to do and why. How is he to react to Mary, to her story of an angel's visit and message, to her baby, or to their friends and families? When trapped in a debilitating dilemma, it is helpful to ask the constructive questions of "How?" and "What?" rather than the unanswerable pleas of "Why?" and "When?" Wrestling with these difficult questions is required because the way to integration and balance is through a season of disintegration. The struggle Joseph faces is instrumental in preparing him to fully support Mary and to receive Christ as his adoptive son.

After Joseph makes a decision, God speaks to him in a dream. Joseph is aware of God and his message, and that *awareness phase* is crucial in transformation. However, his awareness went deeper within his life to tap the greater spiritual component of the soul. God spoke to him during a dream, electing to speak to his unconscious. The resulting product is a total shaping of Joseph's mind, heart, and soul.

True awareness must inspire a response. *Obedience* is an awareness and attentiveness that is sensitive and responsive to God, our world, and ourselves. The interrelationship between obedience and listening suggests that this phase is both the most difficult and most important within the transformation process. Obedience is not a one-step act. Instead, obedience, like awareness, unfolds progressively throughout life. Detachment or surrender further requires us to be cognizant of accountability. Accountability and vulnerability reinforce the communal nature and necessity of Christian transformation.

The four phases of tradition, crisis, awareness, and obedience commonly repeat themselves as we come upon different situations or episodes in our lives. Every crisis is an opportunity to listen with our hearts for "a word from the Lord" and to struggle with the difficult questions that reevaluate our stance and seek a way to move forward with an obedient heart that is committed to

continued ➤

our God and our neighbor. A certain crisis may generate negative outcomes because someone has missed an opportunity and remains unaware and disobedient. One may regress spiritually or move backward on the spiral.

The explanation of Joseph's own maturing suggests that not only the cognitive but also the ethical, volitional, relational, and deepening spiritual factors are present and important. While our belief and trust is intensely personal, it should not become exclusively private because of its impact upon the community in which we live. The transformation displayed through Joseph is a dynamic process where God initiates the spiritual process. Though God makes the genesis move, we are more than robotic manikins. The Holy Spirit, who occasionally appears through the angel of the Lord, is a key participant in the formative process.

Adapted from "Pilgrim's Process" by Tom Schwanda. Used by permission.[11]

judged" (Matt. 7:1), but still live a life marked by racial prejudice and other deformative prejudices. Mere repetition of this command will not cause people to see the connection between Jesus' teaching and their life. In fact, people often use the verse out of context as a defensive weapon to deny the validity of healthy confrontation. The perennial areas of struggle for Christians—racism, doubting God's love, anger, fear, worry, and not seeing their neighbor's pain—need to be addressed in creative ways that allow the message to get past our defenses. An example of this is Nathan's clever confrontation of David through a story. David was certainly aware of the scriptural teaching against adultery, lying, and murder, but when Nathan told a story, it caught David off guard and provided an opening for David to see the error of his way. Similarly, story, drama, testimony, firsthand accounts, and immersion experiences are usually better at getting past our resistance to these very central issues of discipleship than mere direct re-presentations of this truth.

A spiral curriculum has the student constantly revisiting topics and truths, with the aim of working these truths deeper into the fabric of our lives. In the early twentieth century, the field of religious education adopted the linear acquisition curriculum model used in math and science instruction. Educators thought that students mastered basic material and then moved on to more and more complex learning. A linear curriculum has much to commend it in many areas of study, but the wisdom of the ages saw the circular curriculum, analogous to the church year, as far more appropriate for spiritual formation. The circular curriculum re-presents subjects again and again and provides opportunities to go deeper into these subjects.

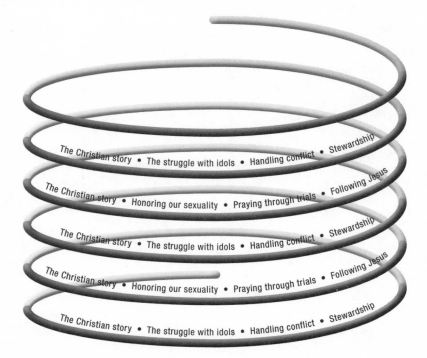

Figure 14. Spiral curriculum

Scripture is very clear about the problem of spiritual blindness. This blindness is an inability to recognize spiritual truth. In Scripture being "blind" describes idolaters (Isa. 44:9–10) and judges whose judgment is perverted because of bribes (Exod. 23:8; Deut. 16:19). Jesus himself characterized the religious leaders and teachers of his own generation in terms of blindness (Matt. 15:14; 23:16–17). Paul changed the metaphor but made the same point: "Don't be so naive and self-confident. You're not exempt. You could fall flat on your face as easily as anyone else. Forget about self-confidence; it's useless. Cultivate God-confidence" (1 Cor. 10:12 Message). Henri Nouwen has advised that "the two main reasons why a preacher often creates more antagonism than sympathy are (1) the assumption of non-existent feelings and (2) the preoccupation with a theological point of view."[12] The problem is that we have set ideas and are resistant to seeing things another way. "In complete contrast to our idea that adulthood means the ability to take care of oneself, Jesus describes it as a growing willingness to stretch out one's hands and be guided by others"[13] (see John 21:18). Nouwen recommends the use of dialogue and availability.

Skills in Teaching

1. **Clarity of communication.** Both the instructional content that is shared and the procedures to be followed in learning require clear communication. In relation to procedures, teachers share with participants the stated purposes, goals, and objectives of the instruction as a means to encourage ownership.

2. **Flexibility and use of a variety of teaching methods.** Openness is called for that compensates for change without losing sight of the original intentions and purposes of the session. Flexibility sometimes signals avoidance of key areas of learning that we should not pass over. Using a variety of teaching methods increases the possibility that the participants will be able to maintain concentration and avoid boredom.

3. **Enthusiasm.** The enthusiasm of the teacher is contagious if the instructional content is owned by the teacher in new ways. This ownership requires diligence in the preparation for teaching. Diligence in the evaluation of teaching provides new possibilities for future presentations.

4. **Maintenance of a task orientation.** Effective teachers are able to keep students focused on the tasks of learning. Sensitivity to persons in terms of care is important in the ministry of teaching, but an equal concern for the content and its potential transformative impact is required. The focus on tasks is the complementary skill to flexibility. In this maintenance of a task orientation, the teacher provides feedback to students regarding their progress in relation to the assigned tasks and reminds them of the ultimate goals of their efforts.

5. **Ability to involve students in the teaching-learning process.** This involvement includes intellectual, psychological, and physical responses. Total involvement of persons encourages the transfer of learning to other situations beyond the immediate instructional setting. In evaluation, participants reflect on and assess the levels of their involvement and suggest alternatives that may have improved their engagement with the instructional content. This skill and its evaluation foster the formation of persons as self-directed learners who have learned how to learn in other settings.

6. **Varying the level of discourse.** Discourses can be at the level of facts, explanations, evaluative judgments, justification, critical analyses and syntheses, concrete realities, and abstract conceptualizations. Variety encourages creative and critical responses. It serves to connect the instructional content with realities outside the immediate setting, and it decreases rote responses from participants.

continued ➤

7. Appropriate use of praise and criticism. The praise shared with participants must be genuine and appropriate to the instruction. This is a real concern in an age of manipulation. The criticism teachers offer to their students must be constructive, particularly in a critical and cynical age that readily dismisses others through negative critique. Affirmation centers on students as persons, and criticism is reserved for their performance or work. With criticism, it is necessary for teachers to suggest alternatives.

8. Self-analysis and self-evaluation. The effective teacher is capable of pursuing continuous self-study and self-analysis so that one's actions improve over time. It requires an integrity that models the teacher's openness toward one's own personal transformation.

Adapted from Basics of Teaching for Christians
by Robert W. Pazmiño. Used by permission.[14]

Dialogue is not a technique or a special skill you can learn in school, but a way of life. . . . Availability is the primary condition for every dialogue that is to lead to a redemptive insight. A preacher who is not willing to make his understanding of his own faith and doubt, anxiety and hope, fear and joy available as a source of recognition for others can never expect to remove the many obstacles which prevent the Word of God from bearing fruit.[15]

Pastoral Care

Personal loss, tragedies, changes, and disruption can contribute to spiritual formation. These events have the effect of stripping away our self-reliance and reminding us of what is truly important in life. They can also be times of great embittering and loss. We need to put structures in place that emphasize deep compassion, care, and empathy as well as formative guidance. In general, our churches are better at providing compassion than formative guidance, and youth programs are far more prone to emphasize diversion over direction. Formation implies in its language that there is a form (an image) to which we are seeking to conform—the character of Christ.

Some years ago an acquaintance of mine was fired during a brutal downsizing of his company. The events traumatized this man, and I remember talking with him about the experience. Members of his small group had come around to provide a listening ear and to provide practical help in terms of childcare and job networking. As we chatted, I asked him what he was doing to guard his heart against becoming bitter. He told me he was not doing anything to guard his heart and spent hours each day thinking negatively about the man who fired him. We talked more, and I warned him about where that path could take him. As we parted, he expressed gratitude for the guidance and mentioned that out of all of the caring members of his church, no one had offered that kind of formative/responsive counsel. Our efforts to avoid the mistake of claiming to know exactly what the person is going through sometimes cause us to miss opportunities to give wisdom and direction where it is desperately needed. In the midst of loss and tragedy, people need to receive not only compassionate and empathetic care but also guidance to understand how to construe the loss that they have experienced.

Community Disciplines That Foster Remembering

It is the main enterprise for every individual to find the way back to his heart. He is an explorer, moving into that unknown, inner region; . . . a pilgrim in search of his heart, of his deepest and his most real being.[16]

André Louf

The community disciplines explored in this section fit into the wider disciplines of teaching and learning. One of the most important steps in establishing a successful, educationally based spiritual formation strategy in a local church is to shift the emphasis from teaching to learning. It's all too easy in a technology-saturated culture to begin to equate teaching with the efficient transmission or publication of material. Spiritual formation contends that there is a need for both informational teaching (teaching that helps ground one in the facts of the Christian story) and formational teaching (teaching that helps one live out the truth of the Christian gospel). An exclusive focus on teaching in many churches tends to give an overemphasis on informational presentations at the expense of those that are more formational.

Story

We use stories to help us understand our world. Christians tell and listen to stories to help bear our sorrows, to prolong our joys, and to gain insights into how we should live. As I listen to people tell their stories of making a tough judgment call, I'm always impressed that it is the stories of Scripture that provide key principles and guidelines for their decision making. Our lack of familiarity with biblical stories leads to impoverished thinking and an inability to appreciate the rich and plentiful biblical allusions and quotes in great speaking. For example, a well-known speech such as Martin Luther King Jr.'s great "I Have a Dream" would be a shell of itself if it were stripped of biblical content. So we need to know the stories of Scripture, and we also need to see ourselves in the large and grand story of salvation. This, in part, requires the need to show that our faith is historically grounded. Here are some stories that people in our churches should be familiar with:

- Historic figures in church history
- Contemporary martyrs
- Missions and ministries of compassion supported by your church
- Local church and institutional history

Small Groups

Problems that seem insoluble when individuals ponder them alone are viewed in a much more optimistic light when the Spirit of God is free to move a group in the direction of God's will.[17]

Lois LeBar

Small groups can provide a marvelous environment for us to remember who we are in the midst of challenges and for the community to love its members. Small groups give us the opportunity to learn and to reflect on our situation. They can be the place where double knowledge (i.e., knowledge of God and self) is refined. Small groups are the perfect environment to provide both the support and challenge that we need to live the Christian life well.

Small groups are a gift of grace from God to a group of people committed to learning and growing together. For many people these small gatherings provide the best examples of Christian community. They are places where Larry Crabb's characteristics of spiritual community are often most clearly seen as: "1) celebrating people as created and forgiven by God; 2) visioning what another is becoming and trusting God to accomplish such; 3) discerning happenings as climates for growth; 4) empowering others to fully become what God is desiring for them to be."[18]

Anointed Teaching

Seek Him! What can we do without Him? Seek Him! Seek Him always. But go beyond seeking Him; expect Him.[19]

Martyn Lloyd-Jones

It is the peculiar ministry of the Holy Spirit to make the outer Word an inner experience. No other teacher can be both an outer and an inner factor.[20]

Lois LeBar

Presenting a curriculum for Christlikeness requires the integration of both anointed teaching and careful curriculum development. Anointed teaching means that the Holy Spirit comes upon the teacher in a special manner. It is God giving insight, power, and enabling, through the Spirit, to the teacher in order that one may do this work in a manner that lifts it up beyond simple human efforts and endeavors.[21] Anointing is not just an optional enrichment to teaching but something that must mark it. The Puritan writer and preacher Richard Baxter used an apt expression when he spoke of the anointing on Christian communication as being a "tincture" or dye that colors the entire communication.[22] The audience does not detect anointing merely in the passion of the speaker or in an insightful application of the text, but also in the very fabric of the message and in the seamless integrity between the life of the speaker and the message.

God's Spirit anointed Old Testament leaders, prophets, and others for special tasks when God needed a witness to proclaim his Word, to show his providential presence, or to lead his people. Such setting-apart was often indicated by actual anointing with oil, beautifully described in Psalm 133:2: "How very good and pleasant it is when kindred live together in unity! It is like the precious oil on the head, running down upon the beard, on the beard of Aaron, running down over the collar of his robes."

Examples of anointing include Bezalel (Exod. 31:1–5), Joshua (Deut. 34:9), Othniel (Judg. 3:10), Gideon (Judg. 6:34), Samson (Judg. 14:6, 19), Saul (1 Sam. 11:6), David (1 Sam. 16:13), Ezekiel (Ezek. 3:14), and Daniel (Dan. 5:14). These passages illustrate and emphasize that God is pleased, from time to time, to sovereignly choose to come upon individuals and enable them to carry out their assigned work by the supernatural power of the Holy Spirit.

The New Testament emphasizes the Holy Spirit's enablement of believers to grow spiritually. Consequently, we can understand the interest Christian teachers have in seeking to teach with the Spirit's enabling. Galatians 5:22 describes the fruit of the Spirit as "love, joy, peace, patience, kindness, goodness, faithfulness, gentleness and self-control" (NIV), and 2 Corinthians 3 links the Holy Spirit with our transformation. Romans 5–8 teaches that the Holy Spirit pours out the love of God into our hearts and bears witness to us of our adoption. In Ephesians 6:17 the Word of God is called "the sword of the Spirit," and Paul instructs Timothy to guard the good deposit of sound teaching "with the help of the Holy Spirit living in us" (2 Tim. 1:14). First John 2:20 assures us that "you have an anointing from the Holy One, and all of you know the truth" (NIV). As the teacher prays over the Scripture lesson, the prayer is that the Holy Spirit would permeate the entire teaching and learning process for the spiritual growth and transformation of both the teacher and the learner.

Spirit Within, Spirit Upon, Spirit Among

It is the work of the Holy Spirit to form the living Christ within us, dwelling deep down in the deepest depths of our being.[23]

R. A. Torrey

It is the Spirit who brings gifts and giftedness for power-ministry to my life.[24]

Jack Hayford

The Spirit of God acts on people through people.[25]

Evelyn Underhill

The privilege of being the dwelling of the Spirit was as much a group privilege as an individual one.[26]

Jack Haberer

When considering the work of the Spirit in anointing our communication, it is helpful to have some categories for analyzing the phenomenon. In this section we identify three dimensions that provide a comprehensive way of viewing the Spirit's work in anointing. The dimensions are the Spirit *within*, the Spirit *upon*, and the Spirit *among*. Robust conceptions of anointing expect that all three are present and active in Spirit-empowered teaching for individual and corporate formation.

The Spirit within is the cornerstone of anointed teaching. This indwelling dimension includes (1) the Spirit's work of transformation, (2) illumination of Scripture, and (3) communication of God's grace. The Spirit works to transform teachers as they are regenerate and open to the Spirit's transforming grace. The spiritual maturity of the teacher is not incidental to the teaching-learning process. Teachers can only effectively teach what they deeply understand and have grasped from experience. The spiritual experience and maturity of the teacher affects what material they have mastered, overall judgment, selection of material, and wisdom in handling class situations. Jesus captured this truth so aptly when he said, "A disciple is not above the teacher, but everyone who is fully qualified will be like the teacher" (Luke 6:40). The teacher's spiritual maturity is not a private matter, because it affects one's students.

The teacher must learn truth and experience transformation by the Spirit dwelling within through prayer. E. M. Bounds makes a strong case for the connection between prayer and preaching and goes so far as to say, "Preaching which kills is prayerless preaching."[27] Bounds argues that unction (a synonym for *anointing*) flows from prayer and is essential to Christian ministry. "This divine unction is the feature which separates and distinguishes true gospel preaching from all other methods of presenting the truth."[28] The ongoing prayer of the teacher is for the anointing of the Holy Spirit and for his instruction in the study and preparation required for teaching Scripture. Prayer is required because of the uniqueness of Scripture and the need for the Holy Spirit in understanding and explaining Scripture (1 Cor. 1–2). The teacher has the assurance that the Father will repeatedly give the Holy Spirit to those who ask him (Luke 11:13).

The Spirit upon, the second dimension of anointed teaching, is perhaps the most common understanding of the Spirit's work in anointing. As at Pentecost, when the Spirit descended on those gathered and they ministered in great power, the Spirit comes upon and brings power and authority, authenticating the message and working miracles that give testimony to God's power.

Spirit upon is a supernatural anointing of God's power, enabling ministry and communication. Jesus taught that the purpose of the power is for witnessing. As he ascended he said, "You will receive power when the Holy Spirit comes on you; and you will be my witnesses" (Acts 1:8 NIV). Peter preached, "God anointed Jesus of Nazareth with the Holy Spirit and power, and . . . he went around doing good and healing all who were under the power of the devil, because God was with him" (10:38 NIV). This summary in Peter's sermon is a paraphrase of Jesus' own statement of purpose. When Jesus preached in Nazareth, he applied Isaiah 61:1–2 to himself and proclaimed: "The Spirit of the Lord is on me, because he has anointed me to preach good news to the poor. He has sent me to proclaim freedom for the prisoners and recovery of sight for the blind, to release the oppressed, to proclaim the year of the Lord's favor" (Luke 4:18–19 NIV). The ultimate purpose of all anointing and all filling of the Holy Spirit is to proclaim and bear witness that Jesus is indeed who he said he is and that he alone is able to free and transform us. The effect of Peter's anointing is thus recorded: "While Peter was still speaking these words, the Holy Spirit came on all who heard the message" (Acts 10:44 NIV). These new believers give witness to the fact that the year of the Lord's favor will include Gentiles as well as Jews.

Zeb Bradford Long and Douglas McMurry note that often writers stress either the Spirit within or the Spirit upon. They encourage both groups to learn from each other and to understand that both elements are necessary. "Those who have matured in the character-building virtues of Christ but lack the power gifts in ministry can learn from those who have developed the power gifts, and vice-versa. . . . God wants us all to grow in both the character of Christ and in power ministry."[29] Rather than emphasizing either the Spirit within or the Spirit upon, anointed teaching must seek to integrate them.

The third dimension of anointed teaching is the work of the Spirit among. Anointing creates a new community where the Spirit is among the participants. The Spirit among is demonstrated as the anointing power and presence of the Holy Spirit becomes evident in the community. The community is transformed into one marked by trust, support, loving challenge, worship, ministry, spiritual risk taking, and transformational learning. The Holy Spirit works to construct the church and classroom into a loving, just, compassionate, and worshipping community that invites openness and dialogue.

Spirit among is based on God's work with his chosen people as a group. His covenant was with a family group and not just with Abraham (Gen. 12:1–3). God tells Haggai, "This is what I covenanted with you when you came out of Egypt. And my Spirit remains among you. Do not fear" (Hag. 2:5 NIV; see also Isa. 63:11). Paul taught that we have received spiritual gifts "for the common good" (1 Cor. 12:7). The fruit of the Spirit (Gal. 5:22–23) is immediately relevant to instructions such as these: "Honor one another above yourselves" (Rom. 12:10 NIV). "Live in harmony with one another" (Rom. 12:16). "Be kind to one another, tenderhearted, forgiving one another" (Eph. 4:32). "Encourage one another and build up each other, as indeed you are doing" (1 Thess. 5:11). Gordon Fee notes that in the trinitarian benediction of 2 Corinthians 13:13 (NRSV) or 14 (NIV), Paul selects "fellowship" to characterize the ministry of the Spirit.[30]

The anointing of the Spirit for teaching and learning is a rich and multifaceted experience. When the Spirit comes in sovereign visitation, these dimensions are present, but often the sense of power is what is most observed. As teachers seek to cultivate the anointing of the Spirit through prayer and spiritual openness, they should be aware of the richness of this empowerment and pray with commensurate breath for his presence and power upon the teaching and among the learners.

Cultivating the Anointing

O Lord of power and grace, all hearts are in thy hands, all events at thy disposal. Set the seal of thy almighty will upon my ministry.[31]

Puritan prayer

By means of intercessory prayer God extends to each of us a personalized, hand-engraved invitation to become intimately involved in laboring for the well-being of others.[32]

Richard Foster

Anointed teaching is first and foremost an indwelling and empowering of the Holy Spirit. There are no formulas that can guarantee its coming or effectiveness, and yet there are patterns, practices, and dispositions that foster the presence of anointed teaching. It is our responsibility to desire it, pray for it, acknowledge our need of it, seek outcomes that require it, build a place for it, and cultivate a community that seeks its truth. Anointed teaching depends on the Holy Spirit as sailing depends on the wind. Every earnest sailor will mend his sail, inspect his rigging, train his crew, watch the sky, and expect the wind. He will be ready when the gust comes. He will take full advantage of even a gentle breeze to move his ship forward.

Teachers and preachers must wholeheartedly desire an anointing. Congregations and students must be open and seeking. They must all proclaim with Martyn Lloyd-Jones, "Seek Him! Seek Him! What can we do without Him? Seek Him! Seek always. . . . This 'unction,' this 'anointing,' is the supreme thing. Seek it until you have it; be content with nothing less."[33]

The desire for an anointing ought to be the strongest in the teacher's prayer closet. The Holy Spirit guides the teacher's prayer life with an eye to the mutual concern that, in all of life, the gospel message is proclaimed and heard, Jesus is glorified, the sinner is freed, the seeker understands Scripture, and the disciple is transformed. When the teacher struggles for words or stamina in prayer, the Spirit "intercedes with sighs too deep for words. And God, who searches the heart, knows what is the mind of the Spirit, because the Spirit intercedes for the saints according to the will of God" (Rom. 8:26–27). Anointing flows out of the prayer closet as the teacher's knowledge of God has been expanded and tested. To pray for unction is to pray for a specific endowment of God. E. M. Bounds wrote, "This unction comes to the preacher not in the study but in the closet."[34] Jesus set a high standard for prayer time, but he probably was tempted like we are to subsist on a scanty prayer diet. He sympathizes with our weakness (Heb. 4:15–16) and is the high priest who prays for the prayers of teachers and preachers.

"Piper is right when he says that all genuine preaching is rooted in a feeling of desperation. The preacher wakes up on the Lord's Day morning and he can smell the smoke of hell on one side and feel the crisp breezes of heaven on the other. He then looks down at his pitiful notes and he says to himself, 'Who do I think I am kidding? Is this all there is?'"[35] The apostle Paul had this exact perspective when he wrote, "Since, in the wisdom of God, the world did not know God through wisdom, God decided, through the foolishness of our proclamation, to save those who believe" (1 Cor. 1:21).

Convinced of the need for complete reliance on the Holy Spirit's anointing, the teacher would be empowered to seek outcomes that require it. There is a healthy expectation and anticipation of openness, listening, and authentic change for those impacted by anointed teaching. We usually define educational outcomes as measurable and reasonable, but "when the preacher proclaims the Word of God something occurs that defies exact definition. Despair gives way to hope, lives are transformed, and changes take place that have the power to reshape history."[36] Anointed outcomes assume that the teacher has asked the hard questions: "Are you expecting it to be the turning point in someone's life? Are you expecting anyone to have a climactic experience?"[37] Anointed teaching needs a home, a truthful and holy place within the teacher's character and the classroom. W. E. Sangster goes so far as to tie both prayer and holiness to his definition of unction. "Prayer is the secret of a holy life. . . . Holiness is the secret of unction."[38]

Furthermore, the confidence that the Holy Spirit is the principal teacher and primary mover of truth must be a collective belief held by a community, in order for anointed teaching to be recognized and valued in that community. Here teaching and learning is relational, and "the moment of anointed preaching is a corporate reality."[39] It is expected that learners can learn from each other and from the teacher. The teacher is humble and teachable as well as courageous, willing to listen and venture into the unknown and untried. Teachers and learners pray and seek truth together in a loving community, upheld by the strength and courage of the Holy Spirit (Acts 9:31).

The Fruit of Anointing

Human love breeds hothouse flowers; spiritual love creates the fruits that grow healthily in accord with God's good will in the rain and storm and sunshine of God's outdoors.[40]

Dietrich Bonhoeffer

In a word, the fruit of anointed teaching is love! "The goal of our instruction is love from a pure heart" (1 Tim. 1:5 NASB). People are secure in the love of God and open to growth and care for others. "For you did not receive a spirit of slavery to fall back into fear, but you have received a spirit of adoption. When we cry, 'Abba! Father!' it is that very Spirit bearing witness with our spirit that we are children of God" (Rom. 8:15–16).

There is no room for pride or abuse in anointed teaching.[41] Pride is the opposite of humility and seeks security in self rather than in the grace of God. Jack Deere warns that "of all people, the proud have the most difficulty hearing God's voice. They seldom seriously ask God's opinion because they are convinced they already know what God thinks."[42] In contrast, "humble people put their confidence in the Holy Spirit's ability to speak, not in their ability to hear, and in Christ's ability to lead, not in their ability to follow."[43] Humility, especially in our study and seeking after truth, provides the opening for the Spirit to do his work.

A curriculum for Christlikeness is grounded in both careful attention to the empowering work of the Holy Spirit in teaching and diligent, thoughtful planning and study. We will miss the goal of spiritual transformation if we neglect either element or expect it to come by a natural or automatic process. Including the construct of anointed teaching in our conceptualizing of a curriculum for Christlikeness represents a step toward maintaining a right focus on the Holy Spirit in spiritual formation. Additionally, such a focus is greatly aided by (1) historical studies of anointed teachers and ministries, (2) theoretic proposals of curriculum that support and create a space for anointed teaching, (3) examinations of the classroom dynamics present when anointed teaching occurs, and (4) studies in educational leadership that contribute to the presence of anointed teaching. Many perceive that Bounds's maxim "prayerless preaching kills" is more than just preacherly hyperbole. A curriculum for spiritual formation in Christlikeness is only effective when it is saturated by a grace received through prayer, humble study, and awareness that we cannot achieve what we seek in our own power.

The Two Great Invitations of Jesus

Jesus Invites Us to Love and Obey God

Remember: "You are accepted!" The love of God is one of the most frequently declared doctrines but one of the least lived out. It is so easy to talk of God's love but so hard to get people to trust that love. Many churchgoers will sing of God's love, talk of God's love, and defend God's love but never trust his love and acceptance of them. If you doubt that, just ask: What do Christians around you do with their guilt and shame? Do they run to God, the source of love? Or are they more likely to expiate it by serving in the church, looking good, and stuffing the feelings inside?

Many of us have experienced the transforming trust that flows out of the unconditional love of another person; a certainty of God's love is even more grounding and assuring. Knowledge that God's acceptance of us is based on the cross must be the foundation of our spiritual life. If it is not, we will use our religion to salve our conscience more than to serve God and others. One of our greatest spiritual maladies is forgetfulness—forgetting who we are and whose we are in Christ. Embracing God's love is a lifelong calling, and we need to regularly present this vision to Christians.

The religious instruction described in the Bible was remarkably God-centered, and yet not God-centered in the way we might first imagine. It was not God-centered in the sense that it focused on theology; rather, the focus was on God himself. Significantly, in several Old Testament occurrences of a common Hebrew word for "teach" and "learn" (*lāmad*), it is the Lord himself who is the teacher. God taught his people through his interactions with them in day-to-day living. Furthermore, the great and powerful teachers of the Bible, like Isaiah and Jesus, always had a message directly related to the life of their learners, but even more important, it was a God-centered message. True spiritual formation constantly shows people that righteous and joyful living is available only to those who look at life from God's perspective rather than, as is the usual case, judging God by viewing him through life.

How can we teach and guide people so that in their remembrances they are drawn to love and obey God? Testimonies are one of the most powerful means of drawing people into a greater love of God. The best testimonies are stories of God at work as a Lover, Healer, Savior, and Friend: good testimonies put God on display. We all love stories, and we love stories that are nothing less than tales of God's grace. Testimonies are one simple way of bringing the reality of brokenness into our Christian communities. In general, we can think of testimonies coming in two varieties. The first are those that are resolved stories, where the person giving the story can put it into a "from, through, to" orientation. This means that some time has passed since the person has gone through the struggle, and he or she is able to identify the lessons learned and to cast them in a way that others can see and learn as well. The second variety of testimony are unresolved stories or so-called "in the midst of." Here the person is saying, "I got knocked off the deck of the ship, and I'm in the water; I'm not certain how much longer I can keep my head up, but in the midst of this, God is faithful." We really need a mix of both types of testimonies for them to have their real effect in the church. While testimonies seem so easy and natural, they benefit from some coaching in structure.

Jesus Invites Us to Love One Another

Love is the overflow of joy in God that meets the needs of others.[44]

John Piper

Guidelines for Coaching Testimonies

We begin with the assumption that a leader of the group where testimony is given might select persons ahead of time and meet with them to help them prepare. The concern is not simply that people "get it right" but that when the proper elements are emphasized, testimonies can be a powerful means of teaching. Some of the best testimonies come from people who are not accustomed to being up front and will feel more comfortable if they receive some help and guidance. Some people are going to be much more comfortable if the testimony is written out and they simply read it. From my experience, in general, the best testimonies are going to be given in the form of an interview, where the person giving the testimony knows the questions ahead of time. Asking people questions allows them to talk about areas of growth and victory that they might be hesitant to identify on their own.

Purpose. Make sure that you and the person giving the testimony are very clear about the purpose and the audience. Are you hoping this is a testimony that will capture the non-Christians in the audience, or is it intended to help move along lethargic Christians to more serious discipleship?

Sufficient Information. It is very important that the person giving the testimony share sufficient information about oneself. The audience needs to feel that they know the person and can understand the context in which this story is set.

Interview Format. A few thoughtful questions may draw out a compelling testimony from people who might not know where to start or what to say on their own.

Inner Feelings. One of the marvelous things about testimonies is that they enable people to reveal inner feelings that might not normally be shared in casual conversations. A coach or leader can help people understand what they were feeling and how that contributed to the decisions that they made.

Former Religion. Testimonies often involve leaving a former religion. However, one's spiritual heritage should be described with respect and not dismissed in a way that might be offensive to people in the audience.

Chronological Order. Do not be slavish to chronological order, because it will not guarantee a compelling and helpful testimony. People are interested in hearing the "then," "now," and a personalized understanding of how this evolved.

Wise Confession. Prudent boundaries need to be set on what is confessed. Confessions ought not to be confessions of the sins of others. Be careful about testimonies that could embarrass family members or others in the audience.

continued ➤

Honesty. Because testimonies are a powerful tool, Satan will seek to supplant and destroy their effectiveness. They should not become opportunities for people to overreach, in terms of what God has done in their life, or for people to become spiritually proud. Be vigilant that testimonies are honest and create a climate and culture of brokenness.

Resolution. Testimonies are often criticized when they are "all wrapped up in a neat little package." The "from, through, to" understanding of a person's predicament and a realistic assessment of where he or she ended up are higher priorities than excessive language of victory. When the stories are told, the human heart yearns for a celebration of grace and a sense of resolution of life's problems. The call is not for more unresolved stories, because many listeners will be able to identify with the "through" or "still in the midst of it" turbulent state of affairs. When stories have a happy ending, an interviewer can ask simple, follow-up questions or make some appropriate comments that help put this in a context of truth.

What we remember about ourselves and God affects how we serve and love. One of the most important ways we can affect what we remember and act on is through teaching and learning. When we remember the love and grace God has shown us through Christ, we are far more likely to pattern our responses after that kind of love.

The emphasis in this section is on how loving our neighbor can flow out of the community disciplines of teaching and learning. As I mentioned earlier, an important step in establishing a successful educationally based spiritual formation program in a local church is to shift the emphasis from teaching to learning.

When we emphasize learning, we highlight the experiences of individuals and communities. C. Ellis Nelson has clearly noted the different concerns of teaching and learning as follows:

> Educators often identify learning as that which a person absorbs, accepts, relates to, or identifies with, out of his or her experiences. The experience is the key to what the person learns. Teaching, however, is a deliberate act in which a leader tries to transmit knowledge, skill, attitude, or insight to someone. The key to teaching is the knowledge and ability of the teacher.[45]

Learning needs to flow from experiences where the truths of the gospel are directly related to ordinary life and work. We should see all the disciplines in this section as aspects of the educational, learning-engendering work of the church.

Learners and Learning

To learn is to integrate our awareness into our behavior in ways that influence and shape our decisions and actions. Learning is a profound event that leads to significant change in our total life. It involves four related steps or stages:

- An awareness of a starting point: a conscious acknowledgment of one's present state and its foundation in past experience.
- A significant experience best taking place away from one's home environment, though shared in community with others. The experience need not always be dramatic but will usually entail a feeling of dissonance. We feel the need for change.
- Reflection: a serious confrontation with our lives as lived demands reflection in order to acquire a new sense of stability and wholeness. Prayer is an obvious integral aspect of reflection. Reflection is best done in community with others who are also striving to resolve their dissonances.
- Assimilation: learning is not complete until we eliminate our old ways and integrate our new understandings. The end of assimilation is a public commitment to our new lifestyle and its particular behaviors.

To be Christian with others in the world through the integration of piety and politics requires such learning. And such learning is at the heart of church reform and renewal.

Adapted from Inner Growth, Outer Change *by John H. Westerhoff III.*[46]

These Invitations Flow out of the Call to Love God and Neighbor

Jesus Invites Us to Tell People about the Good News and Make Disciples

A disciple of Christ is one who (1) believes his doctrine, (2) rests on his sacrifice, (3) imbibes his spirit, and (4) imitates his example.[47]

M. G. Easton

A Focus on the Gospel

In the earlier chapters I mentioned the need for the gospel to be a road map to guide our lives. When we look at Paul's letter to the Galatians, we realize that it is easy for us to follow false gospels of various kinds. We need to remind ourselves that all of us follow and lean on various false gospels. Detecting them is difficult because they often are below our theological radar. Few well-churched Christians would actually claim

Life Together

Is the invisible presence of the Christian fellowship a reality and a help to the individual? Do the intercessions of others carry him through the day? Is the Word of God close to him as a comfort and a strength? Or does he misuse his aloneness contrary to the fellowship, the Word, and the prayer? The individual must realize that his hours of aloneness react upon the community. In his solitude he can sunder and besmirch the fellowship, or he can strengthen and hallow it. Every act of self-control of the Christian is also a service to the fellowship.

On the other hand, there is no sin in thought, word, or deed, no matter how personal or secret, that does not inflict injury upon the whole fellowship. An element of sickness gets into the body; perhaps nobody knows where it comes from or in what member it has lodged, but the body is infected. This is the proper metaphor for the Christian community. We are members of a body, not only when we choose to be, but also in our whole existence. Every member serves the whole body, either to its health or to its destruction. This is no mere theory; it is a spiritual reality. And the Christian community has often experienced its effects with disturbing clarity, sometimes destructively and sometimes fortunately.

One who returns to the Christian family fellowship after fighting the battle of the day brings with him the blessing of his aloneness, but he himself receives anew the blessing of the fellowship. Blessed is he who is alone in the strength of the fellowship, and blessed is he who keeps the fellowship in the strength of aloneness. But the strength of aloneness and the strength of the fellowship is solely the strength of the Word of God, which is addressed to the individual in the fellowship.

From Life Together *by Dietrich Bonhoeffer. Used by permission.*[48]

that good parenting, punctuality, etiquette, physical fitness, and active church involvement would be a way of achieving peace with God, but we live as if these are proven ways of gaining God's love and favor. We need to begin with an assumption that daily appropriating the gospel is going to be a struggle for Christians, and we constantly need to be retrained to rely upon the grace of Jesus Christ as offered in the gospel for our salvation and hope.

Training that appropriates the gospel will require a concrete look at subtle patterns of self-reliance and defensiveness. This really requires cultivating the kind of double knowledge that John Calvin speaks of in the first chapter of his *Institutes of the Christian Religion*. He holds that "without knowledge of self there is no knowledge of God," and "without

The Gospel and Christian Education

Is there an element that will bring the Bible, Christian doctrine, all human problems, life, experience, the child, the person, the church, and the Redeemer
of mankind all into bold relief? I believe that there is such an element and that
it is the gospel of God's redeeming activity in Jesus Christ. My conviction is
that Christian education can center in the gospel and use the gospel as its
guiding principle with assurance of its complete adequacy, both theologically
and educationally, and with assurance of its simplicity and clarity.

The suggestion that the gospel be used as the basic guide for Christian
education theory is supported by five arguments:

1. Revelation—the Word of God—is central in Christian education
   theory.
2. The gospel—God's redeeming activity in Jesus Christ—is the very heart
   and point of the Word he has spoken to men in their self-centered
   helplessness throughout the ages, and the very heart and point of the
   Word he speaks to men today.
3. The gospel is the clue to the meaning of history.
4. The gospel is the clue to the meaning of existence.
5. The gospel is the reason for the church's existence: it brings the church
   into existence; it sustains the church; it informs, directs, and corrects
   the church.

From The Gospel and Christian Education *by D. Campbell Wyckoff.*[49]

knowledge of God there is no knowledge of self."[50] This principle of double
knowledge leads us to conclude that "without self-consciousness there
is no consciousness of God; without consciousness of God there is no
self-consciousness." True spiritual formation does require the growth
and knowledge of self and the knowledge of God.

Since Calvin, other spiritual writers have expressed an awareness
that without a true double knowledge, we will not grow in the joy and
peace of Christian discipleship. An example would be Ruth Barton,
who links one's self-worth in Christ with self-knowledge: "First of all,
he [Christ] wants us to know how much we are worth. . . . Key to a
woman's self-esteem is knowledge of herself as an individual who is
unique and separate from others, balanced by a sense of how she fits
into her community. Many women lack self-esteem precisely because
they know so little about themselves."[51] Similarly, David Benner is concerned for the connectedness and growth of spiritual and psychological

wholeness that is embedded in Calvin's position. Benner claims that "people who are afraid to look deeply at themselves will of course be equally afraid to look deeply and personally at God."[52] Finally, Rice works with Calvin's use of the word *knowledge*. He "maintain[s] that 'experience' is a better word than 'know' to point to the way believers apprehend God's acts in the world."[53] When we aim for a strong double knowledge that highlights experience, we are circling back to a previously stated priority to emphasize learning over teaching because learning involves what "a person absorbs, accepts, relates to, or identifies with, out of his or her experiences."[54] I might say that without learning and experiencing myself, there is no experience of God; and without learning and experiencing God, there is no experience of myself. I define myself as a person in light of experience with the Other Person.

A Focus on Catechesis

We call for a catechetical spiritual formation of the people of God that is based firmly on a Trinitarian biblical narrative. We are concerned when spirituality is separated from the story of God and baptism into the life of Christ and his Body. Spirituality, made independent from God's story, is often characterized by legalism, mere intellectual knowledge, an overly therapeutic culture, New Age Gnosticism, a dualistic rejection of this world and a narcissistic preoccupation with one's own experience. These false spiritualities are inadequate for the challenges we face in today's world. Therefore, we call Evangelicals to return to a historic spirituality like that taught and practiced in the ancient catechumenate.[55]

From: "A Call to an Ancient Evangelical Future"

Catechesis, then—our coming to know who and whose we are—is inseparable from doxology, the worship of Christ, the praise and adoration of Father, Son, and Holy Spirit.[56]

Debra Dean Murphy

Catechesis comes from a Greek word meaning "to teach" but has the implication of a life-oriented curriculum aimed at giving an applied, big-picture instruction in the faith. The early church originally used this word to describe the instruction leading up to the baptism of new converts. In recent times, people have applied the term to describe life-oriented instruction that combines biblical, theological, and ethical perspectives. Also implied in this term is a high degree of congruence between various formative elements in a church. We can never reduce catechesis to a single program; it really refers to a church that is committed to the educationally based spiritual formation of its members.

Catechesis really calls for a theologically, biblically, and ethically informed curriculum in which an entire church or parish participates. This is not something to be left to the experts on Sunday morning: it must be taken into the homes for it to be effective.

COMMUNITY SPIRITUAL FORMATION COROLLARY 9

Christian spiritual formation should always be more than the teaching ministry of the church, but never less. True formational teaching is compressive, deeply orthodox, healthy, and anointed by the Spirit of God.

Jesus Invites Us to Create a Space for God through Solitude

The Word of God is the fulcrum upon which the lever of prayer is placed and by which things are mightily moved.[57]

E. M. Bounds

Christian love between persons is reborn in solitude.[58]

Susan Muto and Adrian van Kaam

Silence has the power to force you to dig deep inside yourself.[59]

Paul Tournier

The quest for spiritual formation has included the development of a disciplined prayer life frequently called "centering prayer." Centering prayer involves a quiet, Scripture-based, meditative prayer designed to replace worry and anxiety with a focus on our ever-present Savior and guide, Jesus Christ. Again, many see centering prayer as something done by an individual in private. Under this view, centering prayer is a quite personal and intimate activity. When people have learned the discipline, they undertake it as a way of casting their cares upon Christ as Scripture admonishes us, and they often do this in a quiet, private setting.

Many of us have found that centering prayer, while practiced often in private, is best learned in a group setting. Quiet, meditative prayer is very countercultural. While it enjoys biblical and historical support, many contemporary Christians find a slight guardedness about it and therefore would be inclined to give it up easily if it does not work when first tried. A retreat setting can be an ideal way to help people become established in this pattern of casting cares upon Christ as they gently and quietly pray over Scripture.

Jesus Invites Us to Study and Meditate on Scripture

"Seek God, not happiness"—this is the fundamental rule of all meditation. If you seek God alone, you will gain happiness: that is its promise.[60]

Dietrich Bonhoeffer

Meditation is the aspect of spiritual reading that trains us to read Scripture as a connected, coherent whole, not a collection of inspired bits and pieces.[61]

Eugene H. Peterson

The Bible itself performs certain actions when told, heard, and remembered.[62]

Craig Dykstra

As people of the book, we are to be growing in biblical literacy. Such a working literacy should include an outline of the flow of biblical history, knowledge of the main characters and stories in the Bible, and a comprehension and internalization of the biblical symbol system. The Christian story found in the Bible should form our lives. An important part of spiritual formation is the systematic teaching of the Bible, equipping people to read the Bible on their own in a thoughtful and spiritually engaging way.

It is difficult to clearly remember our identity in Christ when we only vaguely remember the words of assurance of God's love, given to us by our Savior. One of the most powerful spiritual disciplines that Christians can engage in is a regular memorization of Scripture. We often think of Scripture memory as something that is completely private, but the community can foster and encourage it.

A church can identify key verses that it believes members should commit to memory. A church can also present these in the worship service and provide opportunities and encouragement for people to repeat them from memory. People in church often recite Scripture passages like the Lord's Prayer and the Shepherd Psalm almost from memory, though if asked, some of them would not readily recognize these time-honored words as Scripture. Why not other intentionally memorized passages? Why not a collection of biblical passages that have special meaning to that local congregation? I am aware of a church in Wisconsin that chose one of Paul's prayers for the believers in Ephesus and made it their "church life-verses." Visitors have often admitted to a powerful awareness of God's presence when the congregation spontaneously joins the pastor in the benediction with these words:

We pray that Christ will be more and more at home in our hearts, living within us as we trust in him. May our roots grow down deep into the soil of God's marvelous love. And may we be able to feel and understand as all God's children should, how long, how wide, how deep, how high his love really is. And to experience that love for ourselves, though it is so deep that we will never see the end of it, or fully know or understand it, and so at last we will be filled up with God himself. (Eph. 3:17–19 TLB, adapted)

Another advantage that comes from encouraging memorization in a community context is that people learn truth that they might not have gravitated to on their own. At various points on our journey, we tend to emphasize certain truths that bring us comfort and solace and are compatible with our outlook. Yet as Martin Luther taught us, we need the whole counsel of God. When we learn to memorize passages in a community context, we learn verses that emphasize the love of God, our need to participate in building a just community, the importance of prayer and worship, assurance of our salvation, godly family relationships, and much more.

A church that has learned Scripture is also able to engage in worship in a more meaningful way. A part of worship is a purposeful response to God. When the community knows Scripture, God's Word can have a greater place in the singing, exhortation, comforting, teaching, preaching, and care. Paul encourages believers: "Let the Word of Christ—the Message—have the run of the house. Give it plenty of room in your lives" (Col. 3:16 Message). In that context the emphasis was on a corporate worship that flowed from the group's knowledge of Scripture.

When the community has memorized and "bought" Scripture, the Bible can have a higher authority in our lives. Before hearing a word of correction based on Scripture, we have already committed ourselves to the truth of that Scripture when we memorized it; therefore, we are more likely to abide by an admonition based on a Scripture that we thought was worthy of our time to memorize.

Bible memorization is also foundational to many other key spiritual disciplines. For example, Scripture encourages us to continually meditate on the Word of God, and Scripture-based meditation requires knowledge of Scripture. Praying Scripture has been a source of comfort and guidance for Christians through the centuries and requires an intimate knowledge of the Bible. Using the Bible in a thoughtful way for guidance and discernment also requires an ability to reflect on a wide range of verses that one has come to know and understand through Bible memorization.

In corporate and individual meditation we can revisit passages that we have memorized. This discipline provides opportunities for us to go deeper into the meanings and applications of Scripture. We grow as

Christians by learning and relearning a rather limited set of material and then learning how to live it out. Insight comes from sustained, thoughtful attention rather than occasional glances. Then, through that living out, we see whole new opportunities to apply the gospel and to seek to bring Jesus' perspective to bear on our life situations. Scripture's power to teach repeatedly over a lifetime through a myriad of experiences is inherent within a passage, thus highlighting the fact that Scripture is the fusion of words and Spirit. Jesus reminds us, "The words I have spoken to you are spirit and life" (John 6:63).

Finally, we need to acknowledge that, oftentimes, community-oriented Bible memorization has been quite deformative. Prizes, rewards, and competitions have distorted why we are learning Scripture. It is a tragedy when this good gift is so trivialized and belittled. Community-oriented Scripture memorization need not have these deformative aspects. Through using Scripture in worship, in both singing and congregational responsive readings, people can memorize Scriptures in an effective but subtle way over time.

Jesus Invites Us to a Life of Learning

The discipline of learning helps us to be *intentional* learners, not accidental learners.[63]

Donald S. Whitney

You call me Teacher and Lord—and you are right, for this is what I am.

Jesus, in John 13:13

Remembering is deeply related to the life of learning that Jesus engaged in through his teaching ministry. Jesus' disciples were his students, his apprentices, and he often asked questions that challenged them to remember, to learn, and to form new meanings. He is continually addressed as "Rabbi" and "Teacher" (Matt. 8:19; 12:38; 23:7–8; Mark 9:5; Luke 22:11). He surely was a teacher. The Gospels are filled with his teaching, and he invites his disciples to embrace a life of learning.

Much of the learning Jesus invited his first followers to absorb was decidedly corporate. They were gathered together when he taught them to pray (Luke 11:1–4), and his discipleship program required his learners as a group to "follow me" (Luke 5:27).

In terms of emphasis, learning is the spiritual practice that receives the greatest attention in the Gospels. Jesus is continually teaching and calling his disciples to greater understanding, which is measured by their heartfelt demonstration of embodied responses. The task of learning to

Jesus' Teaching Methods

Jesus is universally accepted as a master teacher. As a communicator he presented truth to people who had heard it before but who had lost the meaning of the truth. The people already had a structure for education, and they had heard five hundred sermons on a given topic before. Jesus and the Pharisees were both building basic theology on the foundation of the Old Testament. However, Jesus injected a new approach for thinking and considering questions.

Jesus used the vocabulary of the people who were listening. He was clear, simple, and direct, and he did not use unfamiliar jargon. When talking with the Pharisees, Jesus used language and jargon that suited them. He knew how to read their questions. Some questions were simple and serious, and others were loaded or trick questions. Jesus adjusted vocabulary to the audience and to his concern that they hear afresh.

Jesus knew that the people were not really listening or thinking deeply and that their minds were "in neutral." He forced them to think and question by speaking truth just below the surface of the language. They would walk away wondering what he really meant and what the truth really was. His parables are a prime example of this approach. Parables reveal and conceal at the same time. To reveal is to draw in and ask questions. To conceal is to encourage searching and thinking and not to spoon-feed. Jesus often called them "parables of the kingdom," and the design is that the Jews are blinded until the Gentiles can be drawn in as well. In an example from Mark 10:13–15, Jesus explains that we are to receive the kingdom as a little child. This is not a call to become immature but to grow up. Jesus says, "Consider carefully how you listen. Whoever has will be given more; whoever does not have, even what he thinks he has will be taken from him" (Luke 8:18 NIV). In the kingdom one is either receiving or losing. There is no neutrality in the kingdom. In another parable Jesus says, "Wherever there is a carcass, there the vultures will gather" (Matt. 24:28 NIV). He is teaching about the second coming. When certain things happen, then certain other things happen. The second coming will happen when the situation is right.

Jesus' vocabulary also made use of highly graphic wordings, paradoxical language, or hyperbole. Jesus used graphic wording to describe faith as being like the very small mustard seed (Luke 17:6). We think bigger is better. Jesus thinks size is irrelevant. There is no correlation between the size of my faith and what happens. Even if we can only rise to the faith of a mustard seed, God can move through it. The issue is the power of God and not the size of my faith. Using paradoxical language makes us think, because the ideas presented sound self-contradictory; Jesus says, "Many who are first will be

continued ➤

last, and the last first" (Mark 10:31), and, "Whoever wants to be first must be slave of all" (Mark 10:44). A hyperbole is an overstatement used for its shock effect. Jesus suggests that if a body part causes one to sin, it ought to be cut off (Mark 9:42–48).

Jesus' teaching methods were much like those of the rabbis. He used the familiar method because he did not want the method to offend or distract. He used parables, illustrations, object lessons, commands, proverbs, quotes from the Old Testament, actions, humor, puns, and riddles. His illustrations and object lessons were authentic, and they dealt with general issues from ordinary life such as animals, work, fields, marriage, trees, children, money, and weather.

Adapted from a lecture by Walter Elwell on Jesus' teaching methods.
Used by permission.[64]

love one another is mastered only when one in fact does love the other (John 13:34–35). The learning he desires is holistic knowledge that leads to obedience.

Jesus Invites Us to Believe He Is Who He Claims to Be

[People] are more eager to hear what the world has to say than to listen to God.[65]

Thomas à Kempis

Studying the Master is a critical part of remembering what we have received. In our information-saturated society, it is easy to believe the most pertinent information for guidance and decision making comes from one of our much-vaunted experts. The sentimentalized picture of Jesus that is so prevalent leaves the impression that he is an expert of weakness and ineffectiveness. That is a far cry from the picture of Jesus in the Gospels. Here is a man who, as a boy, kept the intelligentsia of his day occupied for three days when he paid them a visit. He was a spellbinding speaker, a master at verbal repartee, a conversationalist, a counselor of great skill and insight, and the life of the party. There is much we can learn from this man, and we can only learn to imitate Jesus after we have a grasp of his life and teaching.

Rightly remembering is a basic move in spiritual formation. Remembering requires experiences, content, and a way of seeing the world, as well as opportunity to disengage from the rush of life in order to reflect. Spiritual formation has the twofold task of building up the memories and providing structures for people to reflect on what they know/remember about God's work in their lives and then live out of that reality.

Before moving on to the chapters on responding and relating, it would be helpful to recall what has gone before. Most basically, remembering in community is tied to patterns of communal learning and teaching. Teacher and learners must work together to create and maintain spaces where the truth of the gospel is creatively presented. Wisdom is needed in the search for an expanding self-knowledge based on a clearer knowledge of God. The communal or group effort to learn together enriches pastoral care in times of struggle. The joint effort deepens each personal story as it is connected with the stories of peers and with the stories of spiritual heroes and forebears.

Remembering is critical as it recalls the grace that we have received. The gospel is for spiritual formation as one first understands the call to salvation and then, in a day-to-day recalling of the gospel's power, persistently seeks to grow in Christlikeness. Jesus invites us to love and obey God and also to love one another. We can answer these invitations only as we remember the grace we have received and use that grace as the driving force in a desire to grow and be formed like Christ. Spiritual disciplines help to place one in spiritual, emotional, and physical places where the desire to grow can be watered and nourished.

We strengthen and expand remembering in community as individuals work together in Bible memory and study, storytelling and catechesis. A primary goal of remembering in community is to focus on grace received, with an eye to taking grace as the major driver or impetus in responding and relating in a Christlike manner. Receiving, remembering, responding, and relating are a package. Responding is the work within the individual heart where one remembers and internalizes what one has received. Relating is the outer demonstration or working out of one's responses. Again, it is critical that receiving, remembering, responding, and relating work together to build and reinforce each other. Sharing our lives and effort with each other in community provides connection, challenge, compassion, and celebration. This sharing is built on the premise that we serve as priests to one another and stands in contrast to the culture's preference for individualism.

For Further Reading

Bounds, E. M. *The Complete Works of E. M. Bounds on Prayer*. Grand Rapids: Baker Books, 1990. This brief volume argues that life-giving and anointed preaching flows out of the preacher's prayer life.

Gorman, Julie A. *Community That Is Christian*. 2nd ed. Grand Rapids: Baker Books, 2002. Role, definition, and dynamics of small groups for corporate spiritual formation.

Harris, Maria. *Fashion Me a People: Curriculum in the Church*. Louisville: Westminster John Knox, 1989. A guide to establishing a curriculum for community formation.

Lloyd-Jones, David Martyn. *Preaching and Preachers*. London: Hodder & Stoughton, 1971. The chapter on anointed preaching is a wise, balanced, and compelling presentation by a widely acknowledged, anointed preacher.

Nelson, Carl Ellis. *How Faith Matures*. Louisville: Westminster John Knox, 1989. A person's faith matures when ordinary life experiences are interpreted in the light of the gospel and when the congregation is the context for maturing.

Nouwen, Henri J. M. *Creative Ministry*. Garden City, NY: Doubleday, 1971. A brief book with a thoughtful essay on "Beyond the Transference of Knowledge."

Oden, Thomas C. *Pastoral Theology: Essentials of Ministry*. San Francisco: Harper & Row, 1982. A theologically rich but brief exploration of unction.

Osmer, Richard Robert. *The Teaching Ministry of Congregations*. Louisville: Westminster John Knox, 2005. Sets forth a practical theology of the teaching ministry grounded in the practice of the apostle Paul. The author sees the central tasks of the teaching ministry to be catechesis, exhortation, and discernment.

Palmer, Parker J. *The Courage to Teach: Exploring the Inner Landscape of a Teacher's Life*. San Francisco: Jossey-Bass, 1998. This book argues that good teaching comes from the identity and the integrity of the teacher.

Richards, Larry (Lawrence O.), and Gary J. Bredfeldt. *Creative Bible Teaching*. Chicago: Moody, 1998. Sets forth a time-honored approach to teaching the Bible.

Wilhoit, Jim, and Leland Ryken. *Effective Bible Teaching*. Grand Rapids: Baker Academic, 1988. Calls for teachers to give more attention to their preparation through observing the literary dimensions of the text.

Wyckoff, D. Campbell. *The Gospel and Christian Education: A Theory of Christian Education for Our Times*. Philadelphia: Westminster, 1958. A reminder that the gospel should be the central message of Christian education.

Zuck, Roy B. *The Holy Spirit in Your Teachings: The Relationship That Makes All the Difference*. Rev. and expanded ed. Wheaton: Victor Books, 1984. Simple but comprehensive treatment of the role of the Holy Spirit in teaching.

7

Foundations of Responding

Love and Service to God and Others

What are we to respond to?

> We are to respond to God's gospel of love and forgiveness with love and service to God and to those around us.

How do we do this?

> The gospel changes us, and our responding is an outflow of a changed heart. We also learn that God changes us as we live our lives well and reach out in love and service to God and others.

What attitude and approach does this require?

> Marveling at grace. Realizing we are pipes to carry his grace to others and not buckets content to hoard it. Grace comes to us, to go through us, to others.

Therefore, go and make disciples of all the nations, baptizing them in the name of the Father and the Son and the Holy Spirit. Teach these new disciples to obey all the commands I have given you. And be sure of this: I am with you always, even to the end of the age.

> Jesus, in Matthew 28:19–20 NLT

But the goal of our instruction is love from a pure heart and a good conscience and a sincere faith.

1 Timothy 1:5 NASB

What you have heard from me through many witnesses entrust to faithful people who will be able to teach others as well.

2 Timothy 2:2

The spiritual life, however, is prior to the moral life, for we can love the neighbor as God loves us only if first we have experienced that love affair with God. More important, we cannot love God except in response to God's love for us. This love affair with God is the one and only end of human life.[1]

John H. Westerhoff III

God confronts persons at the level of emotions and uses emotion to motivate response and to bring healing and hope: emotion is at the core of faith and love.[2]

Ray S. Anderson

Many of the spiritualities that we encounter in everyday life base their appeal on personal confidence and power. The practitioners are promised effectiveness in living and in their pursuits; in short, they are very narcissistic. They focus on the individual and empowering the individual, with little regard, unless the individual so chooses, for the good of the community and society. In contrast, Christian spiritual formation ultimately is about enabling people to love others more and to help create a just and well-ordered community.

Appropriate responses to the gospel come in many forms. At times a quiet prayer is the fullest and most appropriate response. At other times the appropriate response may be costly and dramatic. What is crucial is that we see that following Christ requires us to cultivate a lifestyle of response. Well-formed believers do not let circumstances have the final word. They do not merely react to crises but learn to respond with a gospel-grounded response. Most often their response in crisis is not different from their everyday response: telling the truth, though now it is quite costly; loving the outcast, though now that seems to betray one's race/class; praying, though now that is forbidden. The picture of perseverance Paul paints in 2 Corinthians 4:7–12 speaks of being "afflicted in every way, but not crushed; perplexed, but not driven to despair; persecuted, but not forsaken; struck down, but not destroyed." It makes the beautiful point that a clay jar does not do its best work by trying to be something other than a clay jar.

Formed to Serve, Formed by Serving

> Of this gospel I have become a servant according to the gift of God's grace that was given to me by the working of his power.
>
> Ephesians 3:7

Cultivating the instinct to act on gospel teaching is crucial to our transformation. Our teaching is not complete until we have nurtured a tendency to act in learners.[3] Cultivating a tendency toward responsible action and engagement is part of the culture of effective spiritual formation programs. Douglas Hyde has aptly illustrated the reinforcing interplay between doing and being. In his book *Dedication and Leadership*, he describes how the Communists in Great Britain effectively used party service as a way of generating interest in learning. A new convert, for example, was not immediately put into classes to learn about Communism but was assigned to a street corner. As he sold Communist papers and pamphlets, people asked him questions about the Soviet Union and Communism that he could not adequately answer. Inevitably, this green recruit found his defense of Communism to be less convincing to the passersby than he had imagined. He left his curbside propaganda work with a thirst to learn so that he would serve the cause better the next time he had the opportunity. Hyde comments:

> Those who sent him into this form of activity did not expect him to have all the answers. He has let down neither the Party nor himself. In the process he has learned a good deal. When he next takes up his stand at the side of the road, he will come determined to do better. Most probably, he has been reading Communist papers in a different way, looking for the answers to the questions he was asked last time. Gathering shot and shell in readiness for the next fight. This is when he really begins to learn and the desire to learn now comes from within himself.[4]

Service predisposes a person to learn. The Communists at times understood this truth very well. Hyde documents how service leads to teachableness and a genuine motivation to learn. John Dewey well understood this interplay of learning and engagement:

> To "learn from experience" is to make a backward and forward connection between what we do to things and what we enjoy or suffer from things in consequence. Under such conditions, doing becomes a trying; an experiment with the world to find out what it is like; the undergoing becomes instruction—discovery of the connection of things.[5]

As Christians we can take Dewey's phrase "an experiment with the world" and enrich it to "an experiment with the world in partnership with God." I made far more progress in prayer when I realized that while prayer is a powerful spiritual tool, it is not something I could break. Even inappropriate prayer exposes us to valuable lessons. I was encouraged by a spiritual mentor to experiment in an appropriate context and with continual reflection on biblical teaching and spiritual masters' teaching on prayer. In this context, Willard's insight, "Prayer is talking to God about what we are doing together," makes so much sense.[6] Like every significant endeavor in life, we do not know how well we have understood or observed until we try to actually do what we learned.

Woven into the fabric of formation must be an emphasis on the learner discovering their "unique-communal life call."[7] The discovery and attentiveness to guarding and developing one's unique communal call is a lifelong project, not something accomplished fully in a single class or seminar. Adrian van Kaam's construct of "unique-communal life call" captures the twofold truth that our calling is unique to us and compatible with our unique gifting, training, life story, and current situation. Our calling is discovered within, affirmed by, and useful to the community of faith. It also is a life calling, not just a passing whim or intuition, but something that provides a life direction.

Part of the foundation for cultivating a tendency to respond can be seen in communities that provide Christians with a deep sense that they are equipped to respond and serve God at this very moment. Too often new Christians are slow to engage in areas of unique service because they feel inadequate. Satan exploits these natural and understandable hesitancies with his accusations (Rev. 12:10) and his lies. As Jesus said, "When he lies, he speaks his native language, for he is a liar and the father of lies" (John 8:44 NIV). Often an early victory in proper spiritual listening occurs when Christians give attention to the affirming voice of God calling his beloved to creative service, which fits who they uniquely are. They discover relief in ignoring the accusations of Satan, which breed self-doubt and fear. Wise communities of believers do not push new Christians into merely serving out of dutiful obligation in a ministry that "does not fit." A faithful, persistent call to "listen to God" will accomplish more for the kingdom than compiling another list of "tasks that need doing—please check one."

Self-acceptance is often not well understood in many Christian communities. The misuse of statements like Jesus' command to deny ourselves has not helped. Even the linchpin statement in the Great Commandment that the degree of love we must have for our neighbor ought to parallel the love we have for ourselves does not receive much serious attention. Historically, self-acceptance was taught as part of the formation process.

An emphasis was placed on an appropriate patience with oneself. This patience and self-acceptance was grounded in the conviction that God created me to be exactly as he wants me to be. In creating me in this way, he created an inimitably wonderful and magnificent being. Psalm 8:5 instructs, "You made him a little lower than the heavenly beings and crowned him with glory and honor" (NIV). This truth is captured in the popular expression "God don't make no junk!"

Christians have seen the negative effects of the popular self-esteem movement and sometimes discount the importance of teaching self-acceptance, but what should we teach in its place? Certainly not self-hatred, which is simply a rejection of God's providence and a rebellion against the creation that he declared to be good. At times believers have taken Jesus' words "Let him deny himself" as encouragement toward self-hatred when they are emphatically the opposite. I do not hate myself when I deny myself any more than I would hate my child if I said no to her when she made an unwise request. Some of the godliest acts of self-acceptance come at precisely those times when we deny ourselves. Self-acceptance is not something that comes easily, and it is something that must be taught and nurtured because we confront plenty of nega-tive data about ourselves. Negative accusation is one of Satan's most effective tools. I believe Richard Lovelace's assessment is close to the mark concerning God's acceptance of us as a lived reality: "There is end-less talk about this in the church, but little apparent belief in it among Christians." He develops this further:

> It is often said today . . . that we must love ourselves before we can be set free to love others. This is certainly the release which we must seek to give our people. But no realistic human beings find it easy to love or to forgive themselves, and hence their self-acceptance must be grounded in their aware-ness that God accepts them in Christ. There is a sense in which the strongest self-love that we can have, in the sense of agape, is merely the mirror image of the lively conviction we have that God loves us. There is endless talk about this in the church, but little apparent belief in it among Christians, although they may have a conscious complacency which conceals the subconscious despair which Kierkegaard calls "the sickness unto death."[8]

This subconscious despair eviscerates Christian service because it leads believers to doubt that they have a significant contribution to make. Serving has such a formative effect because it provides clear evidence that my contribution matters. At the end of the day one can see the church cleaned, the people fed, the children cared for, and the words of wit-ness spoken. We have actually done something, not because of how we expected to feel but simply because Jesus asks us to do it. Appropriately motivated service affirms our contribution to the body of Christ.

Responding as an Outflow of the Priesthood of All Believers

The doctrine of the priesthood of all believers is central to how I am construing spiritual formation. This ancient doctrine mandates and enables spiritual formation and serves as part of its implicit theological foundation. When properly understood, the biblical principle that all believers are priests has infused spiritual formation with a refreshing vitality and spirit of renewal; at other times, however, it has been used to excuse individualism, intellectual lethargy, and a lack of respect for the offices of the church. A balanced concept of the priesthood of all believers will affirm the personal spiritual responsibility of all Christians, their right and duty to minister in Christ's name, and the truth that one does not abide in Christ apart from abiding in the body of Christ, the church.

Spiritual Responsibility and Responding

It is he whom we proclaim, warning everyone and teaching everyone in all wisdom, so that we may present everyone mature in Christ. For this I toil and struggle with all the energy that he powerfully inspires within me.

Colossians 1:28–29

Luther recognized that if all Christians are called to be responsible servants and worshippers, they must be trained and equipped to fulfill this calling—they must be trained to respond to the gospel. Hence he became involved in Christian education. His famous Small Catechism stands as a reminder of this interest. The Small Catechism was written after he visited nearby country parishes, where he was appalled by the ignorance he found. Luther was keenly aware that each individual believer must ultimately answer to Christ concerning one's own spiritual condition. If these people were to be accountable for their faith, Luther reasoned, then they must be instructed in spiritual matters.

All Christians are called to worship God, utilize their gifts, and minister to others according to God's principles as set forth in Scripture. Good intentions or ignorance of divine requirements does not absolve the believer of the responsibility to live out the gospel.

Philipp Jakob Spener (1635–1705) and a number of like-minded Lutheran Pietists developed further the ramifications this doctrine has for Christian education. Spener was a brilliant and sensitive Lutheran pastor who held a doctorate in theology and was fluent in several languages. He also firmly believed that a vital faith is more important for ministry than is either ordination or formal training. He did not disparage theological training (although he wanted to reform it), but he deeply felt that in order to be fit for ministry, a renewed heart and mind are indispensable. Though Lutheranism taught the ministry of all believers, he was aware that people still looked to the pastor as the spiritual center and theological expert in the church. Most of the laity were passive recipients of sermons and sacraments. To correct this situation, Spener, in his book *Pia Desideria*, called for an increased and "diligent exercise of the spiritual priesthood."[9]

According to Spener, the responsibilities of the spiritual priesthood cluster in three general areas: (1) It is the duty of every Christian "industriously to study in the Word of the Lord." By spending time in study of Scripture, we can order our lives by its priorities and minister the word of truth to those around us. (2) As Christians, all of us have a responsibility "to teach others, especially those under [our] own roof, to chastise, exhort, convert, and edify them, to observe their life, pray for all, and in so far as possible be concerned about their salvation." Spener, like the writer to the Hebrews (5:12), believed that all Christians have a responsibility to teach in the sense of speaking the word of truth and influencing people to walk in the paths of righteousness. (3) "Every Christian is bound not only to offer himself but also what he has, his prayer, thanksgiving, good works, alms."[10] The wonderful privileges of the universal priesthood enable us to serve others with a renewed vigor and enthusiasm and with a full array of spiritual tools. Through intercessory prayer and acts of mercy, believer-priests serve one another and their world.

Spener saw his emphasis on the universal priesthood as a restatement of Luther's emphasis: "Nobody can read Luther's writings with some care without observing how earnestly the sainted man advocated this spiritual priesthood."[11] Spener thought that an emphasis on the universal priesthood of believers is necessary for the church to fulfill its biblical obligations of service, worship, care, witness, and prayer. He did not see such a priesthood as competing with the paid clergy; rather, together they can accomplish what neither one can do alone: "No damage will be done to the ministry by a proper use of this priesthood. In fact, one of the principal reasons why the ministry cannot accomplish all that it ought is that it is too weak without the help of the universal priesthood."[12] Without an emphasis on laypersons teaching other laypersons, modern Christian education would not have developed. The task of Christian education and spiritual formation can never fall entirely upon professionals because the financial cost would be prohibitive and because we gain much through the process of mutual teaching and learning. A somewhat bookish academic has frequently told me how encouraged he is by hearing a faithful layperson teach the Bible. Teachers strengthen their credibility by adding a responsive faithfulness to their teaching.

One-Another Verses

Thus says the LORD of hosts: Render true judgments, show kindness and mercy to one another.

Zechariah 7:9

Have we not all one father? Has not one God created us? Why then are we faithless to one another, profaning the covenant of our ancestors?

Malachi 2:10

So if I, your Lord and Teacher, have washed your feet, you also ought to wash one another's feet.

Jesus, in John 13:14

I give you a new commandment, that you love one another. Just as I have loved you, you also should love one another. By this everyone will know that you are my disciples, if you have love for one another.

Jesus, in John 13:34–35

Love one another with mutual affection; outdo one another in showing honor.

Romans 12:10

Live in harmony with one another; do not be haughty, but associate with the lowly; do not claim to be wiser than you are.

Romans 12:16

Owe no one anything, except to love one another; for the one who loves another has fulfilled the law.

Romans 13:8

Let us therefore no longer pass judgment on one another, but resolve instead never to put a stumbling-block or hindrance in the way of another.

Romans 14:13

Welcome one another, therefore, just as Christ has welcomed you, for the glory of God.

Romans 15:7

continued ➤

I myself feel confident about you, my brothers and sisters, that you yourselves are full of goodness, filled with all knowledge, and able to instruct
one another.

Romans 15:14

Now I appeal to you, brothers and sisters, by the name of our Lord Jesus
Christ, that all of you should be in agreement and that there should be no
divisions among you, but that you should be united in the same mind and
the same purpose.

1 Corinthians 1:10 NIV

With all humility and gentleness, with patience, bearing with one another in
love . . .

Ephesians 4:2

And be kind to one another, tender-hearted, forgiving one another, as God
in Christ has forgiven you.

Ephesians 4:32

As you sing psalms and hymns and spiritual songs among yourselves, singing
and making melody to the Lord in your hearts . . .

Ephesians 5:19

Be subject to one another out of reverence for Christ.

Ephesians 5:21

Bear with one another and, if anyone has a complaint against another, forgive
each other; just as the Lord has forgiven you, so you also must forgive.

Colossians 3:13

Let the word of Christ dwell in you richly; teach and admonish one another
in all wisdom; and with gratitude in your hearts sing psalms, hymns, and
spiritual songs to God.

Colossians 3:16

Therefore encourage one another and build up each other, as indeed you
are doing.

1 Thessalonians 5:11

Equipping to Respond to the Gospel

Crossing cultural boundaries has been the life blood of historic Christianity.[13]

Andrew F. Walls

Few developments in our day have been more striking and less anticipated than the emergence of Christianity as a world religion. . . . By contrast Europe and, to some extent, North America, once considered Christian strongholds are in marked recession or retreat.[14]

Lamin Sanneh

The priesthood of all believers places equipping for spiritual service at the heart of the church's formational ministry. We must emphasize this focus of Christian education and formation for all ages. To live as a Christian entails carrying out the responsibilities of a believer-priest, and this is as true for an elementary-school child as for an adult. Three emphases have historically provided Christians with everyday opportunities to respond to the gospel.

Forming world Christians. When Christians learn to recognize a deep connection with believers around the world, they see the world through a whole new lens. Stories of persecution become stories about family members. We learn to "pray the newspaper" as we see the spiritual implications of the news.

COMMUNITY SPIRITUAL FORMATION COROLLARY 10

True Christian spiritual formation forms Christians with a deep identity and engagement with the church worldwide.

Learning to witness to God's love and provide spiritual care. All Christians should be prepared to speak of God's gracious dealing with them. Too often we speak of this in terms of an "evangelistic witnessing," in terms that only fit highly verbal extroverts. We need to teach and encourage people to have an approach that provides spiritual care for those in their relational network. All of us can learn to pray with and for people, offer spiritual guidance and comfort, and patiently and carefully offer words of discernment. A friend remarked that at a local county hospital the best spiritual care was offered by the Jamaican housekeeping staff, whose open speaking of God brought comfort and guidance to so many. When the bar is set at "present the gospel," many Christians remain silent, but many more will respond if we invite them to offer spiritual care to those who cross their paths.

Cultivating the spirit of hospitality. Christians need to extend hospitality to others, especially those who are lonely, mentally ill, needy, and on the margin (Rom. 12:13). We will read the Bible differently when we keep in mind that hospitality is usually described rather than prescribed. Hospitality was a high cultural expectation in those times. Today it must be intentional. Offering hospitality provides Christians with many opportunities to respond to the gospel's call to love and care.

The consumer emphasis in modern American religion is diametrically opposed to the Reformation concept of the believer-priest. The formational ministry of a church will never be fully effective if people come to the church simply to consume spiritual benefits in exchange for their money and loyalty. By contrast, equipping means training people "to do." In the church we must train people for responsible priestly service. This means that we cannot be content simply to exhort people to pray; instead, we must teach them how to pray. And we must not merely talk about evangelism; rather, we must train people to share their faith.

In equipping for spiritual service, the church should give much attention to the two primary contexts in which people live out their faith: the home and the marketplace. It must enable people to live as Christians bearing witness to their faith and genuinely serving their coworkers. It must also help them minister in and through their families.

God's Transforming Grace

The practices of faith are not ultimately our own practices but rather habitations of the Spirit, in the midst of which we are invited to participate in the practices of God.[15]

Craig Dykstra

Only if we experience the mysterious attraction of God will we be able to impart it to others.[16]

John H. Westerhoff III

In our discussion of the priesthood of all believers, we looked at only one half of the equation: our access to God and its attendant responsibilities. The Old Testament priests not only approached God, but also ministered as agents of God's grace to his people. Priests make God's grace available to others. God has called us as believer-priests to administer his transforming power to others. "Like good stewards of the manifold grace of God, serve one another with whatever gift each of you has received" (1 Pet. 4:10). That we can become agents to minister God's sustaining grace to others should transform our view of everyday activities. Our service in the home, our empathy with coworkers, our prayers, and our challenges to others are not just ways of being kind or speaking words of truth; they also are the way of making God's transforming power available. Paul urged the believers to whom he ministered to adopt this aim in life. In fact, he encouraged them by noting that something as simple as ordinary conversations can be a way of dispensing God's power: "Let your speech always be gracious, seasoned with salt, so that you may know how you ought to answer everyone" (Col. 4:6).

Responding to and through Grace

> It is God who is at work in you, enabling you both to will and to work for his good pleasure.
>
> Philippians 2:13

Spiritual formation must include reminding ourselves and others that "swimming against the stream makes sense." We need to remember the courageous persons of compassion and integrity who have stood against society and called people to live effectively. We need to show trust by living according to the gospel. We can create a community where unity and love is a witness to the world. Grace is also a verb: grace brings change. Grace is God's sustaining and transforming power.

The grace of God that has reconciled us and saved us is not just God's kindness, but also his marvelous power that is able to remake us into new people. In the book of Acts, grace essentially equals power. Those persons who were full of grace were also full of God's power to preach and to work mighty miracles. Notice what is said of Stephen: "Now Stephen, a man full of God's grace and power, did great wonders and miraculous signs among the people" (Acts 6:8 NIV). God's powerful sustaining grace brings about transformation and healing in our lives. In a passage where the writer to the Hebrews is exhorting his readers to walk closely with Christ, he warns them not to try to hasten their Christian development through futile means like ceremonial foods, strange teachings, and mysterious ceremonies. Rather, he advises, "It is well for the heart to be strengthened by grace" (Heb. 13:9). In the church are many ways that we can strengthen our hearts through grace. One of the most effective is wise and biblically grounded personal ministry of one believer to another.

Salvation begins with the new birth and is consummated with our glorification. We must remember that the grace of God is working throughout all of this process to bring about our transformation into Christlikeness.

Transformations of the Heart

As our hearts are transformed by faith, we will move

- from self-absorption to concern for God's kingdom (Matt. 6:33).
- from defiance to submission (1 Sam. 15:19–22).
- from self-reliance to God-reliance (Jer. 17:5–8).
- from squandering resources to stewarding them (Matt. 25:14–30).
- from expecting and taking for granted to accepting and gratitude (Luke 17:11–19).
- from spiritual indifference to spiritual growth and vitality (2 Pet. 1:3–8).
- from concern with externals to concern for character (1 Sam. 16:7).
- from conformity with the culture to conformity to God (Rom. 12:1–2).
- from concern for self to concern for others (Phil. 2:3–4).
- from lording [it] over others to serving others (Mark 10:42–45).
- from quarreling to cooperation (James 3:13–17).
- from independence to community (Eccles. 4:9–12).
- from envy, competition, and self-protection to love (1 Cor. 13:4–13).
- from harboring hurt and resentment to extending forgiveness and seeking reconciliation (Eph. 4:32–5:2).

From "The Art of Voice Recognition" by David Henderson.[17]

Paul, highly disciplined as he was, celebrated the movement of grace in his life: "By the grace of God I am what I am, and his grace toward me has not been in vain. On the contrary, I worked harder than any of them—though it was not I, but the grace of God that is with me" (1 Cor. 15:10). Ultimately God's grace brings about human transformation, and we must avail ourselves of the means that God has established to make his grace available to ourselves and others. We respond to his grace, and we respond through his grace as we minister.

The call in this chapter is that our programs of formation must cultivate the tendency to live out the values implicit in the gospel. Christian formation is not about simply teaching or shaping the beliefs of Christians. It must be about a grace-oriented inculcation of the tendency to respond, through training, in a Christ-imitating way.

For Further Reading

Hays, Richard B. *The Moral Vision of the New Testament: Community, Cross, New Creation: A Contemporary Introduction to New Testament*

Ethics. San Francisco: HarperSanFrancisco, 1996. Comprehensive exposition of the ethical agenda of the New Testament.

Liechty, Daniel. *Early Anabaptist Spirituality: Selected Writings*. Classics of Western Spirituality. New York: Paulist Press, 1994. Good selection of sources that emphasize the need for Christians to be engaged in compassionate service.

Wolterstorff, Nicholas. *Educating for Responsible Action*. Commissioned by Christian Schools International. Grand Rapids: CSI Publications; Eerdmans, 1980. A reminder that Christian education must cultivate tendencies to live out kingdom values.

8

To Foster Responding in Community

Every Christian community must realize that not only do the weak need the strong, but also that the strong cannot exist without the weak. The elimination of the weak is the death of the fellowship.[1]

Dietrich Bonhoeffer

The community of believers represents a prophetic counterculture that challenges the gods and myths of the day with regard to which world and life view best fulfills humanity.[2]

Kevin Vanhoozer

A spiritual community, a church, is full of broken people who turn their chairs toward each other because they know they cannot make it alone.[3]

Larry Crabb

There's a deep yearning within us for wholeness, and we find wholeness in the life of holiness. Holiness does not come simply from avoiding certain actions, but by our becoming a channel for God's empowering presence—living as a pipe, not a bucket. Holiness begins with our being made new by God and grows as we open ourselves to the work of God. When we see holiness as merely avoiding bad action, we become passive and wall ourselves off from the world. True piety leads to service, but false piety leads to self-protection. True piety produces depth of soul;

false piety yields shallow hypocrisy. We have centuries' worth of faithful witnesses to the possibility of authentic piety.

> There came to the Abbot Joseph the Abbot Lott, and said to him, "Father, according to my strengths I keep a modest rule of prayer and fasting and meditation and quiet, and according to my strengths I purge my imagination: what more must I do?" The old man, rising, held up his hands against the sky, and his fingers became like ten torches of fire, and he said, "If thou wilt, thou shalt be made wholly aflame."[4]

In an earlier age, holiness was seen as something possessing substance—a transcendent quality that flowed out of our deep inner essence, from our very souls. Many churches have lost sight of the holy and the soul, and the results are tragic. This change has allowed people to replace the idea of growing in holiness (as the presence and power of God increasingly permeate our lives) with the notion of sin management. As explained earlier in the section on receiving (see "Our Yearnings" in chap. 3), sin management claims that people are basically "okay": they simply need to employ a variety of techniques to reduce the amount of overt sin in their lives because it tends to be personally unpleasant, harms others, stifles their growth, and hampers their witness. Such a view rejects the biblical assertion that the human heart—the core of our beings—is bent away from God and others, and it replaces that biblical insight with the notion of sin as personal impairment. The desire for holiness remains, but the primary means become "cheap" (to use Bonhoeffer's language). We want cheap holiness. We want holiness that relishes God's forgiveness and grace without actually admitting that we have anything for which we need forgiveness. We demand the right to claim holiness (at least internally) without actually having to be holy.

Holiness begins with our being made new by God. Through regeneration we receive spiritual life: we are brought from spiritual death to life. With this new life comes the possibility of spiritual growth and growth in gospel virtues. Through this act we receive a new set of governing tendencies and values, come to perceive and cherish spiritual truths, and seek to live as true followers of Christ.

Responding out of the New Life That Jesus Models and Provides

> Gratitude for life in Christ draws out of the believer a desire for holiness, even as it creates in the believer a healthy hatred of the sin that mars our life and disfigures us.[5]

> Robert M. Norris

The incarnation provides us with the truest picture of holiness. We marvel at Jesus not just because he avoided a certain set of negative actions, but because he avoided all sin ("him who had no sin"; 2 Cor. 5:21 NIV) and lived a life full of spiritual power, vitality, and love. Though he kept the law fully, he was a constant irritation to the religious leaders of his day because of his teachings, challenges to their authority, and refusal to follow all the ritual regulations. He firmly rejected the surrounding shift in the definition of sin and pointed his hearers back to their ultimate spiritual accountability before a holy God. His confrontations were scathing: "And so you break the law of God in order to protect your own tradition" (Mark 7:13 NLT). For guidance, we go back to Jesus' life, in which spiritual power and love shine forth like a beacon across a barren spiritual terrain, and we receive a true picture of holiness.

In his public ministry we see his power demonstrated repeatedly. Jesus resisted Satan's direct attack during his time of wilderness temptation (Matt. 4:1–11) and the subtle assault through Peter's concern (16:22–23). He cast out demons by a simple command, healed various infirmities, quieted a storm, turned water into wine, multiplied the bread, and showed love in the face of brutal opposition and hatred. His insight showed in his penetrating teaching. With perfect accuracy he discerned the motives and longings of those he talked with, predicted future events, and offered words of challenge and direction in strikingly artistic sermons. His love shone forth as he associated with the unpleasant and the marginalized, turned away the unkind word with a gentle response, and forgave those who wronged him. And Jesus' willing sacrifice on the cross stands as the greatest act of love that history will ever know.

A simple event during Christ's last week typifies his genuine and unique holiness. Jesus rode into Jerusalem on a colt that had never before been ridden. Beasts of burden require some process of breaking in and do not immediately take to being ridden or harnessed. Yet Jesus simply rides, apparently without any objection from the colt. He possessed great spiritual power that could calm a sea, quiet a crowd, or assure an untrained animal. Spiritual power for Jesus was not marked by noise and bravado, but by an understated authority. He did not need to raise his voice or give the impression of being in control because *he is in control*. Jesus did not do miracles to prove he is the Son of God but because he is the Son of God. This incarnate example of holiness as flowing out of the depths of a person has been replicated in succeeding generations by those who have responded from regeneration into holiness. It is in marked contrast to the picture of holiness set forth in so many contemporary writings on ministry, where holiness/maturity is simply a cluster of external competencies and others-oriented values.

Receiving the Holiness to Respond

> The problem of the soul, in other words, is not at its essence a lack of knowledge—though knowledge is, after all, important and helpful—but the human will which has been corrupted and enslaved. . . . Put another way, how does one *will* to change one's will?[6]
>
> Kenneth J. Collins

We face a critical question: How do we live so that Jesus' experience of holiness is appropriately present in our lives? The answer: There is nothing we can do to grasp the holiness seen in Jesus, but there are things we can do to receive it. Some of what we can do to receive the gift is set forth in the rest of this chapter. As Christians, we no longer have to do what impulse tells us. These misdirected longings of our heart exert inordinate and persistent influence on us not only by attaching these longings to the wrong objects but also by a profound disordering of our interior.

The biblical teaching about the heart, or the human interior, is very rich. Without a clear connection to the heart, religion will degenerate into legalism (a system of impression management), superstition (a system of external acts designed to control deity), or emotionalism (a system that perceives faith's existence to be positive emotions and a sense of being "inspired"). Within all of us is a tendency to distort our faith in one of these directions. Maturity requires that we understand how we distort our spiritual lives and then cultivate spiritual practices that help us resist this distortion.

In considering how to pattern our lives after Christ, we need to realize the power of our core being (in biblical language, heart, soul, mind, will) to shape our lives. The biblical writers continually give attention to the interior. In fact, "root" is one of the primary images of the hidden but essential spiritual life. Those who trust the Lord are like a well-rooted tree planted by a stream (Jer. 17:7–8). Even during hot weather and drought, the leaves of this deeply rooted tree remain green, and it continues to produce fruit. Believers are to remain rooted in the Lord Jesus (Col. 2:7) and his great love (Eph. 3:17–19) so that they might remain stable. A basic spiritual principle emerges: the aspects of spiritual life that are out of sight deserve our highest attention in that "spiritual growth consists most in the growth of the root, which is out of sight."[7] Jesus certainly taught and demonstrated public prayer, but he also spent extended private times with his heavenly Father and did not hesitate to send his followers alone to the prayer closet (Matt. 6:5–6).

The will is immensely important in our spiritual transformation, but we must realize that it is of very limited power, and we must use it to marshal other spiritual resources at our disposal. Our wills inherently suffer from a kind of spiritual attention deficit disorder; they are unable to sustain long-term direction without training, but they are marvelous at making conscious and informed choices to bring other resources to bear. For example, one may find it difficult to resist the allurement of drugs and alcohol at a party. Untrained willpower alone will often prove ineffective at keeping a person sober in the face of temptation; but whoever uses willpower to relocate oneself (remove self from temptation) may avoid the temptation that seems irresistible when faced for several hours among drinking peers. The important maxim of the spiritual life is that we should never expect our will to work by itself. Do not use your will to simply "say no." Use your will to marshal spiritual resources available to you. Remember: "At the crucial moments of choice most of the business of choosing is over."[8]

The soul as "who we are" but also "capable of being programmed" is evident in the biblical perspectives on meditation. Some passages portray meditation as a thermometer that gauges the temperature of the heart. In Psalm 1 the righteous person meditates on the law. In Psalm 104 the writer portrays the prayer that "my meditation be pleasing to [God]" (104:34) as essentially a prayer that God would find the writer to be righteous. Righteous people think or daydream about God's principles and ways. Finding that a person fixes one's mind on God reveals a warm heart for God. As Jesus told us, "For out of the overflow of the heart the mouth speaks" (Matt. 12:34b NIV).

Teaching and Preaching That Supports Responding

Sermons should shape hearers by bringing the transforming Word to nurture the development of their character in the pattern of Christ.[9]

Marva Dawn

It is a long-acknowledged truth that teachers teach the lessons they most need to learn and writers write about the very things that they are most in need of understanding.[10]

Ruth Haley Barton

One predominant sensation should characterize God's people: active expectation. It is not enough for the congregation to possess a proper view of inspiration. They must gather on the Lord's Day expecting to hear the voice of God through the proclamation of the Scriptures.[11]

Arturo G. Azurdia III

There is a way of viewing life that supports a compassionate response to ourselves and those around us. The teaching and preaching ministry of the church plays a vital role in helping form this life orientation. In this area proper teaching and preaching form a necessary, but not sufficient, foundation to cultivating this disposition to respond. Here are some key themes I have observed in the teaching and preaching ministries of churches that support a widespread responding orientation:

- *Biblical focus*. Not only is the proclamation of these churches grounded in Scripture, but the teaching ministry also has the effect of making the congregation "people of the book." Page after page of Scripture invites us to join the work of God in the world: when people are taught to turn to Scripture for guidance, they are more likely to be people who live out the gospel. The atmosphere is one in which Scripture rather than the interpreter is honored with the last word.
- *It is not all about me*. Through our teaching and preaching, we need to invite people into God's kingdom work and perspective. They have gained citizenship in his kingdom through regeneration and need to see that life in the kingdom may cost convenience, but never joy. It is the life we truly want to live.
- *Grace-based responding*. Our responding to the gospel should flow out of a heart that is grateful for grace and a life that has been transformed by God's grace. A deep-seated gratitude is the best motivation for our serving and witnessing.
- *Empathy*. Christians live as broken people in a broken and hurting world. Our observation and assessment of the dominant culture should emphasize our empathy for the pain and disorientation we see around us. We should not shy away from the prophetic cultural critique, but in speaking out, our emphasis should be on an empathetic understanding of this brokenness rather than merely a judgment of it.
- *Evangelism*. We need to teach Christians how to share the gospel with those in their relational web. Life in the kingdom involves more than personal witness to the reality of Christ; that reality is a core disposition on which we need to build a life of responding.

The Two Great Invitations of Jesus: Love and Obey God and Love One Another

Responding out of love is foundational to accepting these two great invitations of Jesus. Ironically, love is a topic that church teaching often dodges. In my thirty years as an adult Christian, I do not recall a single course or small-group series that specifically explored the nature of Christian love. We seem to have an approach-avoidance toward love: we are attracted to the lofty ideal and our glimpses of its presence, but we are repelled by the sentimentality and naive judgments that are born of "love." The fact that it is a challenge and struggle to differentiate the two is no excuse for evasion. The approach of avoidance is spiritually deadly because, through it, we have hardened our hearts to the Bible's clear message to love. Scripture always places a call to love in balance with other virtues: "This is my prayer, that your love may overflow more and more with knowledge and full insight" (Phil. 1:9).

These Invitations Flow out of the Call to Love God and Neighbor

Jesus Invites Us to Tell People about the Good News and Make Disciples

Enthusiasts just cannot help talking about what they are into. One can have enthusiasm for a particular breed of dog, or for a new piece of technology, or for a sports team. The human spirit desires to complete the joy of our experience by not only sharing that joy with others but also seeking to have others enter into our appreciation and experience. Christians act on this very basic human tendency to share what we have found beneficial when we evangelize. Evangelism should not be so much a task for us to accomplish as a natural outflow of a life excited about the Savior. Christ has called us and invites us to tell the good news. His emphasis is upon the need for his followers to make disciples.

A practice that some churches follow to foster evangelism is to conduct a series of listening sessions. Members learn to listen to the competing spiritual views in our society, sometimes through invited guests and other times through texts or media. They practice the respectful discipline of seeking to truly understand and cogently state the other position. Respectful listening coupled with a clear understanding of one's own faith is a good foundation for evangelism.

COMMUNITY SPIRITUAL FORMATION COROLLARY 11

Evangelism is an essential part of spiritual formation. Evangelism, as people are called to faith in Christ, is the initial act of Christian formation. The act of evangelism is a powerful means of formation for the believer who reaches out in love to share the good news.

Disciples are to be set apart from the world through baptism and by learning to obey all that Jesus commanded. The basic response to growing in Christ's love is to invite other people to follow the path of wisdom that he has given. His invitation comes with personal assurance: "My yoke is easy, and my burden is light" (Matt. 11:30). It is not an invitation to a life of drudgery that is rewarded only by a blessed afterlife, but an invitation to a blessed life in the kingdom of God for all eternity, beginning now.

The underlying theme of this book is that the gospel of Christ should bring us great joy. To the extent that we live our lives in the grace of Christ, with his cross growing ever larger, then we will be excited by his life, message, and gospel so that we will present his teachings to others.

Jesus Invites Us to Practice Discernment

A durable yearning for learning characterizes all those who are truly wise.[12]

Donald S. Whitney

Covetousness we call ambition. Hoarding we call prudence. Greed we call industry.[13]

Richard Foster

Responding to the gospel in healthy, loving, and life-giving ways means that we will follow the path of wisdom and practice the discipline of discernment. We would do well to learn from the half-truths of the human-potential movement that flourished in the mid-twentieth century. This movement discovered that human performance, especially seen in Olympic athletes, could be dramatically improved by the proper use of one's imagination. No Olympic coach suggested that one replace physical training with visualization, but we learned the power that came when athletes devoted part of their training to their detailed imagining of them performing in superior ways.

As Christians, we need to understand that one of the first ways we respond to the gospel well is by practicing discernment over what we hear about ourselves. In the course of the day, it is easy for a person to attend to a myriad of negative messages: advertisements that remind us that we are not wearing the right clothes, we do not smell just right, our hair is not the way it should be, our car is not sporty enough, and we have not gone to the right place on vacation. When this is coupled with work and family situations marked by negativity, it is easy for a person to take in harmful negative messages. The gospel calls us to see ourselves as sinners but never calls us to embrace self-hatred. The first step of discernment is to learn to listen to the voice of God, who sings a song of affirmation and love over us. This is something that the community must foster. Coming to church should not load one with guilt, but leave one marveling at God's grace and standing in awe at the wisdom of his love.

Another important pattern of discernment is to learn the gracious application of the Ten Commandments to our lives. These laws bring health and vitality to those who follow them, and we can easily memorize them and apply them to our life situations. Instilling a knowledge and tendency to follow the Ten Commandments should be central to the ethical teaching of the church. We should be more concerned that the Ten Commandments be learned and followed by ordinary Christians than that they be posted in public buildings. The concern that adherence to the Ten Commandments will lead to legalism is simply not true. Legalism is an innate tendency in humankind, and we will tend to subvert any system of grace into legalism because, in our pride, legalism emphasizes our importance. The Reformers deeply understood that a proper emphasis upon the Ten Commandments would continually make people aware of their sin and continually draw them to the Savior, while providing wise guidance for corporate and personal living.

Another important practice in discernment is that of encouraging people to reflect on their life in solitude and to seek the prayer and counsel of wise persons and elders in the church. The path of wisdom is hard to walk alone; the book of Proverbs reminds us that the counsel of others can provide wisdom and guidance. In informal and semiformal ways, churches should let people know that there are opportunities to pray and to seek the counsel of those who will bring an independent perspective and some years of life experience to the struggles and decisions they are facing. It is important for the church to model a Scripture-based and prayerful decision-making process in times of ministry planning.

Jesus Invites Us to Keep Relational Commitments

The first service that one owes to others in the fellowship consists in listening to them.[14]

Dietrich Bonhoeffer

Our society usually thinks of justice as fair play or equal treatment; the Bible portrays justice or righteousness as fulfillment of one's relational responsibility. The just or righteous person carries out the responsibilities of one's relationships. Since fulfillment of relational responsibility is a mark of righteousness, we must model and teach integrity, respect, and commitment in relationships. Achtemeier comments that in the

Bible each relationship "brings with it specific demands, the fulfillment of which constitutes righteousness. The demands may differ from relationship to relationship. . . . When God or man fulfills the conditions imposed upon him by a relationship, he is, in Old Testament terms, righteous."[15] Carrying out the obligations of family and community life is more than being nice; it is doing justice.

Jesus Invites Us to a Life of Compassion for the Poor and Marginalized and to the Elimination of Prejudice

The message of the gospel is that when we were far from God, when we were seeking to manage our lives to bring the pleasure and peace we desired, when we were utterly lost in our plans and self-protection, God reached out to us and all humanity collectively through Jesus Christ. The message of the gospel is that of God reaching out to us, and that invites us to reach out to those who are on the margins. The human instinct is to seek to find the inner circle in a group, to break in and be part of the group that is affirmed and is seen as the center of things. Life teaches us that the "inner circle" is illusory, and being there is seldom worth the price extracted to get there. Christians should cultivate a disposition of not seeking to break into the inner circle but of reaching out to those who are at the margins—those who are lonely or struggling with mental illness, whose education and poverty leave them vulnerable.

A Philippine-American pastor said that our society views most of the members of his congregation as "machine people." Such people are invisible to the busy professionals, who view them as simply an extension of service machinery that performs the duties we want done. They are an extension of dish cleaning, dry cleaning, or hotel services. He challenged me to simply pay attention to these invisible "machine people" that I, as he correctly predicted, encounter every day and yet overlook. He urged me, as an act of following Jesus, to engage these people with eye contact, affirmations, and questions about their life and well-being. Part of the call here for compassion is simply developing a way of seeing. The early desert writers of Christianity were willing to say that the essence of spirituality was adopting a new way of seeing. Particularly, to regard or show compassion and cultivate an ability or disposition to see those who are lonely and in need—these are the first great steps toward loving them.

Racial and ethnic prejudice is endemic to the fallen human race. It creates needless divisions, fuels hatred, and when present among Christians, destroys the kingdom community of Christ. The problem of our prejudice is illustrated by the godly prophet Samuel, whom God told to anoint the new king of Israel. He searched for a king and looked for what he thought would be a "kingly type." But God had something different in mind; his choice was the youngest boy, whom his father had not even called to meet Samuel. Samuel was ready to choose for physical prowess, but God told him, "Do not look on his appearance or on the height of his stature, because I have rejected him; for the LORD does not see as mortals see; they look on the outward appearance, but the LORD looks on the heart" (1 Sam. 16:7). Christians need to be taught to walk free of prejudices, which distort our ability to see people's worth and discern their hearts. Our dream should be that of Martin Luther King Jr.: "I have a dream that my four little children will one day live in a nation where they will not be judged by the color of their skin but by the content of their character."[16]

Days of service and missions trips are an excellent way of introducing people to the joy of service and showing them agencies and strategies that work in the community. A friend who has led several trips to rebuild houses in storm-damaged areas has remarked that the best spiritual formation takes place on a twenty-hour van ride. The power of community combined with tangible hands-on, community-based care for the poor in the context of prayer and worship is very formative.

Jesus Invites Us to Weep

As a young Christian I was nurtured in a faith tradition that subtly communicated that a mark of spiritual maturity was an increasing emotional disengagement. The hidden curriculum of this discipleship orientation emphasized that emotions could not be trusted, and we would do well to follow the example of Paul and Jesus, who did not display emotions. Somewhere along the line we simply overlooked passages that speak of Jesus and Paul's humanity and the reality of their emotions. Jesus' humanity is clearly imaged in his emotional states. In his ministry we see a full range of human emotions and physiological responses.

Jesus experienced hunger and weariness and deep fatigue. He experienced and displayed raw human feelings. He was angered by stubborn hearts (Mark 3:5) and felt deep compassion for the crowds that followed him (Matt. 9:36; 14:14; Heb. 4:15). He was moved to tears at the death of his friend Lazarus (John 11:35), and yet experienced joy in the Spirit at various times (Luke 10:21). He was overwhelmed with sorrow in the Garden of Gethsemane (Matt. 26:37–38; Mark 14:33–34); Luke records that he agonized to the point that "his sweat became like great drops of blood falling down on the ground" (Luke 22:44; cf. Heb. 5:7). And finally, at the agony of the cross he felt forsaken by God (Mark 15:34) and vented that agony.

Jesus' example teaches us that weeping is often the most appropriate response to the brokenness that we find in the world. His was a ministry and life marked by joy and laughter and times spent with beloved friends. His view of God's providence and care did not hold him back from entering into the sufferings of others with deep empathy, even to the point of tears. Paul describes his ministry at Ephesus as one of visiting houses and marked by tears. One of the gospel responses to the brokenness of the world is to allow ourselves to enter into the sorrow (the groaning of creation) and to weep for how things are not the way they should be. Christians have a reason to hope because of God's providence and rule, but we also have a reason to be sorrowful because we know that this groaning is not what God intended. The sorrow of the world is not an accident; the sorrow of the world represents a marring of God's good creation.

How can we foster weeping? (1) Do not try to fix everything. At times the most sensible response is to weep and pray. (2) Honor empathetic emotional responses as appropriate and truthful. (3) Learn to enter into the sufferings of others with a desire to love, not fix the problem, fully aware that sometimes the problem will not be fixed this side of eternity.

Jesus Invites Us to a Life of Integrity

One of the most unique teachings of Jesus involved his confrontation of hypocrisy. Some have asserted that Jesus essentially coined a new ethical construct. The Greek word *hypokrisis* (hypocrisy) was really a term for acting. Jesus publicly confronted this deceptive acting, where a person's heart and values and actions do not align and where a person manipulates others by giving a false impression of himself or herself. Exposing hypocrisy and the lack of integrity was a foundational concern for Christ. Once we have moved to a place where we routinely live with our lives and souls out of sync, it becomes difficult to receive the feedback that is necessary to live out a gospel-oriented life. Three invitations of Jesus summarize the essence of gospel integrity.

The first invitation is in the Golden Rule: "In everything do to others as you would have them do to you" (Matt. 7:12). This speaks of a basic, ethical life orientation where we always imagine ourselves to be subject to the ethical requirements that we place on others. We do not ask people to do what we would not do. It strikes at an entitlement mentality that would have us believe we are somehow so uniquely wounded or so uniquely in need of attention that we can demand of others what we would never deliver ourselves.

The second invitation comes in Jesus' call for us to keep our word (Matt. 5:37). We are to be people whose word can be counted on. I know from painful personal experience that we do not achieve this simply by pledging to speak the truth; it also requires soul-searching and reflection over what is so valuable to us that we are willing to lie so that we are not deprived of it. Idols of personal peace and inner-personal, tension-free living are often valued in churches far more than truth telling. We need to be people who tell the truth and who are committed to keeping our word.

The third great invitation is the call of Jesus for us to avoid hypocrisy (Matt. 7:5). We often practice hypocrisy unknowingly, and it is a spiritual disease that kills our soul. Its essence is when we put on a front and seek to show ourselves as someone that we truly are not. Jesus warned about seeking to show off spiritually so that we appear to be more pious than we are. It also comes when our financial giving is made public, or when we engage in veiled theological boasting, or when we talk about our theological beliefs and give the impression that those beliefs guide our lives more than they actually do. In our times hypocrisy often shows up in demands for blanket tolerance that, if actually applied, would leave a person incapable of discerning right from wrong and good from evil. The great disciplines that help to safeguard one from hypocrisy are practices of living in secret what we live in public and guarding oneself from boasting. Integrity is akin to a foundation for the spiritual life. It is not a spiritual or righteous life, but it forms the foundation that allows a life to be built that will not end up tilting and collapsing upon itself.

Jesus Invites Us to Use Our Money Wisely

Jesus' references to money and its spiritual implications form his number one topic of practical faith. He talks about money more frequently than heaven, hell, or prayer. This is not because Jesus is a legalist or a cosmic spoilsport descended to earth. Jesus is plainly aware that our use of money reflects our deep values, and more important for spiritual formation, our use of money can affect our soul. Our use of money, then, is a thermometer in the sense that it tells much about the condition of our heart; our money also can become a means of affecting the temperature of our heart. Our prayers and actions will be drawn to ministry that our money has supported, and our hearts are warmed in compassion toward people we show compassion to through finances. Jesus knew that our heart and our treasure will always be close to each other (Matt. 6:21). In a consumer-oriented society, there is such an emphasis on what our money can buy; the emphasis in spiritual formation needs to be on what money cannot buy.

In the past two decades, a number of wise and balanced resources on financial stewardship have become available to churches. Some observers have stereotyped the church as driven by self-interest in addressing financial issues; hence, we need to highlight these resources as holistic while we teach about the role of finances throughout life. There is a call in the Gospels, as well, for us to lay up treasures in heaven because as we put a focus on giving money to God, our hearts are also going to be drawn to God. Using our money well is a tough subject to teach because we all wrestle with what it means to be a faithful steward of our finances. Here is a place where, in our brokenness, we need to honor the fact that Jesus' invitation contains a call to a more sensible life than the one that comes from grasping our money.

Jesus Invites Us to Handle Conflicts Well and Forgive One Another

Therefore, in response to God's love and in reliance on his grace, we commit ourselves to respond to conflict according to the following principles. Glorify God, Get the Log out of Your Own Eye, Go and Show Your Brother His Fault, Go and Be Reconciled. By God's grace, we will apply these principles as a matter of stewardship, realizing that conflict is an assignment, not an accident. We will remember that success in God's eyes is not a matter of specific results but of faithful, dependent obedience.[17]

Ken Sande

Practicing forgiveness is applying the gospel to our lives. We have received much grace and are called to learn to be stewards of this great grace to others. As Matthew Linn and Dennis Linn write, "God's forgiveness toward me and my forgiveness toward another are like the voice and the echo."[18] If we cannot provide the echo of forgiveness, then we have not heard the voice of forgiveness clearly and deeply enough. The provision of hope within God's grace and love provides us with the strength and energy to be open and real about the need for ready and repeated forgiveness within relationships. In the Lord's Prayer we petition the Father: "Forgive us our sins, for we also forgive everyone who sins against us" (Luke 11:4 NIV). Forgiving others and receiving forgiveness shapes us into magnanimous stewards, where grace has come full circle and we respond to others as God has responded to us.

COMMUNITY SPIRITUAL FORMATION COROLLARY 12

Conflict has a unique way of forming us. In conflict our natural patterns of defensiveness arise, and in this vulnerable place we can experience much growth as we learn that Jesus' teachings are so sensible.

In conclusion, we need to cultivate the disposition for members of our community to respond to the gospel invitations. The spiritual practices we have discussed here will incline us to respond to the gospel, to respond to the call to imitate the values of our King. In every age cultural pressures seek to deform the gospel. The pressures today tend to make the gospel into merely a message of personal peace and self-sufficiency. One pastor put it well when he said that he struggles daily so that at the end of his life he would not find that the only thing he and God have in common is that "we both love me." Therefore, we aim to foster a climate that makes an others-oriented response to the gospel seem natural and reasonable.

Before moving to the last *R* (*relating*), a bit of review may be useful. *Responding* is our construct for appraising how we view what we have received and what we are remembering over time. The purpose and intent of our response is to render service to our Lord and to those around us. Service to others is only possible as we access Christ and his work on our behalf and as we focus on God's transforming grace. Our actions and thoughts toward others demonstrate our service to the Lord. Responses toward others and toward the Lord depend upon each other and cannot be separated.

For Further Reading

Baxter, Richard. *The Reformed Pastor*. 1656. Reprinted, Edinburgh and Carlisle, PA: Banner of Truth, 1974. A classic work concerned with the spirituality and practice of the pastor's personal life and his ministry to others.

Farnham, Suzanne G., Stephanie A. Hull, and R. Taylor McLean. *Grounded in God: Listening Hearts Discernment for Group Deliberations*. Harrisburg, PA: Morehouse, 1996. Brief, helpful work includes theoretical foundation and practical method for cultivating intentional listening and prayerful discernment with groups.

Hestenes, Roberta. *Turning Committees into Communities*. Colorado Springs: NavPress, 1991. Refreshing call to get around the usual divide between task groups and community groups.

Jacobsen, Steve. *Hearts to God, Hands to Work: Connecting Spirituality and Work*. Bethesda, MD: Alban Institute, 1997. Informative and personal account of a pastor's efforts to address the spiritual needs in the family and work situations of his people through preaching, pastoral care, education, and vision casting.

McNeill, John Thomas. *A History of the Cure of Souls*. New York: Harper, 1951. Well-regarded study of the history of pastoral care.

Nouwen, Henri J. M. *In the Name of Jesus: Reflections on Christian Leadership*. New York: Crossroad, 1989. Reminds us that followers of Jesus are too often seduced by power into a style of ministry or leadership that is decidedly not redemptive.

Torrance, James B. *Worship, Community, and the Triune God of Grace*. Downers Grove, IL: InterVarsity, 1996. This is a careful study of the theological and practical implications of a trinitarian stance in worship, prayer, sacraments, and gender concerns. It includes operational definitions for person, individual, community, and society.

Ward, Benedicta, ed. and trans. *The Desert Fathers: Sayings of the Early Christian Monks*. Penguin Classics. London and New York: Penguin Books, 2003. An accessible collection of the aphoristic writings of these early Christians who provide much wisdom concerning living in community.

9

Foundations of Relating

Spiritually Enriching Relationships of Love and Service

What role do our relationships play in spiritual formation?

> Our Creator designed us to live and grow in relationship with him and in human community. Other people are one of the most important sources of God's grace in our lives.

How do we do this?

> We need to seek out spiritually enriching relationships of love and service. We should put ourselves in places such as small groups and service units where the formation and growth of these relationships is encouraged. We need to invest in community.

What stance does this require?

> It requires a commitment to fellowship and a deep recognition that we need the church far more than the church needs us.

And let us consider how to provoke one another to love and good deeds.

Hebrews 10:24

The test of the character and quality of our relationship with God is measured by the character and quality of all other relationships.[1]

John H. Westerhoff III

The identity of the self is not so much determined by self-reflection as by intentions and actions through which the self is related to others.[2]

Ray S. Anderson

The church is always more than a school, but the church cannot be less than a school.[3]

Jaroslav Pelikan

I am increasingly convinced that most North American churches—conservative or liberal, orthodox or non-traditional—actually sponsor an education more dependent on popular understandings of psychology, therapy, and marketing.[4]

Charles Foster

In corporate worship the lives of Christians are formed and transformed, Christian identity is conferred and nurtured.[5]

Debra Dean Murphy

The biblical way of life is decidedly centered on others. Christian service is a pathway of great joy and not one of self-annihilation. Our service begins with giving ourselves to God. All Christian service starts by acknowledging God's claim on all our property, talent, and time. We serve God in our worship, in our giving, in our study, and in our concern for others. Springing from a heart given to God, service always involves doing. The doing may be kind words, time spent with another, sacrificial giving, or teaching; but in any event, the servant, like Jesus, goes about doing kind and good deeds.

Our Confession "Jesus Is Lord" Calls Us to Action

In some circles, one has the impression that the relational aspect of Christianity is just supposed to happen, almost by magic. While there is spontaneity in the best of relationships, this does not minimize the fact that healthy communities arise out of people who are committed to a certain way of being; they possess certain settled dispositions and habits of the heart that consistently prompt community-supportive disciplines. In Genesis 1 and 2, immediately after creating Adam and Eve, God delineated humankind's major responsibilities. The focus of God's concern was on action. Later in Scripture an emphasis on affections and intentions also appears, but in the final analysis God requires properly motivated action, not just good intentions or a warm heart. For this reason true spiritual formation must cultivate not just knowledge or skills but service of God through responsible action. Nicholas Wolterstorff, in his book *Educating for Responsible Action*, makes this point clear: "Education must aim at producing alterations in what students tend (are disposed, are inclined) to do. It must aim at tendency learning."[6] Christianity must touch all areas of a person's life: thinking, feeling, and doing. That touch must be true, clear, and firm enough to provoke or promote an active response.

We can never reduce this emphasis on action to behaviorist strategies. The responsible actions commanded in Scripture are not simply reflex reactions to certain stimuli. We cannot produce the fruit of the Spirit by mere behavior modification. Rather, this fruit of the Spirit flows from the Spirit's work in us. We reap what we sow. We can cultivate Spirit-born virtues and practices by favoring the Spirit's work: "If you sow to your own flesh, you will reap corruption from the flesh; but if you sow to the Spirit, you will reap eternal life from the Spirit" (Gal. 6:8). Sickly trees do not produce abundant fruit. "Make a tree good and its fruit will be good" (Matt. 12:33 NIV). Only the spiritually whole person produces abundant spiritual fruit.

Christians obey the call to responsible action not simply because responsible living is more satisfying than self-indulgence or hedonism, but because loyalty to Christ demands it. He calls Christians to obey his invitations and walk humbly with him. The guidelines are not ambiguous: "If you love me, you will keep my commandments" (John 14:15). The daily walk of the Christian should reflect our declaration "Jesus is Lord," which speaks of complete surrender and obedience to him. The confession "Jesus is Lord" is one of the oldest creeds of the church (1 Cor. 12:3). "With this call the NT community submitted itself to its Lord, but at the same time it also confessed him as ruler of the world."[7] The confession speaks of the Christian's willingness to have a unique worldview and value system. The Christian desires to follow God's commands for example, "What does the Lord require of you but to do justice, and to love kindness, and to walk humbly with your God?" (Mic. 6:8) because that is what the Lord Jesus Christ desires. True acknowledgment of Jesus as Lord leads to a lifestyle based on love and obedience, not on self-satisfaction. To acknowledge Jesus as Lord means to acknowledge oneself as a servant of Jesus and of others and to witness to the kingdom of God.

Attributes of the Forming Community

The church is Christ's body on earth. When Jesus confronted Paul on the Damascus Road, he questioned his persecutor, "Saul, Saul, why do you persecute me?" (Acts 9:4). What a remarkable identification with the church! To persecute the church is to persecute Christ. Paul uses the natural impulse to care for one's body to show Christ's care for the church: "For no one ever hates his own body, but he nourishes and tenderly cares for it, just as Christ does for the church" (Eph. 5:29). As we consider the church and spiritual formation, we must remember that spiritual formation is always an outflow of the church following Christ. When formation is put as a preliminary goal or a means to an end— "We follow Jesus so our kids will turn out okay"—we obtain neither the formation we seek nor a church that embodies (lives out the reality of being his body on earth) Christ's values. Julie Gorman writes: "True community issues out of a realization that God has placed us and held us together as he wants. . . . Community becomes God's nurturing, caring, revealing, supportive means of displaying himself as a personal, relational being in our culture."[8] A church in which God reigns, in which the kingdom of God is manifest, will demonstrate four attributes: meaningful worship, compassionate service, public witness, and disciple making. These attributes do not appear in isolation; they function in harmony, reinforcing each other.

First, meaningful worship will characterize such a church. The church was born at Pentecost by the power of the Holy Spirit when the disciples had gathered together to worship. The book of Acts regularly describes the church as a vibrant worshipping community. The believers broke bread, gathered at the temple, sang, rejoiced, and prayed. They were grateful to God for their salvation, and when they gathered together they ascribed to him worth and honor. The church was born in worship, and likewise, at the consummation of this age, the church will give itself over to the worship of God (Rev. 7:9–17). Faithful servants will worship God alone. We respond to God's grace with gratitude, and his character draws us to worship. The worship of the church is also formative. Doxological formation should make us less likely to bow before the idols of money, power, and security instead of the one living and true God.

The second characteristic is compassionate service. God has called Christians to be instruments of his compassion and service in the world. We love God wholly in worship, and we love our neighbor in service. The model of such service is Jesus, who "came not to be served but to serve, and to give his life a ransom for many" (Matt. 20:28), and who "emptied himself, taking the form of a slave, being born in human likeness. And being found in human form, he humbled himself and became obedient to the point of death—even death on a cross" (Phil. 2:7–8). This example of service is to guide the church as it not only ministers to an aching world, but also strives to eliminate the sources of injustice, oppression, and degradation. In service, the church is to use all of the gifts and resources it possesses as it seeks to minister to the entire person.

Third, the church in which the Lord reigns bears public witness to its Lord. The church has a message of joy and hope that we must tell to a troubled world: the message of divine-human reconciliation and true freedom through Jesus Christ. Loving God and neighbor in its deepest sense leads us to share the good news with our neighbor. Witness must be in both word and deed. The faithful church must confirm the validity of its spoken and written message through its life. It must live its doctrines and show forth a contagious love. Jesus indicated that outsiders could legitimately test the truth of our message by our actions: "Everyone will know that you are my disciples, if you have love for one another" (John 13:35). Christ here asserts that true love is to be the mark of the Christian community, and he assures us that its presence will be a powerful witness. "Jesus turns to the world and says, 'I've something to say to you. On the basis of my authority, I give you a right: you may judge whether or not an individual is a Christian on the basis of the love he shows to all Christians.'"[9] The Lord mandates the church to take this message of salvation to all people.

Finally and most important for Christian spiritual formation, the church has the responsibility of discipling its members and people of all nations who call upon the Lord for salvation. Loving God and neighbor comes full circle when the neighbor joins us in loving God and neighbor as a fellow disciple. The church is to develop individuals who will "lead a life worthy of God" (1 Thess. 2:12), who will bear witness through their lifestyle of gentle obedience to Christ and imitation of his character. Jesus' disciples exhibited just such an obedience to and imitation of him. Recall that when the disciples of John the Baptist noticed that Jesus' followers did not fast, they went to Jesus and asked, "Why do we and the Pharisees fast often, but your disciples do not fast?" (Matt. 9:14). Here we see that Jesus' disciples had patterned their lifestyle after their Teacher. This is the heart of discipleship. A disciple's thoughts and deeds reflect those of one's master. Like Jesus' first disciples, we should pattern our behavior after our Master and seriously study the curriculum for Christlikeness (review the section on the invitations of Jesus in chap. 2). Then with Paul we will be able to say, "Be imitators of me, as I am of Christ" (1 Cor. 11:1).

How Churches Encourage Formational Relationships

One cannot despise oneself and truly love God or the neighbor.[10]

Ray S. Anderson

The link between emotional health and spiritual maturity is a large, un-explored area of discipleship.[11]

Peter Scazzero

The groaning we all experience living this side of Eden shows itself painfully in relationships. Domination, distance, and self-interests have so often replaced the trust, the true partnership, and the intimacy of Eden. We catch glimpses of how things are supposed to be in healthy marriages, committed friendships, the healing community of good churches, and effective work groups. But we also see much pain and ugliness in relationships.

Part of our yearning for heaven is a yearning for a whole and open relationship in which we are fully known and understood. When things are set right, we will stand before God and for the first time be fully known by someone and yet not afraid because "there is no fear in love. But perfect love drives out fear, because fear has to do with punishment" (1 John 4:18 NIV). When another person learns something about our deepest thoughts and fears, they hold a certain power over us. We are very careful to whom we open up for fear we might be rejected when our true selves are revealed. So imagine standing before God, being fully known and yet feeling more completely loved than we ever have before. When Eden is restored, the children of God will know the reality of being fully known and having no fear, only a deep sense of finally being at home and fully understood.

We live in a remarkably future-oriented culture. We are a culture of savers and planners and people who only uneasily enter into the present moment, except for brief hedonistic retreats into mindless activities, and we are impatient when it comes to seriously reflecting on the past. At a friend's suggestion I have begun to ask students in my classes to name their great-grandparents' first and last names, and I have yet to have a student identify all of their great-grandparents. The sobering thought is that we live just two generations away from extinction in the collective memory. There are wonderful benefits of a future orientation in terms of its support of long-term research and careful planning about public works projects. However, an excessive orientation upon the future robs us of some of the deepest joys that we were designed to know. For it makes it hard for us to dwell in the present time—the time where we meet and enjoy God.

The spiritual life requires that we step out of the future orientation where we ask, what does this present activity do for me in terms of the future? and simply live our present. We get a sense of the difference between a future orientation and a present orientation when we think about friendships in our culture. One simple definition of friendship says, "Friends are the people we waste time with." Think about a brief commercial encounter that seems interminable. The actual time spent is not the issue as much as our perception of its value and necessity, and what we are receiving from this meeting that will help meet our goals. Yet we eagerly prolong pleasant conversations with friends and leave pleasant gatherings far later than we had planned because we enjoy spending time with friends. At some level, we can only enjoy friendships when we enter into the present and simply enjoy the reality of talking and sharing and supporting one another. For a little while we lose track of time. Our excessive future orientation robs us of relational depth and makes enjoying God's presence nearly impossible.

The deep joy promised in the gospel is only available if we learn to switch out of a driven, future orientation and are willing to waste time with God. To have a sense of the joy of coming home and being known. To feel God's embrace. To enjoy the pleasure of his company. Part of the dynamic of the spiritual life is forming and deepening a friendship with God. God desires to be our friend! He wants us to live in relationship with him so much that he chose to die rather than live without us as friends. As I began to learn to sit quietly before God, I began to experience the caress of God. With this experience of God's tender love, I began to find in Scripture a whole new teaching about God's extravagant and alluring love. Words like Zephaniah's beautiful picture of God quieting us with his love and rejoicing over us with singing (Zeph. 3:17; cf. Isa. 62:5) have become favorites of mine. On my best days, I increasingly see that if indeed "God is love," then he can only respond to me out of love.

Community First, Growth Second

Faith and the life of faith are communal before they are individual.[12]

Craig Dykstra

People need two sorts of relationships to grow: the divine and the human. . . . No matter what the issue or struggle, relatedness must come first.[13]

Henry Cloud and John Townsend

The conversation with Jose was like so many I have had over the years. He was young, married, and successful, but his life was showing the signs of stress and loneliness. He and his wife were many states removed from their parents and extended family. He had opened up to a friend at a church social event about his wife's nagging him about his long work hours, his ineptitude with the children, and his weekly Saturday golf game. His friend encouraged him and his wife to join a small group and assured him that they could find friends and support. I first talked with Jose when things had worsened in his marriage and his emotional state. I inquired about how their small group was responding, and he said, "Oh, we stopped going after a few weeks. We weren't getting anything out of it; it didn't help us at all, and it was a real nuisance to get a sitter for the kids." We need to be aware that no single program or spiritual activity will be a means of healing grace for everyone. Perhaps Jose's friend had made it seem like all he had to do was show up or perhaps the experience revealed a quick-fix mentality. There must be a willingness to engage—a willingness and desire to love—that makes grace available in these settings.

We know the maxim: "If you pursue happiness, you'll never find it." We discover happiness as the by-product of other pursuits. Happiness will forever elude us when we pursue it directly. Likewise, we generally find healing and support in community when that is not our primary aim. Much hope and healing can come through participation in true Christian community, but only if we relate to the community in a receptive and investing way. As Bellah and his colleagues ask, "Are friends that one makes in order to improve one's health really friends enough to improve one's health?"[14] We generally find help and healing through community when we are willing to commit to being part of community, period. The commitment to others does begin to put us in a place where we are more open to the healing and change that communities truly offer.

Spiritual formation is concerned with facilitating spiritual change in people. People change most readily when they are in environments that foster change as they learn to live out their unique communal calling. Such environments supply both support and challenge, and participants accept community responsibility as a way of life. We think of being responsible for others and of allowing others to care for us. There is a shift from independence to healthy interdependence. We begin to let go of our disgust for self-disclosure, vulnerability, and weakness. Commitment is upheld instead of being feared as binding or controlling.[15]

At the heart of transformational Christian formation is the working of God's grace. True formation opens the student to God's transforming power. The atmosphere must be permeated by a reverence for God, a respect for persons, and a deep sense of mission. Through moments of worship, prayer, and openness to God's work, the teacher must seek to create a community anointed by God.

For Further Reading

Bellah, Robert Neelly. *Habits of the Heart: Individualism and Commitment in American Life*. Berkeley: University of California Press, 1985. Now a bit dated, but in its day was startlingly revealing of the pervasive individualism and resulting alienation and isolation in modern American life.

Foster, Charles R. *Educating Congregations: The Future of Christian Education*. Nashville: Abingdon, 1994. Argues that our dependence on a public school model of education has caused our Christian education to lack the corporate and spiritual focus that is needed.

Hauerwas, Stanley, and William H. Willimon. *Resident Aliens: Life in the Christian Colony*. Nashville: Abingdon, 1989. Explores the ramifications of discipleship and ethics for a church that considers itself "a colony of heaven" in an ever-changing, secular culture.

Schaeffer, Francis A. *The Mark of the Christian*. Downers Grove, IL: InterVarsity, 1970. Argues that love is to be the distinctive mark of the Christian and the church.

Spener, Philipp Jakob. *Pia Desideria*. Philadelphia: Fortress, 1964. A historic call for honoring the priesthood of all believers.

Volf, Miroslav. *Exclusion and Embrace: A Theological Exploration of Identity, Otherness, and Reconciliation*. Nashville: Abingdon, 1996. A highly academic book; a moving reflection on his struggle to understand and deal with the effects of the genocide in his native Croatia as he lives out God's radical embrace of sinful humanity.

10

To Foster Relating in Community

A true religious community is only possible when presence to Christ is central in each of our lives.[1]

> Susan Muto and Adrian van Kaam

People cannot be introduced to or incorporated within a repenting, praying, and serving community unless there is one.[2]

> Craig Dykstra

Spiritual friendship is a relationship devoted to paying attention to the invitations of God in our lives and supporting one another in making a faithful response.[3]

> Ruth Haley Barton

When we listen to people's journeys of faith, we cannot help but recognize the presence and impact of other people in these stories. E. M. Bounds's maxim is right: "People are God's method. The church is looking for better methods; God is looking for better people."[4] In fact, most of us can attest to God's persistent practice of taking people who were not much "better"—but available—and growing them into better people through whose lives God could work. The people who enter our lives for our spiritual good relate to us in a variety of roles. Some are mentors. Generally these are people older than ourselves, who have had more experience in the faith, and who come alongside for a season, giving some direct guidance as to how to follow Christ more closely. At times mentors or examples may not even be aware of the impact they are having. For example, certain authors have had a powerful influence in my life.

There are also spiritual friendships. These are marked by more reciprocity in the relationship and may go on for decades or may mark a special season, especially in transition times like college or military service. The key words for these relationships are *sharing* and *support*. Family members provide another important source of spiritual guidance. Whether through parents, siblings, grandparents, or aunts and uncles, we are influenced spiritually in our families, often in quite positive ways, through godly role models who care for us, love us, and pray for us. Finally, we need to mention what we would simply call those serendipitous encounters. Usually these are memorable moments when a stranger speaks or models, often unknowingly, a word that proves to give shape to our current situation and guides us in our spiritual life.

Part of the task of leaders in spiritual formation is to encourage the formation of spiritually challenging and supportive relationships in the Christian community. This is not a call for some grand social engineering scheme of trying to match people up, but providing a climate where relationships that are spiritually nourishing can flourish and are valued. It is also important that leaders give attention to what types of relationships seem available to persons at different places on their spiritual journey. Viewed from the vantage point of history, we need to renew our commitment to a role that previous generations called "spiritual direction."

For example, I have spoken with many people who feel spiritually forsaken: to them, God is silent and distant. Generally, these people believe that there is no one in their church to turn to at such a time. Church leaders should do an informal audit by asking what resources are available for these different parts of the journey. What wise and healing relationships are available to those in a dark night? Who can help disciple a new Christian? What resources are available to the adult Christian who is growing weary in service? How intentional are our efforts to identify and encourage spiritual directors? In what ways are we training the congregation as a whole about steps to take and people to contact when someone is feeling disconnected? How are we speaking openly to these issues so that people are not blindsided by the ebb and flow of spiritual experience?

Time: A Necessity for Community

Time surely does not guarantee positive relationships, but without time they cannot develop and mature into deep spiritually forming

Evangelism, Discipleship, Mentoring, and Spiritual Guidance

Evangelism is the ministry that introduces a pre-Christian to Jesus Christ and launches the new convert on a lifelong spiritual journey. The essential message of evangelism is, "Here is what you must do in order to become a child of God." Evangelism focuses on issues of sin, conversion, and trust in Christ as Savior and Lord. Every Christian helping ministry builds on this foundation.

Spiritual formation concerns the shaping of our life after the pattern of Jesus Christ. It is a process that takes place in the inner person, whereby the Spirit reshapes our character. Many Scriptures describe this lifelong process of spiritual formation, including 2 Corinthians 3:18; Galatians 4:19; Ephesians 4:13, 22–24; Colossians 3:9–10; and 1 Thessalonians 5:23.

Discipleship is the ministry that seeks to teach new believers essential Christian beliefs and also to train us in practices that are normal in the unfolding spiritual journey. Richard V. Peace, a professor at Fuller Seminary, tells of being discipled by a program that included church attendance, Bible reading, believing the right things, prayer, and witnessing. "We did pretty well at the *knowing*, okay at the *doing*, but the whole question of *being* was fraught with difficulty. The real issue was internal. Something else was needed." Peace concludes that in order to *become*, true disciples of Jesus will benefit greatly by supplementing helpful, short-term discipleship programs with lifelong patterns of spiritual formation and direction.

Mentoring is the process whereby someone who is more experienced at a given skill teaches, models, and imparts essential knowledge, skills, and strategies to someone less experienced. The spirit of the mentoring relationship is that the mentor imparts these things freely, in order to help the protégés attain goals that are their own. It is not mentoring, but something else, if we try to re-create people in our own image, or to accomplish goals that are ours, not theirs. Gordon Shea describes a mentor as one of those special people in life who, through his deeds and words, helps another person move toward the fulfillment of his individual potential.

Spiritual guidance refers to any help given individually or in a group that advances the process of spiritual formation. The essential message of spiritual guidance is, "Together, we're going to pay prayerful attention to God's gracious working in your life."

continued ➤

Spiritual friendship is the most basic ministry of spiritual guidance in which two or more friends—on a relatively equal basis—support, encourage, and pray for one another on their journeys.

Spiritual counsel refers to the occasional helping ministry in which a godly Christian offers focused help to another person who seeks to know God and his will. One may offer spiritual counsel through a personal conversation, letter, or sermon.

Spiritual direction refers to the ministry of soul care in which a gifted and experienced Christian helps another person to grow in relationship with and obedience to God by following the example of Jesus Christ. Spiritual direction is a highly personalized ministry, respecting individual life histories, temperaments, levels of maturity, and vocations. The goals of spiritual direction are threefold. In the area of knowing, the spiritual director helps the directee understand God's will as revealed in Scripture and illuminated by faithful spiritual writings. In the realm of being, the director prays for the transformation of the directee's inner world after the image of Christ. In the realm of doing, the director encourages the directee to faithfully live out the gospel in the power of the Spirit.

Psychological counseling is the ministry that seeks personality growth, resolution of inner conflicts, and more efficient interpersonal functioning. This kind of counseling is initiated by an anxiety-laden problem or crisis, advances through personal discovery and growth, and ends with the resolution of the presenting problem. An important healing factor is the client-counselor relationship.

Adapted from Soul Guide *by Bruce Demarest. Used by permission.*[5]

relationships. In parenting, we make a distinction between quantity and quality of time, the premise being that a few hours of focused attention may be worth more than many hours of distracted mutual presence. While that distinction may be a bit dubious, we need to see that there are differences in the type of time we spend together in a church. In practice, we discover that in parenting and fellowship, quality times often show up unannounced in the middle of quantity times. Announcing to our children or fellow believers that we are about to focus solely on quality time for the next hour may be greeted with less than enthusiastic approval. The question is, Are we eager and willing to inject or derive quality from our times together? To get a sense of how the quality of our time in community varies, consider the following examples.

Task time. Many churches carry out their work through small committees or task groups. It is possible to work side by side with people, week after week, and not know much about them. You may find yourself completely surprised when a struggle in their life surfaces in another context, because during the task time there was not the opportunity to expose those areas of struggle.

Large gathering time. Whether in business meetings or worship services, most churches are going to call people together to meet where the focus is not primarily upon making connections but upon conveying information or some stated spiritual end. After such a meeting, a friend quipped that all of us had our elbows together but our hearts apart.

Large social time. These provide an opportunity for people to connect with acquaintances and meet new people on a personal affinity basis. Here is an opportunity for people to talk and share their lives and catch up on news with each other.

Midsize congregational time. These are intentionally relational groups that number less than 150 people and may be the congregation of the church or a selected subgroup of the congregation. Often there is an emphasis on teaching, worship, and spiritual formation activities. There is an opportunity for people to engage with one another at a personal level and do this in a context of prayer and worship.

Small formational study-group time. Small groups meeting in a home or comfortable environment, where people have made a commitment to study and pray together, provide an opportunity for in-depth sharing and support.

Spiritual friendship time. These may be one-on-one meetings with a peer, respected spiritual mentor, or a small prayer group. The people are committed to Christ and one another. Meeting together, they urge "one another to love and good deeds" (Heb. 10:24).

The purpose of the above list is to remind us that the effects of the time together are going to be different depending on how it is spent. A person whose entire time in Christian community is in large, impersonal gatherings is going to leave with the knowledge and orientation that was provided in that group but is going to lack the kind of interpersonal support and challenge that is found in smaller formation groups. Likewise, a person who is simply in a small formation group is going to lack the connection with the larger body of Christ and will miss some of the opportunities for worship and proclamation that can occur in such venues. A minimum quantity of time is necessary to be really engaged in the task of community formation, but it is also important that we experience community in a rich variety of ways.

Another important venue that comes into the time equation of spiritual formation concerns our time orientation. As previously mentioned, we in North America are a very future-oriented lot. We tend to measure our lives in terms of productivity and think of time as something to be saved and spent. For many of us, we are able to identify who our friends are by recognizing that they are the small subset of people that we are quite willing to "waste time with." But our rigid connection to a future-time orientation can limit our ability to truly engage in community. There is much practical wisdom in the longtime Christian practice of having shared meals together because eating a meal is one thing that pulls us out of our future orientation and causes us to dwell for a time in the present. It is only when we are in the present that we can enter into the spiritual realm and engage in true friendship activities.

The Two Great Invitations of Jesus: Love and Obey God and Love One Another

> God continually calls us to take steps that are just one degree beyond our current ability.[6]
>
> Charles Stanley

> We have many people who are passionate for God and his work, yet who are unconnected to their own emotions or those around them.[7]
>
> Peter Scazzero

Formation takes place in life. Our classes, small groups, reading, and worship equip us to respond well to the forming events of our lives. Most of the deeply forming events of our lives will come in the midst of relationships. All of the R's of formation are important, but relating has unique power both to show our formation (Are we patient in the face of interpersonal tensions? Do we display long-suffering love? Do we exhibit relational integrity?) and to form us (the forming power of love, the "rocks my world" effects of a mentor, the soothing effects of a parent). Relating is where the rubber of formation teaching and longing meets the road of life.

Those seeking to foster spiritual formation in churches need to encourage interpersonal connecting, but there must also be an emphasis on learning to follow Jesus' wisdom in relationships. Jesus' invitation to us to live a life of love is not simply a call to benign acceptance and tolerance. Love calls us to seek the best for another—it calls for wisdom, self-awareness ("First take the log out of your own eye"; Luke 6:42), knowledge, empathy, and the ability to discern the heart rather than mere appearance. True love requires training and practice. In a society filled with interpersonal pain, the church must offer "Love 101" as part of its spiritual formation. Believers must model and teach love.

These Invitations Flow out of the Call to Love God and Neighbor

Jesus Invites Us to Depend More and More on God and His Grace

Faith as the residue of experience with God is not a doctrine but a feeling or a sense of confidence that one is related to an unseen holy Will that is concerned for the conditions of human life everywhere.[8]

C. Ellis Nelson

The secret of all life-giving relation to others, and of all that is social, lies in the fact that the primary other for a human being, whether he wants it or not, is always God.[9]

Dallas Willard

Connection refers not only to the development of spiritual friendships and interpersonal bonds that allow for formational relationships to operate, but also to a deep commitment to the reality that "two are better than one" (Eccles. 4:9). People who care for us and hold us accountable are one of God's greatest means of grace. This level of connecting is encouraged when churches affirm that relationships are vital to spiritual growth. "Truth-model" churches, which place the emphasis exclusively on learning truth to change, occasionally downplay the value of relationships. We need to underscore the place that spiritual friendships and supportive relationships can have in our nurture and seek to foster their presence in our community. Jesus calls us to become more and more dependent on God and interdependent with other people, with whom we are forming relationships. These are one of God's greatest means to becoming more and more dependent on him. Never support the false dichotomy that drives a wedge between knowing God and being in relationship with people. The two great invitations in the commandment make our relationship with God and people inseparable.

Jesus Invites Us to the Joy and Freedom of Practicing Spiritual Disciplines

Joy in God is both the root and fruit of faith.[10]

John Piper

These practices, when engaged in deep interrelation with one another, have the effect of turning the flow of power in a new direction.[11]

Craig Dykstra

A healthy community is a truly spiritual forming community. Community spiritual health can be encouraged by practicing community disciplines as a means of being open and transparent before God. This corporate life is important, for communities must embody humility as well as individuals. The reality of the Lord's promise, "My grace is sufficient for you, for power is made perfect in weakness" (2 Cor. 12:9), is true for churches. We practice the disciplines because they allow us to access the grace and strength needed to cultivate the community we want. God builds true community through grace, which we access through our disciplined, grace-filled living.

The disciplines needed for grace-bathed community are those of abstinence (those practices like refraining from gossip, where we give up or abstain from a destructive pattern), empowerment (practices like confession, where we actively embrace truth that will guide), and discernment (practices that allow godly wisdom a central place in our community). Historically, many communities have found it useful to develop a "community rule of life" that provides concrete guidance about how to live together in a grace-oriented way. Wise groups consult and learn from the experiences of previous generations. Spiritual formation is not a wheel for us to reinvent but a badly neglected part of the vehicle that we need to grease. In their own traditional documents and history, many denominations can find the outlines for community rules. From the ancient monastic rules, the catechisms of the Reformation, the journals of Wesley, and the statements of community standards common to Christian colleges and camps, to the "new monastic" movement—sources of insight and wisdom abound. Confession, participation in church life, secrecy, and the avoiding of gossip were common elements in a community rule of life.

Confession. Confession is a basic discipline in the spiritual life, not for us to dread but for us to accept as a good gift. The old maxim that tells us, "There is no stronger sin than the sin that remains hidden," is indeed true. There is also a place for us to offer confession and find accountability among other Christians. There is a fear of confession in some circles because of abuses that have appeared, but this does not diminish the Bible's call for us to confess to one another and its spiritual importance: "Therefore confess your sins to one another, and pray for one another, so that you may be healed" (James 5:16). The reality of these abuses should encourage us to train others for this pastoral ministry and to be very wise in how we encourage the practice of confession in our congregations.

Participating in church life. Jesus said, "For where two or three are gathered in my name, I am there among them" (Matt. 18:20). Christ is present with us as we gather, and in fellowship we can have an experience of the Lord's presence as we engage with one another for spiritual growth. At its heart, fellowship is a commitment to be with one another through the thick and thin of things and to recognize the importance of using our giftings in such settings. Earlier we talked about the God of formation, and we identified the force of entropy that is constantly seeking to tear us apart. Adam was not complete without Eve (Gen. 2:18), and sadly, sin brought isolation from Eve and from God. Jesus came to restore our relationships with God and to create the possibility of a new community. Finally, at the end of history, we see in the book of Revelation a perfect fellowship among the saints of God.

Secrecy. Secrecy refers to the discipline that Jesus advocated in terms of our giving money and care. Secrecy works in tandem with confession; confession highlights the level of openness we seek with each other, and secrecy emphasizes the care with which we treat each others' confidences. Often in community groups we hear of needs, and at times it is quite appropriate for us to respond in public ways as we join together to help someone. At times, it is also important for us to practice secret help, which may protect the dignity of the person who is receiving help and certainly protects us from vainglory. This is an important discipline that deserves clear and sustained instruction. We can encourage the practice of secret help without making it the sole means by which we show compassion in our community. This is best left to individuals' discretion, as they realize how the person receiving aid and they themselves will benefit most when it is done in secret.

Avoiding gossip. Society generally understands gossip to mean the spreading of rumor and misinformation. Consequently, I have heard sincere persons justify their gossiping by saying, "It was true, so it is not gossip." From a Christian perspective, gossip is the public revelation of another person's sins, generally for self-oriented reasons. Gossip tears at the fabric of community and is part of a long list of community vices that we need to set aside and guard against. Paul pointed to these when he wrote, "I fear that there may perhaps be quarreling, jealousy, anger, selfishness, slander, gossip, conceit, and disorder" (2 Cor. 12:20).

Jesus Invites Us to Practice Discernment

The habit of discernment is a quality of attentiveness to God.[12]

Ruth Barton

Focus upon the kingdom produces the inward reality, and without the inward reality we will degenerate into legalistic trivia.[13]

Richard Foster

One of the outstanding features of Christian community is that, as we share our stories and struggles, a continual process of discernment and guidance is going on; we receive words of encouragement and perspective from other people. We express a corporate desire to seek God's direction for personal and group decisions. Ruth Barton has identified three beliefs necessary for discernment: belief in the goodness of God, in our primary calling to love, and in God's communicating with us through the Holy Spirit.[14] The Holy Spirit helps us to wait with an open heart that desires to give up all that would keep us from seeing and accepting the invitations of love in our personal or group situations.

We often call it "guidance" when people need help in making will-of-God decisions about employment, marriage, major life choices, and so forth. That is certainly true, but another form of guidance happens through receiving counsel that contains a gospel perspective on a situation that we face. It is rather easy for us to lose track and to fall into negative patterns of thinking or patterns learned when we were far from the gospel, in terms of relying on power or escape in hard times. The faithfulness of a brother or sister in Christ who has experienced a similar situation can be a powerful form of guidance as he or she simply shows us another way of dealing with the circumstances. Also, the gentle words of hope and assurance that we are offered as we tell of our struggle and as a person reminds us that this too can be used of God for our sanctification, that God can use even this seemingly ordinary event to transform our lives—such very indirect gospel speech can be a powerful form of guidance in our lives.

Jesus Invites Us to Practice Detachment

The modern hero is the poor boy who purposefully becomes rich rather than the rich boy who voluntarily becomes poor.[15]

Richard Foster

The practice of detachment is more something Jesus assumed would be true of his disciples than an explicit theme of his teaching. When he addresses detachment, his words are direct and even shocking. Using his typical hyperbole, he calls for a commitment to himself and detachment from others. "Whoever comes to me and does not hate his father and mother, wife and children, brothers and sisters, yes, and even life itself, cannot be my disciples" (Luke 14:26). The detachment he calls for is not just relational. He insists that you cannot be "my disciple if you do not give up all your possessions" (14:33).

The detachment to which Jesus invites us is not indifference. This detachment is to enable us to love God and neighbor more fully. An indifferent person appears to be unattached but actually is uncaring and ultimately is deeply attached to self-protection. Similarly, Richard Foster writes:

> Asceticism and simplicity are mutually incompatible. Asceticism renounces possessions. Simplicity sets possessions in proper perspective. Simplicity is the only thing that sufficiently reorients our lives so that possessions can be genuinely enjoyed without destroying us. Without simplicity we will either capitulate to the "mammon" spirit of this present evil age, or we will fall into an un-Christian legalistic asceticism. Both lead to idolatry. Both are spiritually lethal.[16]

The detached person cares appropriately because one is ultimately serving an Audience of One.[17] Detachment, as Jesus invites us to it, is the freedom to love. Detachment calls us to rightly order our lives and to set our loves in order.

To varying degrees, we are ensnared by three kinds of attachment: possessions (things), people (inordinate attachment, compulsive approval needs, various fears), and thoughts (lust, depreciative thoughts, jealousy, anger, food and drink). The setting aside of false attachments is really the work of a lifetime. Most will find that detachment comes far easier in one of these three areas. In and through community we learn the need for detachment in the areas to which we are blind and see models of what true detachment means in those around us. Our desire for detachment grows as we seek the freedom to love.

A community can help foster detachment by clear teaching about the power of things to possess us. Also, we must give and hear clear teaching on the nature of undue attachments. We must guide each other to see that the fault or defect is not in the object—it is not merely "too attractive"—but in the self: my disordered loves draw me to this.

Jesus Invites Us to Worship and to Celebrate the Sacraments

> Essentially mysterious but entirely accessible, the sacraments are pure genius for teaching us what we need to know and, paradoxically, what we can never know about our relationship with God. . . . In every case, the first thing they teach us is that we do not worship God alone. We need other people in our lives to feed us and forgive us, to touch us and bless us and strengthen our resolve. There are no solo sacraments. We need one another.[18]
>
> Barbara Brown Taylor

Christians have every reason to celebrate, and our worshipful celebration is the central forming event in our community life. The single most important event in our spiritual formation is participating in worship that evokes awe, draws forth a loving response to others, and leaves us certain that isolated individualism is not compatible with the gospel. We are loved by God and adopted as his children. The new spiritual life we have received, the continuing redemptive work of God, and the very beauty of God should call forth our celebration. In celebration we strengthen one another through our corporate rejoicing. The doxology of God's people is an end in itself and does bear healing fruit. Many struggling persons have found themselves strengthened and their life vision renewed simply by experiencing the celebration of God's people.

When reading the Gospels, we are struck with how central celebration was to the life of Christ. Paul goes so far as to command us to "rejoice in the Lord always" (Phil. 4:4). Celebration is not merely a feel-good, group-building activity; instead, it should be a response to God's gracious deliverance of us. So the celebration called for here is one of celebrating the jubilee that Christ has given us. We might speak of this as having parties for a purpose, where we seek to enjoy one another and remind ourselves of the great gifts God has given us.

Jesus Invites Us to Extend Hospitality

Just as the human need for hospitality is a constant, so it seems, is the human fear of the stranger.[19]

Ana Maria Pineda

In both word and deed, Jesus invites his followers to show hospitality. In the Gospels, Jesus was the frequent recipient of hospitality (Matt. 13:1, 36; Mark 1:29–31; 14:3–9; Luke 7:36–39; 10:38–42; 14:1–6; John 2:1–10), and he seemed to assume that hospitality would be extended to him. He also clearly extends hospitality in his mass feedings (Matt. 14:15–21; 15:32) and especially for the Last Supper (John 13). Here he serves as the host who provides the space and food and breaks social convention by washing the feet of his guests.

The early church took to heart Jesus' invitation and placed special emphasis on showing hospitality to strangers. Opening the fellowship of reading and interpreting Scripture and prayer to friends and strangers widens the circle of fellowship and breaks down the barriers that had previously left strangers on the outside. In three summary lists of virtuous actions, hospitality to the stranger is highlighted (Rom. 12:13; 1 Tim. 5:10; Heb. 13:2). Additionally, one of the qualifications of a church leader is a hospitable nature (1 Tim. 3:2; Titus 1:8). The call for hospitality goes beyond simply entertaining guests and allows believers to work corporately with several disciplines simultaneously.

Hospitality is a practical outworking of the call to love and creates a space for formation. Creating a space for food, spiritual conversation, and the warmth of acceptance are so important to our formation. The New Testament writers first gave these commands in cultures where hospitality was already a social norm. How much more we need this urging today, when we treasure privacy and acknowledge that "we are short not only of tables that welcome strangers but even of tables that welcome friends."[20]

Jesus Invites Us to Keep Relational Commitments

We need to acknowledge that people and, indeed, the whole of creation are not objects for us to engage but subjects that engage us. People are always best understood as mysteries and surprises.[21]

                                                            John H. Westerhoff III

Self-consciousness arises through authentic encounter and interchange with another person: the self is intrinsically social.[22]

                                                                  Ray S. Anderson

The calling of community is to lure people off the island onto the mainland where connection is possible and to provide it.[23]

                                                                      Larry Crabb

Certain relational activities have more spiritual leverage in the way they affect our souls. Keeping and honoring relational responsibilities should be a gospel-driven priority in our lives. Scripture understands justice largely as a matter of carrying out our relational responsibility. These relationships extend beyond immediate friends and family and include the family of God: those whom the Bible calls our neighbors, our nation, and our environment. When considering spiritual formation, we place an emphasis on relational responsibilities because doing so is an important ethical principle and because honoring or breaking these uniquely affects our soul.

Part of the preoccupation of the church with sex comes from the wisdom that sexual transgressions, which are a violation of our relational commitments, have a unique power to deform the soul. Paul warns: "Run from sexual sin! No other sin so clearly affects the body as this one does. For sexual immorality is a sin against your own body" (1 Cor. 6:18 NLT). Chastity speaks about the discipline of living and relating to other people so that we see them primarily as persons and not objects of sexual fantasy or manipulation. Our sexuality is a good and perfect gift that we need to celebrate. Nevertheless, we need to discipline ourselves in Christian community so that we are careful not to sexualize our interactions in ways that distract us from our spiritual tasks. At the practical level, it means that men need to watch the wandering eye and any flirtation, and women need to watch their dress and demeanor, so that both relate to one another as brothers and sisters in Christ with full integrity.

Jesus Invites Us to a Life of Compassion for the Poor and Marginalized and to the Elimination of Prejudice

A spiritual friend is a sensitive, caring, open, flexible person of faith and prayer who listens well and maintains confidentiality.[24]

John H. Westerhoff III

Lifestyles and choices that love and value people more than things is the litmus test of faith.[25]

Adele Ahlberg Calhoun

Compassion complements the previous mark of formative community. Here we are called to care for one another, but even more important, the community looks outward. Some of my most memorable times of community building have been when the church worked together to show compassion for others. Community forms at its deepest when it is not simply seeking to form relationships as an end in themselves, but when enlightened task groups aim at showing compassion for the surrounding community.

In the context of an ongoing ministry of teaching the Word, we need specific instruction because we are a forgetful people; we must continually remind each other of God's love. We are also a highly prejudiced people, and we must continually train each other to set aside our racial prejudices and our innate tendency to assign persons to a status different from ourselves. We additionally need to remind people that God will work in their life circumstances, if invited, and emphasize the importance of learning to handle conflict as a true peacemaker. We need to give the call to love God and neighbor both as a challenge and as a lived reality that brings support and safety. Without the challenge, we often will retreat to self-protective strategies that make it difficult for us to give and receive love.

Jesus Invites Us to Handle Conflicts Well and to Forgive One Another

Being forgiven requires an ongoing willingness to honor a new claim that has been made on us, to speak with a new truthfulness, and to live in a new way with one another.[26]

L. Gregory Jones

Conflict ranges from interpersonal irritations, based in pride and pettiness, to deep-seated ideological conflicts; from genuine differences between high-minded people over allocating scarce resources for a good cause, to systemic patterns of institutionalized conflict. Handling conflict properly was certainly one of Jesus' major concerns, and every New Testament epistle addresses it. Forgiving is a powerful witness to our personal and corporate ability to recognize the forgiveness that we have received in such a way as to be able to use it: to multiply it by extending it to others. "The experience of forgiveness makes us forgiving. Once we see ourselves as people who need God's mercy, we will be more likely to show mercy to others."[27]

Offense and conflict are inevitable and come in all shapes and sizes. The bottom-line questions should point first to the reality of the resources available in the love and sovereignty of God, and then to the uniqueness or difficulties of particular cases. Our churches need to guide groups and individuals aggressively through reconciliation by together taking grace that has been received and owned with positive responses and extending that grace to others in healthy, forgiving relationships. Jesus sternly summarized the parable of the unmerciful servant: "So my heavenly Father will also do to every one of you, if you do not forgive your brother or sister from your heart" (Matt. 18:35). As we forgive and extend mercy, we relate as Jesus has invited us to do, and the gospel is evident both to ourselves and to all within our circle of influence. Here the power of the gospel shines because forgiveness is often extremely difficult and counted as beyond human expectation in a culture of individualism and self-preoccupation.

To implement this *R* of *relating*, we need to realize our "natural" resistance to enter into the kind of formative relationships that are truly essential. These relationships require vulnerability and expose us to the challenge of connection and the disappointment that comes whenever we have extended ourselves in love. As leaders in formation, we are not able to—nor should we try to—manipulate things so that people experience formative relationships. However, we do have a responsibility to see that we do all that is in our power, through prayer and diligent work, to create a climate that supports formative relationships. Perhaps the first fatal mistake people make in seeking to foster formative relationships is to think that certain programs carry this out. At their best, programs create a place where formative relating can take place, but they do not guarantee it. In my experience, we do best at cultivating these kinds of relationships when we seek to encourage a robust presence of the major formative interpersonal qualities. The major formative qualities that appear to mark forming communities are connection, challenge, compassion, and celebration.

Insights on Forgiveness

Forgiveness takes brokenness seriously and affirms that guilt is real but also affirms that guilt is not the last word.

The possibility of forgiveness is rooted in the character and actions of God.

Forgiving is not forgetting. . . . Forgiving is not excusing. . . . Forgiving is not ignoring. . . . Forgiving is not necessarily to offer unconditional trust.

Along the way to accomplishing forgiveness, you will need to: (1) Consider how you were forgiven. (2) Be realistic. Name the sin against you for what it truly is. Limit your expectations of what will result from forgiveness. (3) Share the pain (Isa. 53:4; Matt. 8:17; Gal. 6:2). (4) Accept the time forgiving may take. (5) Understand what it means to "forgive and forget." God cannot forget our sins in the sense that he loses them from his memory. By forgetting them, he must mean that he sets aside the punishment we deserve. So when we "forget" the offense done to us, it means we will not in the future "use" the offense as reason to punish the offender. (6) Finally learn ways to break the chain of self-enslavement to bitter thoughts.

For healing to occur, our perceptions must be brought into line with reality, with truth. The essence of this reinterpretation of my hurt is seeing those who hurt me as separate from what they did to me and *seeing myself as more than my wound.*

To forgive is not necessarily to extend unconditional trust. Additionally, I must realize that the perceived value from the empowerment that anger seems to give me must be put in perspective with the possible ultimate cost to my own spirit of abiding malice (Heb. 12:15).

The other set of difficulties in forgiveness is in receiving it. The hard-work miracle may be hard to believe as a miracle. Who qualifies for a miracle? The answers and solutions may lie in following three steps: (1) Realize the hidden motives you may have in fearing to rest in God's sheer mercy. (2) Remember the tactics of the enemy of your soul's peace and learn how to overcome them. (3) Reexamine the reality and integrity of the forgiveness provided for you in Jesus Christ.

I also need to realize that a *refusal to accept forgiveness can be a form of idolatry* and pride. Boldly put, am I such a unique exception in the world that I can handle my redemption better than God?

In his accusations *the devil always points us away from Christ*, either to get us to excuse self or dwell upon self. On the other hand, the Holy Spirit points us to Christ, and if he convicts of sin, he also seeks to convince us of grace. Satan twists Scripture. Satan confuses doctrine. How do we meet his accusations? (1) Address the power of sin instead of the shame of sin. Study

continued ➤

what it is doing to you more than how it makes you feel (Rom. 2–8). (2) Work to keep your conscience clean through confession (Acts 24:16; 1 Tim. 1:19; Heb. 9:14). (3) Fix your eyes upon the evidences of grace in your life, past and present. (4) Share your struggle over guilt with another believer, and ask that friend to pray for your assurance of forgiveness. (5) Above all, realize that Satan cannot accuse you, a Christian, before God! God may convict you of sin in order to bring you to confession and cleansing, but he will not listen to the accusations of Satan and change his mind about your salvation (Rom. 8:33–34).

Adapted from Understanding and Facilitating Forgiveness *by David G. Benner and Robert W. Harvey. Used by permission.*[28]

Finally, it is the answering of Jesus' invitations to love and obey God, to love one another, and to do what naturally flows from those two invitations that we give evidence to having *received* grace and gospel, *remembered* those blessings, *responded* to them, and *related* to others in a manner directed by them (the four *R*'s). Our goal is a spiritual formation that, by the receiving of God's grace and the empowering of the Holy Spirit, moves a curriculum for Christlikeness from a teaching approach to a living, breathing, gospel-directed life of shared community. Such a mission will fill our deepest longings for home and holiness. The journey is one for us to take together and to engage in with an eye to our eternal home, because going it alone or seeking out other temporary homes will never satisfy. We belong together in our Father's home.

For Further Reading

Augustine. *Love One Another, My Friends: St. Augustine's Homilies on the First Letter of John; An Abridged English Version*. Translated and abridged by John Leinenweber. San Francisco: Harper & Row, 1989. Simple and attractive writing style invites readers to follow the path of love in their relations.

Benner, David G., and Robert W. Harvey. *Understanding and Facilitating Forgiveness*, Strategic Pastoral Counseling Resources. Grand Rapids: Baker Books, 1996. An in-depth exploration of necessity and implications for forgiveness that is helpful for the lay reader as well as those involved in pastoral care.

Bonhoeffer, Dietrich. *Life Together*. Translated by John W. Doberstein. New York: Harper, 1954. This description of an underground seminary during the Nazi years provides a compelling and now-classic exploration of faith in community.

Dougherty, Rose Mary. *Group Spiritual Direction: Community for Discernment*. New York: Paulist Press, 1995. An experienced spiritual director shares her insights on discernment, prayers, silence, listening, and awareness. She provides practical advice for implementing and caring for a ministry of group spiritual direction.

Snyder, Howard A. *The Community of the King*. Downers Grove, IL: InterVarsity, 1977. A practical guide for church life based on the relationship between the kingdom of God and the church.

Symeon. *Symeon the New Theologian: The Discourses*. Translated by C. J. de Catanzaro. Classics of Western Spirituality. New York: Paulist Press, 1980. Originally given as sermons in his monastery, this work captures the core distinctive of Eastern Christian spirituality.

Appendix

Assessment Questions

My purpose has been to set forward a curriculum for Christlikeness grounded in the gospel and the grace that it makes available. Without a constant appropriation of the grace extended, it would be foolish to pursue such an involved and demanding purpose as imitating Christ. Grace sets us on our way and accompanies us to the finish. The framework for this curriculum is the lifelong practice of *receiving, remembering, responding*, and *relating*. These are verbs and not nouns. These categories call for believers to take action and to do so in the ordinary circumstances of everyday life. The four *R*'s invite us to intentional activity, to live out—in both the public and the most private aspects of daily life and thought—the wise invitations of Jesus to kingdom living. The goal of Christlikeness has been well-articulated by Dallas Willard:

> This process of "conformation to Christ," as we might more appropriately call it, is constantly supported by grace and otherwise would be impossible. But it is not therefore passive. Grace is opposed to earning, not to effort. In fact, nothing inspires and enhances effort like the experience of grace.
> Yet it is today necessary to assert boldly and often that becoming Christlike never occurs without intense and well-informed action on our part. This in turn cannot be reliably sustained outside of a like-minded fellowship. Our churches will be centers of spiritual formation only as they understand Christlikeness and communicate it to individuals, through teaching and example, in a convincing and supportive fashion.[1]

As we work with this curriculum, it will be necessary to take some time for evaluation and planning. Are we getting it? Are we doing better or worse? Why? What has helped and what has hindered our work with the curriculum? The questions in the following section are intended to assist us in the process of self and group evaluation regarding our progress in *receiving, remembering, responding,* and *relating.* I have constructed the questions to use broad group language terms of "we" and "our church" and thus facilitate a group assessment setting.

If spiritual formation is the mission of the church, then thoughtful evaluation is necessary to insure that we are carrying out the mission as our priority. Since any curriculum for Christlikeness takes concerted resolve, we should also understand that assessments are profoundly difficult due to the human vulnerability to self-deception and blind spots. Here it is immensely important to be open to the work of the Holy Spirit, not to rush, to pray, and to plead for the grace and humility to see what God sees. What follows are two sets of questions designed to look at the formation process from two distinct perspectives. Each perspective is important in evaluating the formational ministry of a church.

Assessing the Presence of the Four *R*'s

I. Examining the four main components of the curriculum for Christlikeness
  A. Receiving: Where do people receive God's grace and love?
    • In what ways does our church encourage the application of the gospel to everyday situations?
    • How do we encourage the cultivation of awe for God's beauty, mystery, or wonder?
    • Which corporate disciplines support our longing for God and for Christlikeness?
    • Where and when do people receive grace in our church?
    • Where do we cultivate the desire to receive God's love?
  B. Remembering: Where are people encouraged to remember who they truly are as children of God and whose they truly are?
    • Where do we practice spiritual remembering through testimony, journaling, and thanksgiving?
    • Where are learners receiving a comprehensive presentation of the Bible?
    • How well is our overall curriculum teaching people to actually adopt Jesus' lifestyle?
    • Where are they learning to practice the spiritual disciplines that marked Jesus' life?

- How well are we teaching people to live out the great invitations of Jesus? Review the list of the invitations below and list places where we are teaching people to live these out.
  1. Invitations to steward Christ's gospel
     - Jesus invites us to tell people about the good news and make disciples.
     - Jesus invites us to practice discernment.
     - Jesus invites us to a life of integrity.
     - Jesus invites us to use our money wisely.
     - Jesus invites us to practice detachment.
  2. Invitations to extend Christ's compassion
     - Jesus invites us to pray for and bless others.
     - Jesus invites us to keep relational commitments.
     - Jesus invites us to a life of compassion for the poor and marginalized and to the elimination of prejudice.
     - Jesus invites us to weep—a call to empathy.
     - Jesus invites us to handle conflicts well and forgive one another.
     - Jesus invites us to extend hospitality.
  3. Invitations to worship
     - Jesus invites us to worship and to celebrate the sacraments.
     - Jesus invites us to create a space for God through solitude.
     - Jesus invites us to use our body in prayer and worship.
  4. Invitations to think rightly about God
     - Jesus invites us to depend more and more on God and his grace.
     - Jesus invites us to the joy and freedom of practicing spiritual disciplines.
     - Jesus invites us to study and meditate on Scripture.
     - Jesus invites us to repentance and to draw close to God and himself.
     - Jesus invites us to believe he is who he claims to be.
     - Jesus invites us to a life of learning.
C. Responding: In what ways do we foster a disposition to be people of love and "right living"?
  - Where do we provide specific training to live well: in relationships, in families, at work?
  - Where do we provide training on Christian conflict resolution?

- Where do we help people to learn to set aside racial and ethnic prejudices?
- Where do we help people learn to be good stewards of creation?
- Where do we equip people to evangelize?

D. Relating: Where do we provide opportunities to grow in and through relationships?
   - In what ways does our community support an attitude or outlook of brokenness before one another and before God?
   - Where do we show hospitality to one another? Where do we show hospitality to the stranger?
   - How well do we discipline or confront known patterns of sin within our church?

II. Where does formation happen in the church?

These questions are a parallel way of evaluating the formational patterns and programs in a church or ministry. Here the focus switches to look at "resources for the journey."

Goal: Provide rich formative opportunities for all stages of the Christian life.

Evaluative task: Identify life phases that are under-resourced.

Process: Observe and then brainstorm a description of the experience of a church member at each of these stages on the spiritual journey.

A. New Christian
   - What education or discipleship program is in place to train a new believer? In what ways does the program reflect the curriculum of Christlikeness in the ordinary aspects of individual lives?
   - How do we enfold new believers into the fellowship of the larger group?
   - Do we give new believers service opportunities that match their abilities and maturation?
   - When new believers ask hard questions or seek to change the status quo, how do we respond?
   - How well are we doing at providing mentors for new Christians?

B. Christians struggling with addictions, temptations, crises, grief
   - Where in our church do we allow or encourage the troubled to share their brokenness and tell their story?
   - How does our church respond to these admissions of need both initially and over the long term?

- In what ways and by whom are the struggling or broken identified and cared for?
- Where are the struggling or troubled allowed to contribute or serve within our church?
- What is our protocol for referring the troubled to professional help or community services?

C. Christians struggling with doubting
- Where in our church do we allow or encourage the doubter to ask difficult and disturbing questions?
- In what ways does our church seek to engage with the ordinary day-to-day life of the doubter?
- How do we identify and care for the doubters?
- In what ways do we assure doubters that we still accept and value them?
- What are the usual long-term outcomes for those who have come to our church with difficult questions? Do these individuals usually stay or disappear over time?
- What resources are available in the form of books, sermon tapes, or other study materials for doubters?

D. Christians experiencing a dark night of the soul
- What efforts are we making to instruct all members of our church regarding the dark night of the soul?
- Is there a conscious effort on the part of the leadership to be watching for cases of spiritual depression and spiritual dryness among themselves and those for whom they care?
- What is our general attitude and response to those who express that they fear they are losing their faith?
- What methods do we make available to answer the questions and concerns of those in this condition?

E. Christians wearied by ordinariness of faithfully following Jesus
- In what ways do we review and assess the educational curriculum of the church for freshness and effectiveness?
- What kind of vision do we have to inspire the long-term faithful members?
- How do individuals or small groups usually present their visions or challenges to the larger group?
- How does the larger group usually respond to the visions or challenges of individuals or small groups?

F. Christians in need of restorative discipline
- In what ways do we approach an individual or group of individuals and motivate them to cooperate with restorative discipline?

- When restoration requires reconciliation between two members within the church, who usually initiates discussions—the offended party, the defending party, or a leader who has a heart that sees and responds to trouble in early stages?
- How do we incorporate accountability into a restorative process?

Remember that prayer is our leading ally for the work of assessment. In prayer we can find rest from our striving and be strengthened in God's love. As R. A. Torrey has instructed:

> God does not demand of us the impossible, He does not demand of us that we imitate Christ in our own strength. He offers to us something infinitely better, He offers to form Christ in us by the power of his Holy Spirit. And when Christ is thus formed in us by the Holy Spirit's power, all we have to do is to let this indwelling Christ live out his own life in us, and then we shall be like Christ without struggle and effort of our own.[2]

Notes

Chapter 1 Formation through the Ordinary

1. Dallas Willard, "Spiritual Formation in Christ: A Perspective on What It Is and How It Might Be Done," *Journal of Psychology and Theology* 28, no. 4 (2000): 256.

2. Richard F. Lovelace, *Dynamics of Spiritual Life: An Evangelical Theology of Renewal* (Downers Grove, IL: InterVarsity, 1979), 143.

3. Centers for Disease Control and Prevention, "Ten Great Public Health Achievements—United States, 1900–1999," *Morbidity and Mortality Weekly Report* 48, no. 12 (1999): 241–43.

4. Ibid.

5. Dallas Willard, *Renovation of the Heart: Putting on the Character of Christ* (Colorado Springs: NavPress, 2002), 10.

6. David G. Benner, *Care of Souls: Revisioning Christian Nurture and Counsel* (Grand Rapids: Baker Books, 1998), 95–108.

7. Leland Ryken, James C. Wilhoit, and Tremper Longman III, eds., "Race" in *Dictionary of Biblical Imagery* (Downers Grove, IL: InterVarsity, 1988), 693.

8. Ibid., 697.

9. Kenneth J. Collins, *Soul Care: Deliverance and Renewal through the Christian Life* (Wheaton: Victor Books, 1995), 110.

10. Patric Knaak, whose clear gospel teaching has helped me immensely, suggested the diagrams on the gospel and spiritual growth.

11. John Ortberg, "True (and False) Transformation," *Leadership* 24, no. 3 (2002): 102.

12. Lovelace, *Dynamics of Spiritual Life*, 101.

13. Millard J. Erickson, *Christian Theology*, 2nd ed. (Grand Rapids: Baker Academic, 1998), 1072.

14. World Harvest Mission, *Discipling by Grace* (Jenikstown, PA: World Harvest Mission, 1996), 1.3.

15. Quoted in Jim Berkley and Kevin Miller, "Vital Signs," *Leadership* 8, no. 1 (1987): 12–21, esp. 15.

16. Dallas Willard, *The Divine Conspiracy: Rediscovering Our Hidden Life in God* (San Francisco: HarperSanFrancisco, 1998), 308.

17. Craig R. Dykstra, *Growing in the Life of Faith: Education and Christian Practices*, 2nd ed. (Louisville: Westminster John Knox, 2005), 78.

18. M. Scott Peck, *The Road Less Traveled: A New Psychology of Love, Traditional Values, and Spiritual Growth* (New York: Simon & Schuster, 1978), 268.

19. Ryken, Wilhoit, and Longman, "Chaos" in *Dictionary*, 136.

20. Willard, *Renovation*, 19.

Chapter 2 Curriculum for Christlikeness

1. Willard, *Divine Conspiracy*, 348–49.

2. Robert P. Meye, "The Imitation of Christ: Means and End of Spiritual Formation," in *The Christian Educator's Handbook on Spiritual Formation*, ed. Kenneth O. Gangel and James C. Wilhoit (Grand Rapids: Baker Books, 1994), 199.

3. Willard, *Divine Conspiracy*, 282–83.

4. John R. W. Stott, *God's New Society: The Message of Ephesians* (Downers Grove, IL: InterVarsity, 1979), 193.

5. Mark I. Pinsky, *The Gospel according to the Simpsons: The Spiritual Life of the World's Most Animated Family* (Louisville: Westminster John Knox, 2001), 22.

6. The number of Jesus' devotional acts recorded in the Gospels can be computed as 129; though this was carefully ascertained, one must be cautious about using this number too freely. This is a simple counting of "devotional acts" (a partial list includes prayer, fasting, solitude, service done in secret, anointing, meditation, solitude, Scripture memory); some acts occurring in more than one Gospel may be counted twice. Also in arriving at this number, the primary discipline highlighted in the text was counted, and thus secondary disciplines may be underrepresented.

7. Richard J. Foster, *Prayer: Finding the Heart's True Home* (San Francisco: HarperSan-Francisco, 1992), 135.

8. Kallistos Ware, *The Orthodox Way*, rev. ed. (Crestwood, NY: St. Vladimir's Seminary Press, 1995), 74.

9. Willard, *Divine Conspiracy*, 320.

10. E. J. Tinsley proposes a solution. He wants to hold together the sense of active imitation with the idea that God is actively conforming us to Christ's image. He sees that maintaining this tension is vital to a robust understanding of imitation. "In a fully developed theology of the Christian life as imitation of Christ both the terms *conformitas* and *imitatio* would need to be used. The imitative life of the Christian involves both God's activity, through the Spirit, in conforming man to his image in Christ (*conformitas*), and man's forming of his moral and spiritual attention on the exemplar, Christ (*imitatio*)." E. J. Tinsley, "Some Principles for Reconstructing a Doctrine of the Imitation of Christ," *Scottish Journal of Theology* 25, no. 1 (1972): 47.

11. Marguerite Shuster, "The Use and Misuse of the Idea of the Imitation of Christ," *Ex auditu* 14 (1998): 79.

12. Quoted by Dallas Willard, *The Spirit of the Disciplines: Understanding How God Changes Lives* (San Francisco: Harper & Row, 1988), 265.

13. Andrew Murray, *Like Christ: Thoughts on the Blessed Life of Conformity to the Son of God* (London: James Nisbet, 1896), 11.

14. Willard, *Divine Conspiracy*, 320.

15. In this section concerning six myths, I am indebted to the work of Henry Cloud and John Sims Townsend, *Twelve "Christian" Beliefs That Can Drive You Crazy: Relief from False Assumptions* (Grand Rapids: Zondervan, 1995).

16. Carol Lakey Hess, "Educating in the Spirit" (PhD diss., Princeton Theological Seminary, 1990), 221.

17. Larry Richards, *Creative Bible Teaching* (Chicago: Moody, 1973), 75.

Chapter 3 Foundations of Receiving: Formation by Grace for the Broken and Thirsty

1. Howard L. Rice, *Reformed Spirituality: An Introduction for Believers* (Louisville: Westminster John Knox, 1991), 42.

2. J. Harold Ellens, "Sin or Sickness: The Problem of Human Dysfunction," in *Seeking Understanding: The Stob Lectures, 1986–1998*, ed. The Stob Lecture Endowment of Calvin Theological Seminary (Grand Rapids: Eerdmans, 2001), 481.

3. John H. Westerhoff III, *Spiritual Life: The Foundation for Preaching and Teaching* (Louisville: Westminster John Knox, 1994), 36.

4. J. Harold Ellens, "Sin and Sickness: The Nature of Human Failure," in *Counseling and the Human Predicament: A Study of Sin, Guilt, and Forgiveness*, ed. LeRoy Aden and David G. Benner (Grand Rapids: Baker Academic, 1989), 74–75.

5. Ellens, "Sin or Sickness: The Problem of Human Dysfunction," 489.

6. André Louf, *Tuning in to Grace: The Quest for God*, trans. John Vriend (Kalamazoo, MI: Cistercian Publications, 1992), 16.

7. C. S. Lewis, *The Last Battle*, illustrated by Pauline Baynes, Collier Books ed. (New York: Collier Books, 1970), 162.

8. C. S. Lewis, *The Problem of Pain*, Macmillan Paperbacks ed. (New York: Macmillan, 1962), 145.

9. Augustine, *Confessions*, trans. Henry Chadwick (Oxford and New York: Oxford University Press, 1991), 3.

10. Hess, "Educating in the Spirit" (1990), 214–15.

11. Dan B. Allender and Tremper Longman III, *The Cry of the Soul: How Our Emotions Reveal Our Deepest Questions about God* (Colorado Springs: NavPress, 1994), 25–26, 44–53, 221–36, 245–46.

12. Ryken, Wilhoit, and Longman, "Fall from Innocence" in *Dictionary*, 263.

13. George MacDonald, *Unspoken Sermons: First Series* (London: Longmans, Green, 1897), 106.

14. Julie A. Gorman, *Community That Is Christian*, 2nd ed. (Grand Rapids: Baker Books, 2002), 198.

15. Gerald Lawson Sittser, *A Grace Disguised: How the Soul Grows through Loss*, expanded ed. (Grand Rapids: Zondervan, 2004), 185.

16. Alan Medinger, "A Deep Longing for Purity," *Mission and Ministry* 10, no. 4 (1993): 12–20.

17. Adapted from Ryken, Wilhoit, and Longman, "Brokenness" in *Dictionary*, 123–24.

18. Victor Mihailoff, *Breaking the Chains of Addiction: How to Use Ancient Eastern Orthodox Spirituality to Free Our Minds and Bodies from All Addictions* (Salisbury, MA: Regina Orthodox Press, n.d.), 17.

19. Lawrence J. Crabb, "Longing for Eden and Sinning on the Way to Heaven," in *Christian Educator's Handbook on Spiritual Formation*, ed. Kenneth Gangel and James Wilhoit (Grand Rapids: Baker Books, 1997), 95.

20. John R. Cole, *Pascal: The Man and His Two Loves* (New York: New York University Press, 1995), 153.

21. Peter L. Berger, *The Sacred Canopy: Elements of a Sociological Theory of Religion* (Garden City, NY: Doubleday, 1967), 45, 46.

22. Ryken, Wilhoit, and Longman, "Ashes" in *Dictionary*, 50.

23. Jean Calvin, *Calvin's Institutes: A New Compend*, ed. Hugh T. Kerr (Louisville: Westminster John Knox, 1989), 108.

24. James Bryan Smith, *Embracing the Love of God: The Path and Promise of Christian Life* (San Francisco: HarperSanFrancisco, 1995), 21.

25. Ibid.

26. Louf, *Tuning in to Grace*, 10.

27. Eugene H. Peterson, *A Long Obedience in the Same Direction: Discipleship in an Instant Society*, 20th anniversary ed. (Downers Grove, IL: InterVarsity, 2000), 201–2. Used with permission of InterVarsity Press, PO Box 1400, Downers Grove, IL 60515, www.ivpress.com.

28. Philip Yancey, *Rumors of Another World: What on Earth Are We Missing?* (Grand Rapids: Zondervan, 2003), 149.

29. Willard, "Spiritual Formation in Christ," 257.

30. Ole Hallesby, *Prayer* (Minneapolis: Augsburg, 1994), 16–17.

31. Richard J. Foster, *Celebration of Discipline: The Path to Spiritual Growth*, rev. ed. (San Francisco: Harper & Row, 1988), 33.

Chapter 4 To Foster Receiving in Community

1. Susan A. Muto and Adrian van Kaam, *Commitment: Key to Christian Maturity* (Pittsburgh: Epiphany Association, 2002), 209.

2. Rice, *Reformed Spirituality*, 166.

3. Ray Sherman Anderson, *Self-Care: A Theology of Personal Empowerment and Spiritual Healing* (Wheaton: Victor Books, 1995), 236.

4. Peter Scazzero and Warren Bird, *The Emotionally Healthy Church: A Strategy for Discipleship That Actually Changes Lives* (Grand Rapids: Zondervan, 2003), 74.

5. Quoted in Gloria Goris Stronks and Doug Blomberg, *A Vision with a Task: Christian Schooling for a Responsive Discipleship* (Grand Rapids: Baker Books, 1993), 58.

6. Charles F. Melchert, *Wise Teaching: Biblical Wisdom and Educational Ministry* (Harrisburg, PA: Trinity Press International, 1998), 269–70.

7. Alan Nelson, *Broken in the Right Place: How God Tames the Soul* (Nashville: Nelson, 1994), 7.

8. Henri J. M. Nouwen, *The Return of the Prodigal Son: A Meditation on Fathers, Brothers, and Sons* (New York: Doubleday, 1992), 21–22.

9. Stronks and Blomberg, *Vision*, 59.

10. Anderson, *Self-Care*, 236.

11. Lauren F. Winner, *Real Sex: The Naked Truth about Chastity* (Grand Rapids: Brazos, 2005), 14.

12. Scazzero and Bird, *Emotionally Healthy Church*, 110.

13. Lois E. LeBar, *Education That Is Christian: The Classic Bestseller* (Wheaton: Victor Books, 1989), 281.

14. Tom F. Schwanda, "Pilgrim's Process: Some Pansophic Reflections on Christian Transformation and Worship," (DMin thesis, Fuller Theological Seminary, 1992), 244–66.

15. *The Westminster Confession of Faith* (Glasgow: Free Presbyterian Publications, 1976), 252–53.

16. Kenneth Boa, *Conformed to His Image: Biblical and Practical Approaches to Spiritual Formation* (Grand Rapids: Zondervan, 2001), 79.

17. Thomas à Kempis, *Imitation of Christ*, trans. and ed. William Creasy (Notre Dame, IN: Ave Maria, 2004), 52.

18. Dykstra, *Growing in the Life of Faith*, 16.

19. Willard, *Spirit of the Disciplines*, 20.

20. Thomas à Kempis, *Imitation*, 38.

21. Frank Rogers Jr., "Discernment," in *Practicing Our Faith: A Way of Life for a Searching People*, ed. Dorothy C. Bass (San Francisco: Jossey-Bass, 1997), 114–16.

22. E. M. Bounds, *The Complete Works of E. M. Bounds on Prayer* (Grand Rapids: Baker Books, 1990), 369.

23. Carl Ellis Nelson, *How Faith Matures* (Louisville: Westminster John Knox, 1989), 142.

24. Boa, *Conformed to His Image*, 86.

25. Nelson, *How Faith Matures*, 175.

26. Ruth Haley Barton, *Sacred Rhythms: Arranging Our Lives for Spiritual Transformation* (Downers Grove, IL: InterVarsity, 2006), 86.

27. Rice, *Reformed Spirituality*, 194.

28. Richard J. Foster, *Freedom of Simplicity*, 1st ed. (San Francisco: Harper & Row, 1981), 3.

29. Dietrich Bonhoeffer, *Life Together*, trans. John W. Doberstein (New York: Harper, 1954), 114–15.

30. Robert M. Norris, "Introduction," in Jonathan Edwards, *Pursuing Holiness in the Lord*, ed. T. M. Moore (Phillipsburg, NJ: P & R, 2005), 7.

31. Timothy J. Keller, "The Centrality of the Gospel" (sermon on Gal. 2:6–14; Redeemer Presbyterian Church, 1359 Broadway, New York, November 2, 1997; www.redeemer2.com/resources/papers/centrality.pdf).

Chapter 5 Foundations of Remembering: Letting the Cross Grow Larger

1. Robert J. Wicks, *Everyday Simplicity: A Practical Guide to Spiritual Growth* (Notre Dame, IN: Sorin Books, 2000), 55.

2. Jerry Bridges, *The Pursuit of Holiness* (Colorado Springs: NavPress, 1978), 20.

3. Lewis, *Problem of Pain*, 57.

4. G. K. Chesterton, *Orthodoxy*, Wheaton Literary Series (Wheaton: H. Shaw, 1994), 25.

5. Willard, *Renovation*, 93–94.

6. For a number of years I have used a modification of the bridge diagram as a way of talking about the difference between our perceived distance from God and the reality of the chasm. I am indebted to the insights provided by the presentation of the "The Cross Chart" in *Discipling by Grace*, by World Harvest Mission, 2.2 (p. 1).

7. Horace Bushnell, Williston Walker, and Luther Allan Weigle, *Christian Nurture*, new ed. (New York: Scribner's Sons, 1916), 4.

Chapter 6 To Foster Remembering in Community

1. Thomas H. Groome, *Christian Religious Education: Sharing Our Story and Vision* (San Francisco: Harper & Row, 1980), 271.

2. Jack Haberer, *Living the Presence of the Spirit* (Louisville: Geneva, 2001), 28.

3. Parker J. Palmer, *The Courage to Teach: Exploring the Inner Landscape of a Teacher's Life* (San Francisco: Jossey-Bass, 1998), 102–3.

4. Parker J. Palmer, *To Know as We Are Known: Education as a Spiritual Journey*, HarperCollins paperback ed. (San Francisco: HarperSanFrancisco, 1993), 69.

5. Boa, *Conformed to His Image*, 210.

6. A. W. Tozer, *The Knowledge of the Holy: The Attributes of God; Their Meaning in the Christian Life*, HarperCollins gift ed. (New York: HarperSanFrancisco, 1992), 93.

7. John Piper, *Desiring God: Meditations of a Christian Hedonist* (Portland, OR: Multnomah, 1986), 47.

8. Daniel J. Estes, *Hear, My Son: Teaching and Learning in Proverbs 1–9* (Grand Rapids: Eerdmans, 1997), 43.

9. F. Clark Power, Ann Higgins-D'Alessandro, and Lawrence Kohlberg, *Lawrence Kohlberg's Approach to Moral Education: Critical Assessments of Contemporary Psychology* (New York: Columbia University Press, 1989).

10. Henri J. M. Nouwen, *Creative Ministry* (Garden City, NY: Doubleday, 1971), 97.

11. Schwanda, "Pilgrim's Process," 137–61.

12. Nouwen, *Creative Ministry*, 29.

13. Ibid., 34.

14. Robert W. Pazmiño, *Basics of Teaching for Christians: Preparation, Instruction, and Evaluation* (Grand Rapids: Baker Academic, 1998), 89–94 (repr., Eugene, OR: Wipf & Stock, 2002).

15. Nouwen, *Creative Ministry*, 37.

16. André Louf, *Teach Us to Pray; Learning a Little about God*, trans. Hubert Hoskins, US ed. (Chicago: Franciscan Herald Press, 1975), 18.

17. LeBar, *Education*, 286.

18. Gorman, *Community*, 82 (Gorman is summarizing Crabb).

19. David Martyn Lloyd-Jones, *Preaching and Preachers* (London: Hodder & Stoughton, 1971), 325.

20. LeBar, *Education*, 284.

21. Lloyd-Jones, *Preaching and Preachers*, 305; Thomas C. Oden, *Pastoral Theology: Essentials of Ministry* (San Francisco: Harper & Row, 1982), 139.

22. Richard Baxter, *The Reformed Pastor* (Richmond: John Knox, 1956), 120.

23. R. A. Torrey, *The Person and Work of the Holy Spirit*, rev. ed. (Grand Rapids: Zondervan, 1974), 122–23.

24. Jack W. Hayford, *The Power and Blessing: Celebrating the Disciplines of Spirit-Filled Living* (Wheaton: Victor Books, 1994), 21.

25. Evelyn Underhill, *Concerning the Inner Life* (Oxford: Oneworld Publications, 1999), 55.

26. Haberer, *Living the Presence of the Spirit*, 112.

27. Bounds, *Complete Works*, 453.

28. Ibid., 478.

29. Zeb Bradford Long and Douglas McMurry, *Receiving the Power: Preparing the Way for the Holy Spirit* (Grand Rapids: Chosen Books, 1996), 139.

30. Gordon D. Fee, *God's Empowering Presence: The Holy Spirit in the Letters of Paul* (Peabody, MA: Hendrickson, 1994), 872.

31. In Arthur Bennett, *The Valley of Vision: A Collection of Puritan Prayers and Devotions* (Edinburgh: Banner of Truth Trust, 1975), 186.

32. Foster, *Prayer*, 210.

33. Lloyd-Jones, *Preaching and Preachers*, 325.

34. Bounds, *Complete Works*, 479.

35. Arturo G. Azurdia III, *Spirit Empowered Preaching: The Vitality of the Holy Spirit in Preaching* (Fearn, Ross-shire, UK: Mentor, 1998), 92.

36. Don Allen McGregor, "The Anointed Pulpit" (DMin thesis, Asbury Theological Seminary, 2000), 17.

37. Lloyd-Jones, *Preaching and Preachers*, 325.

38. W. E. Sangster, *Power in Preaching* (New York: Abingdon, 1958), 109.

39. James A. Forbes, *The Holy Spirit and Preaching* (Nashville: Abingdon, 1989), 86.

40. Bonhoeffer, *Life Together*, 37.

41. For a full discussion of spiritual abuse, see Charles H. Kraft, *I Give You Authority* (Grand Rapids: Chosen Books, 1997); and David Johnson and Jeff Van Vonderen, *The Subtle Power of Spiritual Abuse* (Minneapolis: Bethany House, 1991; repr., 2005).

42. Jack Deere, *Surprised by the Voice of God: How God Speaks Today through Prophecies, Dreams, and Visions* (Grand Rapids: Zondervan, 1996), 243.

43. Ibid., 319.

44. Piper, *Desiring God*, 114.

45. Nelson, *How Faith Matures*, 163.

46. John H. Westerhoff III, *Inner Growth, Outer Change: An Educational Guide to Church Renewal* (New York: Seabury, 1979), 61–62.

47. This quotation is attributed to various authors. Taken from M. G. Easton, *Illustrated Bible Dictionary* (Grand Rapids: Baker Books, 1978), 204.

48. Dietrich Bonhoeffer, *Life Together*, translated by John Doberstein, 88–89. English translation copyright © 1954 by Harper & Brothers, copyright renewed 1982 by Helen S. Doberstein. Reprinted by permission of HarperCollins Publishers.

49. D. Campbell Wyckoff, *The Gospel and Christian Education: A Theory of Christian Education for Our Times* (Philadelphia: Westminster, 1958), 92, 98, 108.

50. Calvin, *Institutes*, 35, 37.

51. Ruth Haley Barton, *The Truths That Free Us: A Woman's Calling to Spiritual Transformation* (Colorado Springs: Shaw Books, 2002), 26–27.

52. Benner, *Care of Souls*, 99–100.

53. Rice, *Reformed Spirituality*, 26–27.

54. Nelson, *How Faith Matures*, 163.

55. David Neff, "Together in the Jesus Story," *Christianity Today* (September 2006), 54–58. "A Call" was developed under the leadership of Robert Webber and Phil Kenyon.

56. Debra Dean Murphy, *Teaching That Transforms: Worship as the Heart of Christian Education* (Grand Rapids: Brazos, 2004), 112.

57. Bounds, *Complete Works*, 66.

58. Susan Annette Muto and Adrian van Kaam, *Tell Me Who I Am: Questions and Answers on Christian Spirituality* (Denville, NJ: Dimension Books, 1977), 16.

59. In Richard J. Foster and Emilie Griffin, *Spiritual Classics: Selected Readings for Individuals and Groups on the Twelve Spiritual Disciplines* (San Francisco: HarperSanFrancisco, 2000), 161.

60. Bonhoeffer, *Life Together*, 84.

61. Eugene H. Peterson, *Eat This Book: A Conversation in the Art of Spiritual Reading* (Grand Rapids: Eerdmans, 2006), 100.

62. Dykstra, *Growing in the Life of Faith*, 58.

63. Donald S. Whitney, *Spiritual Disciplines for the Christian Life* (Colorado Springs: NavPress, 1991), 219.

64. Walter Elwell, class lecture, Wheaton College, Wheaton, IL, November 2002.

65. Thomas à Kempis, *Imitation*, 86.

Chapter 7 Foundations of Responding: Love and Service to God and Others

1. Westerhoff, *Spiritual Life*, 1.

2. Anderson, *Self-Care*, 77.

3. Nicholas Wolterstorff, *Educating for Responsible Action*, commissioned by Christian Schools International (Grand Rapids: CSI Publications; Eerdmans, 1980), 4–6.

4. Douglas Arnold Hyde, *Dedication and Leadership: Learning from the Communists* (Notre Dame, IN: University of Notre Dame Press, 1966), 44–45.

5. John Dewey and Jo Ann Boydston, *1916*, vol. 9 of *The Middle Works, 1899–1924* (Carbondale: Southern Illinois University Press, 1980), 147.

6. Willard, *Divine Conspiracy*, 243.

7. Adrian van Kaam and Susan Muto, *Foundations of the Christian Heart*, Formation Theology Series 3 (Pittsburgh: Epiphany Books, 2006), 201–10.

8. Lovelace, *Dynamics of Spiritual Life*, 212.

9. Philipp Jakob Spener, *Pia Desideria*, trans. and ed. T. G. Tappert (Philadelphia: Fortress, 1964), 92.

10. Ibid., 94.

11. Ibid., 92.

12. Ibid., 94.

13. Andrew F. Walls, *The Cross-Cultural Process in Christian History: Studies in the Transmission and Appropriation of Faith* (Maryknoll, NY: Orbis Books, 2002), 32.

14. Lamin O. Sanneh, "Introduction: The Changing Face of Christianity: The Cultural Impetus of a World Religion," in *The Changing Face of Christianity: Africa, the West, and the World*, ed. Lamin O. Sanneh and Joel A. Carpenter (New York: Oxford University Press, 2005), 3–4.

15. Dykstra, *Growing in the Life of Faith*, 78.

16. Westerhoff, *Spiritual Life*, 76.

17. David Henderson, "The Art of Voice Recognition," *Discipleship Journal* 150 (November/December 2005): 58–66.

Chapter 8 To Foster Responding in Community

1. Bonhoeffer, *Life Together*, 94.

2. Kevin J. Vanhoozer, *First Theology: God, Scripture and Hermeneutics* (Downers Grove, IL: InterVarsity, 2002), 334.

3. Lawrence J. Crabb, *The Safest Place on Earth: Where People Connect and Are Forever Changed* (Nashville: Word, 1999), 32.

4. Helen Waddell, trans., *The Desert Fathers* (London: Constable, 1936), 157–58.

5. Norris, "Introduction," in Edwards, *Pursuing Holiness*, 3.

6. Collins, *Soul Care*, 104.

7. Robert Jamieson, A. R. Fausset, and David Brown, *A Commentary, Critical and Explanatory, on the Old and New Testaments* (Grand Rapids: Zondervan, 1934), 663.

8. Iris Murdoch, *The Sovereignty of Good* (New York: Schocken Books, 1971), 37.

9. Marva J. Dawn, *Reaching Out without Dumbing Down: A Theology of Worship for the Turn-of-the-Century Culture* (Grand Rapids: Eerdmans, 1995), 211.

10. Barton, *Truths That Free Us*, xviii-xix.

11. Azurdia, *Spirit Empowered Preaching*, 158.

12. Whitney, *Spiritual Disciplines*, 216.

13. Foster, *Celebration of Discipline*, 81.

14. Bonhoeffer, *Life Together*, 99.

15. Elizabeth R. Achtemeier, "Righteousness in the OT," in *The Interpreter's Dictionary of the Bible*, ed. George Arthur Buttrick (New York: Abingdon, 1962), 4:80.

16. Martin Luther King Jr., *A Testament of Hope: The Essential Writings of Martin Luther King, Jr.*, ed. James Melvin Washington (San Francisco: Harper & Row, 1986), 219.

17. Ken Sande, *The Peacemaker: A Biblical Guide to Resolving Personal Conflict* (Grand Rapids: Baker Books, 2004), 259–61.

18. Matthew Linn and Dennis Linn, *Healing Life's Hurts: Healing Memories through Five Stages of Forgiveness* (New York: Paulist Press, 1978), 151.

Chapter 9 Foundations of Relating: Spiritually Enriching Relationships of Love and Service

1. Westerhoff, *Spiritual Life*, 1.

2. Anderson, *Self-Care*, 32–33.

3. Jaroslav Jan Pelikan, *The Christian Tradition: A History of the Development of Doctrine* (Chicago: University of Chicago Press, 1971), 1.

4. Charles R. Foster, *Educating Congregations: The Future of Christian Education* (Nashville: Abingdon, 1994), 27.

5. Murphy, *Teaching*, 16.

6. Wolterstorff, *Educating*, 15.

7. Hans Bietenhard, "*Kyrios* [Lord]," in vol. 2 of *The New International Dictionary of New Testament Theology*, ed. Colin Brown (Grand Rapids: Zondervan, 1975), 514.

8. Gorman, *Community*, 15.

9. Francis A. Schaeffer, *The Mark of the Christian* (Downers Grove, IL: InterVarsity, 1970), 13.

10. Anderson, *Self-Care*, 106.

11. Scazzero and Bird, *Emotionally Healthy Church*, 19.

12. Dykstra, *Growing in the Life of Faith*, 39.

13. Henry Cloud and John Sims Townsend, *How People Grow: What the Bible Reveals about Personal Growth* (Grand Rapids: Zondervan, 2001), 81.

14. Robert Neelly Bellah, *Habits of the Heart: Individualism and Commitment in American Life* (Berkeley: University of California Press, 1985), 135.

15. Gorman, *Community*, 16.

Chapter 10 To Foster Relating in Community

1. Muto and van Kaam, *Tell Me*, 25.

2. Craig R. Dykstra, *Vision and Character: A Christian Educator's Alternative to Kohlberg* (New York: Paulist Press, 1981), 122.

3. Barton, *Truths That Free Us*, xviii.

4. Adapted from Bounds, *Complete Works*, 447.

5. Bruce A. Demarest, *Soul Guide: Following Jesus as Spiritual Director* (Colorado Springs: NavPress, 2003), 35–41.

6. Charles F. Stanley, *Walking Wisely: Real Guidance for Life's Journey* (Nashville: Nelson, 2002), 108.

7. Scazzero and Bird, *Emotionally Healthy Church*, 37.

8. Nelson, *How Faith Matures*, 127.

9. Willard, *Renovation*, 185.

10. Piper, *Desiring God*, 55.

11. Dykstra, *Growing in the Life of Faith*, 56.

12. Barton, *Sacred Rhythms*, 111.

13. Foster, *Celebration of Discipline*, 87.

14. Barton, *Sacred Rhythms*, 116–18.

15. Foster, *Celebration of Discipline*, 81.

16. Ibid., 84–85.

17. Os Guinness, *The Call: Finding and Fulfilling the Central Purpose of Your Life* (Nashville: Word, 1998), 74.

18. Barbara Brown Taylor, *The Preaching Life* (Cambridge, MA: Cowley Publications, 1993), 66.

19. Ana Maria Pineda, "Hospitality," in *Practicing Our Faith: A Way of Life for a Searching People*, ed. Dorothy C. Bass (San Francisco: Jossey-Bass, 1997), 31.

20. Ibid., 32.

21. Westerhoff, *Spiritual Life*, 49.

22. Anderson, *Self-Care*, 52–53.

23. Lawrence J. Crabb, *Connecting: Healing for Ourselves and Our Relationships: A Radical New Vision* (Nashville: Word, 1997), 38.

24. Westerhoff, *Spiritual Life*, 69.

25. Adele Ahlberg Calhoun, *Spiritual Disciplines Handbook: Practices That Transform Us* (Downers Grove, IL: InterVarsity, 2005), 195.

26. L. Gregory Jones, "Forgiveness," in *Practicing Our Faith: A Way of Life for a Searching People*, ed. Dorothy C. Bass (San Francisco: Jossey-Bass, 1997), 135.

27. Sittser, *A Grace Disguised*, 147.

28. David G. Benner and Robert W. Harvey, *Understanding and Facilitating Forgiveness*, Strategic Pastoral Counseling Resources Series (Grand Rapids: Baker Books, 1996), 33–83.

Appendix: Assessment Questions

1. Dallas Willard, "The Spirit Is Willing: The Body as a Tool for Spiritual Growth," in *The Christian Educator's Handbook on Spiritual Formation*, ed. Kenneth O. Gangel and James C. Wilhoit (Grand Rapids: Baker Books, 1994), 225.

2. Torrey, *Person and Work of the Holy Spirit*, 123.

Scripture Index

Genesis

1 178
1:1 33
1:1–2:25 34
1:2 34
1:31 34
2 178
2:7 34
2:8 34
2:18 194
2:19 34
3:7 65
3:8 65
6–9 22
9:20 22
12:1–3 128

Exodus

20:3–5 73
23:8 120
31:1–5 125
32:4 35

Deuteronomy

16:12 105
16:19 120
34:9 125

Judges

2:10 105
3:10 125

6:34 125
14:6 125
14:19 125

1 Samuel

2:21 42
2:26 41, 42
11:6 125
15:19–22 159
16:7 159, 171
16:13 125

2 Kings

6:17 83

Job

13:12 75

Psalms

1 165
8:5 151
23:5 93
34:17–18 70
51 63
63:1 67
81:16 74
104 165
104:34 165
111:10 116
119:18 83

133:2 125
147:2–3 70
147:3 25

Proverbs

3:4 42
4:23 21, 24
9:10 116

Ecclesiastes

4:9 192
4:9–12 159
12:1 105

Isaiah

29:13 44
42:16 116
42:20 84
44 75
44:9–10 120
44:13–20 75
44:18 74
44:19 74
44:20 74
46:8–9 105
53:4 201
55:1 93
55:1–2 67
57:20 79
61:1 70
61:1–2 127

Subject Index